John Russell

Essays on the Rise and Progress of the Christian Religion in the West

of Europe

From the Reign of Tiberius to the End of the Council of Trent

John Russell

Essays on the Rise and Progress of the Christian Religion in the West of Europe
From the Reign of Tiberius to the End of the Council of Trent

ISBN/EAN: 9783337130305

Printed in Europe, USA, Canada, Australia, Japan

Cover: Foto ©Lupo / pixelio.de

More available books at **www.hansebooks.com**

ESSAYS

ON THE RISE AND PROGRESS OF

THE CHRISTIAN RELIGION

IN THE

WEST OF EUROPE

FROM THE REIGN OF TIBERIUS

TO THE END OF THE COUNCIL OF TRENT

BY

JOHN EARL RUSSELL.

'Scripture, say the Protestants, is the only rule of faith in matters pertaining to revealed religion, and they say well. There is no other Christianity than this; no other centre of union than this. Whatsoever is not clearly delivered there, may be true, but cannot be important. HÆC MEA EST SENTENTIA, NEQUE ME EX EA ULLIUS UNQUAM AUT DOCTI AUT INDOCTI MOVEBIT ORATIO.'—*Dr. Jortin.*

LONDON:

LONGMANS, GREEN, AND CO.

1873.

PREFACE.

The able authors who wrote the work entitled 'The Pope and the Council,' by Janus, have said in their preface, 'For many reasons no names of authors are placed on our title-page. We consider that a work so entirely made up of facts and supporting all its statements by reference to the original authorities, must and can speak for itself, without needing any names attached to it.' It is for an opposite reason, it is because the present work is not entirely made up of facts and that its statements are not supported by reference to the original authorities, that I have thought it necessary to place my name before the public and to explain in this preface what are the works upon which I have relied and who are the men whose opinions I have adopted.

The chief works then upon which I have relied are, (1), 'The History of Latin Christianity, including that of the Popes to the Pontificate of Nicolas V.', by Dr. Milman, late Dean of St. Paul's; (2), 'Remarks on Ecclesiastical History,' by John Jortin, D.D. The first of these authors says, ' As it is my own confident belief that the words of Christ, and His words alone (the

primal, indefeasible truths of Christianity), shall not
pass away; so I cannot presume to say that men may
not attain to a clearer, at the same time more full and
comprehensive and balanced sense of those words, than
has as yet been generally received in the Christian
world.'

Another work of far less bulk than that of Dean
Milman's is called 'St. Paul and Protestantism,'
written by Mr. Matthew Arnold. The object of
the author is to give a view of St. Paul's teaching
very different from that of the Calvinists, but, as
it appears to me, far more in accordance with the
real doctrine of St. Paul than that which persons
who have failed to comprehend his real intentions
have attributed to him. The error of Mr. Arnold
appears to me, not that he has failed to comprehend
St. Paul's meaning, but that he has omitted to notice
the political circumstances, and the violence of the
conflict in which the Puritans of England appeared
as the aggressors, when they were in reality fighting
against a revival of Popery, and the spiritual tyranny
of Archbishop Laud.

Among Roman Catholic writers, Dr. Newman has
greatly distinguished himself. His latest work, 'The
Grammar of Assent,' deserves to be deeply studied.
Of those who, on the other side, have taken a very
large and friendly view of the Reformation, there is
no work more deserving of attention than the 'History
of the Rise and Influence of Rationalism in Europe,'
by Mr. Lecky. Mr. Lecky has given a favourable
view of the opinions originally espoused by Origen,

and afterwards adopted by Zuinglius. Origen had expressed his hope that Pythagoras and Plato might be
saved by the merciful decree of the Almighty from
eternity of punishment. Gibbon has recorded, as his
manner is, the intolerance of Justinian, who would not
leave undisturbed the soul of a great Christian writer
who had died three hundred years before. 'It was
now three hundred years since the body of Origen had
been eaten by the worms; his soul, of which he held
the pre-existence, was in the hands of its Creator, but
his writings were eagerly perused by the monks of
Palestine. In these writings the piercing eye of Justinian descried more than ten metaphysical errors;
and the primitive doctor, in the company of Pythagoras and Plato, was devoted by the clergy to the
eternity of hell-fire, which he had presumed to deny.'[1]

Fortunately, we live in happier times, and the damnatory decrees of Justinian have not been extended to
the ecclesiastics of the Church of England by the pro-
vident care and the enlarged learning of the Judicial
Committee of Privy Council, to whom Parliament has
wisely entrusted the authority to fix the sense of the
Articles of Religion and the Book of Common Prayer,
which have been sanctioned by the authority of Parliament with the assent of Convocation.

Among the works which have lately appeared,
four volumes, called the 'New Testament for English
Readers,' by the late Dean of Canterbury, Dr. Alford,
are well worth study.

---

[1] Gibbon's *Roman Empire*, vol. viii. p. 325, 326.

It is surely desirable that men thoroughly conversant with the Greek and the English tongue should enable the English nation to understand and take to heart, the lessons which Paul delivered to the various nations of the Roman Empire at the beginning of the propagation of Christianity upon earth.

Thus we find in the authorized version of the 13th chapter of the 1st Epistle to the Corinthians, that ' charity suffereth long, that charity vaunteth not itself, beareth all things, believeth all things, hopeth all things, endureth all things ; ' so likewise in the end, ' and now abideth faith, hope, charity, these three ; but the greatest of these is charity.' [1]

But as the word charity has in these days a much narrower meaning than it had when the Bible was first translated, Dean Alford in this chapter, and Dean Stanley in his translation of St. Paul's Epistles to the Corinthians, use the word love, so that we read, ' and now abideth faith, hope, love, these three ; but the greatest of these is love.' Liddell and Scott, in their Greek Lexicon, use the word ' brotherly love,' which is, perhaps, the best version. At all events, the word charity is here inadequate and insufficient.

In these Essays I have purposely avoided the work of controversy, and leave it to others to defend the miracles of Christ and his Apostles. I rest in the faith of Jeremy Taylor, of Barrow, of Tillotson, of Hoadley, of Samuel Clarke, of Middleton, of Warburton, of Arnold, without attempting to reconcile points of difference among these great men.

[1] S. Paul's First Epistle to the Corinthians, c. xiii. v. 13.

Gibbon has spoken of the arguments which satisfied, or subdued, the reason of such men as Grotius, Pascal, and Locke.

These were not bigoted or illiterate thinkers. Grotius has branded with just hate the persecutors of the Netherlands, whose victims he computes at 100,000, double the number estimated by Paolo Sarpi. He says finely, that the sins of the body can be reached by punishments which affect the body; but the soul, as it is free and immortal, cannot be made subject to the fire and steel which torment the body.

Pascal, in his Provincial Letters, has thoroughly exposed the evasions and insincerity of the Jesuits.

Locke, in his argument for Religious Liberty, fails only in refusing to allow to Roman Catholics the freedom he claims for the Protestants.

Still Grotius and Pascal and Locke may well be claimed by those who believe in Christianity as men of intellects equal to those of the philosophers of the present age.

Galileo Galilei has related in a letter to a friend, that the only argument used against him when he contended for the motion of the earth, was a quotation from the words of Scripture :—Whether the Bible contains all the truths concerning Astronomy, Physiology, and Anatomy, or whether its Divine authority be confined to faith .and morals, is still a matter of dispute between the Church of Rome and Protestant Communions.

The opinion, that Scripture is the only rule of faith in matters pertaining to revealed religion, might be supported by extracts from the works of Erasmus, who employed his great learning in the translation of the Bible; by the authority of Luther, who with more firmness and consistency maintained a similar opinion; by Chillingworth, who considers the Bible as the religion of Protestants.

On the other hand, Paolo Sarpi, who wrote the best history of the Council of Trent, says, 'That if it were not for Aristotle, we (meaning the Church of Rome) should be wanting in many articles of faith.' It is, therefore, a part of my business to distinguish the theories of Aristotle as expressed in what is falsely called the Athanasian Creed, from the declarations made in the Holy Scriptures, and while I fully admit the ingenuity and the subtlety of reasoning, which distinguished the Greek philosopher, I am entitled to refuse to him that Divine authority which is willingly attributed by all Protestants to Christ and his Apostles.

Sydney Smith, who squandered the arrows of his wit on every side, takes occasion from a passage in Waterton's account of South America, describing a bird, who from its peculiar note is called the cathedral bird, to say that it puts him in mind of the bell of an English cathedral, ringing in a·new dean, promoted on account of good birth, shabby politics, and moderate understanding.

It occurred to me when I had the privilege of recommending to the Crown persons worthy of the dignity of dean, that this part of the Royal patronage might be bestowed in a better manner than that which

Sydney Smith has commemorated. Among those whom I recommended to Her Majesty were Dr. Tait, to whom I offered the Deanery of Carlisle, and whose union of the liberal opinions of the present age with judicious moderation, has induced my successors to recommend him for the Bishopric of London in the first place, and finally to the highest post in the English Church, the Archbishopric of Canterbury. Another selection, namely, that of Dr. Milman, who by my advice was made Dean of St. Paul's, affords an instance of the fruits that may be derived from the devotion of learning and of leisure to Ecclesiastical History. The History of the Latin Church, by Dean Milman, is a work replete with accurate information and judicious criticism; but it is in six bulky octavo volumes, and while I have drawn largely from their contents, I expect that, in this busy age, the readers of poetry and of novels will hardly make themselves masters of so voluminous a work. I have, therefore, endeavoured to condense the details which have given to Dean Milman's History its great and unenvied reputation.

Another person whom I recommended to a deanery was Dr. Dawes, whose school at King's Somborne showed how agreeably the dry lessons of reading, writing, and arithmetic might be relieved by interesting facts of natural history and some information of other kinds. Mr. Lowe, who is proud of being the author of the Revised Code, may despise the information in history and geography which can be acquired at an elementary school; but such elementary knowledge may point the way to graver studies. I remember pointing out to Mr. Baines, the member for Leeds, who at that time refused the Parliamentary grant, that boys of the humbler classes, who benefited by Government grants in a primary school, might, if they had abilities, rise high in the State or in the more liberal professions and occupations. It is to be hoped that in spite of Mr. Lowe's prejudices, the progress of the English people in liberal education will hereafter be as large as that which prevails in Scotland, in Saxony, and in Switzerland. In fact there are two great measures, which all the nations of Europe, if they value their rights and are fit judges of their interests, ought to demand. The first of these is a large and liberal education, giving to every boy and girl, termed in the language of English law infants, large and liberal instruction, neither shackled by the sacerdotal power, nor restrained by the narrow prejudices of a Minister of Finance.

The next postulate on which the nations of Europe should insist is real liberty of the Press, or, as it may be more properly termed, real liberty of the human mind. If this be not obtained, the decline and the fall of national power is sure to follow. The story of Ancient Rome is told by Tacitus with his usual insight into human nature, and his usual brevity of expression. He gives this abstract as his reason for not attempting to relate the history of the Republic :—
' Nam post conditam urbem, octingentos et viginti prioris ævi annos multi auctores retulerunt ; dum res populi Romani memorabantur, pari eloquentia, ac

libertate ; postquam bellatum apud Actium, atque
omnem potestatem ad unum conferri pacis interfuit,
magna illa ingenia cessere.'

Of course, these men of great minds ceased to exist
when they could not write with liberty as well as with
eloquence. The battle of Cannæ and the military genius
of Hannibal did not produce the fall of Rome : 'Can-
narum vindex, Romani sanguinis ultor Annulus.' The
Roman state survived Cannæ—it could not survive
Actium. The personal government of Nero (such is
the modern phrase) and the personal government of
Vitellius showed what cruelty and sensuality could do
to ruin the State. A long succession of Emperors
ended with the triumph of a Turkish conqueror.

The history of Modern Europe is not wanting in
similar examples. Personal government has had its
sway in Austria, in Prussia, and in Russia—it has not
had the power to save from conquest Vienna, Berlin,
or Moscow. On the other hand, neither the wonderful
military genius of Napoleon I. nor the sagacity and
prudence of Napoleon III. could give duration to
the reigns of those two monarchs, and in each case
despotism, to call things by their right name, has
had to yield its capital to the cannon of the invader.
Neither ancient nor modern history is without its moral.
Cæsar was preferred to Pompey by the democratic
faction of Rome. Cromwell overcame the Presbyterian
party by the help of more violent democrats. Napoleon I., the greatest tyrant of our times, prevailed by
his preference of the extreme to the moderate democrats. Passing from this subject I resume the questions

of our own day. It is the duty of the State to provide for the education of every child under its control. It is also the duty of the State to grant to its adult population the utmost liberty to think what it pleases, and to utter what it thinks.

Of course in speaking thus generally, I do not intend to condemn measures necessary for safety. 'Ne quid detrimenti respublica capiat' is a maxim which all states must observe.

The President and Congress of the United States of America observe it no less than the Emperor and Senate of Russia.

To Christianity for their religion, to liberty for their political institutions, the nations of the world must look, abjuring Superstition, Persecution, Intolerance in their religion ; Injustice, Inequality, Despotism in their political institutions.

CONTENTS.

HISTORY

OF THE

CHRISTIAN RELIGION.

I. PRELIMINARY ESSAY.

STATE OF ROME UNDER AUGUSTUS.

AT the period when Christ came into the world, the human race, which was almost comprehended in the Roman Empire, was afflicted, after a series of fierce and pitiless wars, by the loss of liberty and the degeneracy of morals. Augustus, by the victory of Actium, had put an end to the rivalry by which, since the first triumvirate, the world had been given up to slaughter, proscription, and division. The great poet Lucretius had put up his prayer for peace :—

Funde potens placidam Romanis inclyte pacem.

Virgil and Horace, the adroit flatterers of Augustus, had endeavoured to instil the belief that, along with the cessation of civil war, there would arise an age not only of civil tranquillity, but of domestic purity. It was the fiction of these two sweet singers, that Augustus was about to open an age of felicity upon earth, founded upon the strength of the Roman arms and the restoration of the ancient Roman manners.

2·6

B

Virgil, with some modesty, confines this era of domestic happiness to the rural population :—

> Interea dulces pendent circum oscula nati :
> Casta pudicitiam servat domus.

Horace, with a bolder flight of imagination, adorns in Venetian colours the happiness of the Roman Empire under his generous patron :—

> Tutus bos etenim rura perambulat :
> Nutrit culta Ceres, almaque Faustitas :
> Pacatum volitant per mare navitæ :
>   Culpari metuit fides.
> Nullis polluitur casta domus stupris ;
> Mos et lex maculosum edomuit nefas :
> Laudantur simili prole puerperæ :
>   Culpam pœna premit comes.
> Quis Parthum paveat ? Quis gelidum Scythen ?
> Quis Germania quos horrida parturit
> Fœtus, incolumi Cæsare ? Quis feræ
>   Bellum curet Iberiæ ?

In this and twenty other passages, Horace endeavours to infuse the belief that purity of domestic life, with security from foreign foes and civil discord, were to be the happy inheritance of the subjects of Augustus Cæsar. Yet he himself has given us a picture as disgusting as any that Juvenal or Tacitus has drawn of the connubial fidelity of the Roman wives :—

> Fœcunda culpæ sæcula nuptias
> Primum inquinavere, et genus, et domos :
> Hoc fonte derivata clades
>   In patriam populumque fluxit.
> Motus doceri gaudet Ionicos
> Matura virgo, et fingitur artubus
> Jam nunc, et incestos amores
>   De tenero meditatur ungui.

> Mox juniores quærit adulteros
> Inter mariti vina : neque eligit
>   Cui donet impermissa raptim
>   Gaudia, luminibus remotis ;
> Sed jussa coram non sine conscio
> Surgit marito, seu vocat institor,
>   Seu navis Hispanæ magister,
>   Dedecorum pretiosus emptor.
>
> .   .   .   .   .   .
>
> Damnosa quid non imminuit dies ?
> Ætas parentum pejor avis tulit
>   Nos nequiores, mox daturos
>   Progeniem vitiosiorem.[1]

Ovid is not a whit behind his brother bards in the task of adulation and false auguries of peace and purity. First commemorating the victories of Octavius—

> Illius auspiciis obsessæ mœnia pacem
> Victa petent Mutinæ : Pharsalia sentiet illum
> Æmathiæque iterum madefacti cæde Philippi
> . . . quodcunque habitabile tellus
> Sustinet hujus erit, Pontus quoque serviet illi—

the poet proceeds to commemorate the blessings of peace :—

> Pace datà terris, animum ad civilia vertet
> Jura suum, legesque feret justissimus auctor ;
> Exemploque suo mores regit ; inque futuri
> Temporis ætatem, venturorumque nepotum
> Prospiciens prolem sanctâ de conjuge natam,
> Ferre simul nomenque suum curisque jubebit.

I need hardly say how little Horace and Ovid illustrated in their conduct the 'casta domus' and the 'prolem sanctâ de conjuge natam' which they celebrated in their harmonious numbers. But that is of little consequence. The important fact for us is, that

---

[1] Hor. Odes, lib. iii. 6.

B 2

the reformation of manners, so confidently predicted,
did not happen, and that, on the contrary, never was
there so rapid a dissolution of morals, such a violation
of the respect due to virtuous matrons and innocent
daughters, as that which took place during the reign
of Augustus and his immediate successors. Augustus
himself was doomed to see and to condemn, in the
person of his daughter Julia, an example of extreme
vice. Julia, married in the bloom of her beauty
to Marcellus, the son of Octavia, was, after the pre-
mature death of the youth (so poetically celebrated
by Virgil), bound by her father's authority, and against
her own inclinations, to Agrippa in a second, and to
Tiberius in a third marriage. Exulting in her charms,
and vain of her wit, she gave way to the most un-
bounded profligacy, and degraded the forum and the
senate by making them the scenes of her licentious-
ness. The current stories may have been exaggerated,
but it is certain that Augustus adopted the belief that
the guilt of his daughter was shared with several of
the young nobles of Rome. Julius Antonius, son of the
triumvir, one of Julia's lovers, was accused of treason-
able conspiracy, and put to death.[1] But is there any
need of proving the utter failure of such projects as
Augustus may have had for the regulation of morals?

> Quid leges sine moribus
> Vanæ proficiunt?

is the exclamation of Horace himself.

Further, the very reign in which Christ first taught,
the reign of Tiberius Cæsar, was marked by the

---

[1] Seneca, *De Benef.* vi. 32.

profligate habits of the Emperor. The caustic satire of Juvenal, and the grave narrative of Tacitus, all bear witness to the degeneracy of Roman manners. Tacitus contrasts the virgin purity and conjugal fidelity of the German women with the temptations of the theatres of Rome ; he observes sarcastically, ' Nec corrumpere et corrumpi sæculum vocatur.'

The purity of the early ages of Rome and of the barbarous ages of Germany was due no doubt to a state of society which had much of the rudeness of ignorance. The Epistle of St. Paul to the Romans shows how the simplicity of the Roman Republic in its early days had been succeeded in the flourishing period of the Empire by the prevalence of vice the most gross, and crimes the most unnatural.

The time was come to place the respect due to the sanctity of marriage on other grounds than those of rudeness of manners and absence of civilisation.

Such was one task which, in the name and with the authority of the Almighty, our Saviour undertook.

But there was another task, not less necessary, and not less calling for a revelation from Heaven—the worship of the true God. The gods and goddesses of the Homeric Olympus, whether they were names intended to represent the sun, the dawn, the dew, and other powers of nature, or whether they were meant to be real objects of worship, had, before the advent of Augustus, lost all credit with the people of Greece and Rome. Socrates was content to die, rather than profess a real belief in the gods of his country.

Cicero laughed at the ceremonies of the augurs in
which he pretended to share. Ovid has told in beautiful poetry the stories of Cadmus and of Phaeton, of
one nymph changed into a laurel, of another into
a fountain, of Danae, of Europa, of the birth of
Bacchus, and the despair of Niobe. But no one could
ever pretend to suppose that these stories of mythology were other than fictions of admirable invention. The poet Lucretius never pretended to pass off
his Venus and Mars as more than 'airy nothings' to
which 'the poet's pen' gave 'a local habitation and a
name.' He relates in solemn and sublime strains the
doctrines of his own Epicurean philosophy :—

> Humana ante oculos fœdè quum vita jaceret,
> In terris oppressa gravi sub religione,
> Primum Graius homo mortales tollere contra
> Est oculos ausus primusque obsistere contra.

So, when he has beautifully and pathetically related
the sacrifice of Iphigenia, he adds :—

> Tantum religio potuit suadere malorum.

Virgil, while he worships the Muses, does not restrict
their dominion to woods and lakes :—

> Me vero primum dulces ante omnia Musæ,
> Quarum sacra fero, ingenti perculsus amore,
> Accipiant; cœlique vias et sidera monstrent.

In another passage he exults that hell does not really
exist :—

> Felix qui potuit rerum cognoscere causas,
> Atque metus omnes et inexorabile fatum
> Subjecit pedibus, strepitumque Acherontis avari !

Thus rendering a timid homage to the earlier and
perhaps the greater poet.

At length, in a succeeding reign, Juvenal spoke of the ancient superstition as almost universally exploded :—

> Esse aliquos Manes, et subterranea regna,
> Et contum, et Stygio ranas in gurgite nigras,
> Atque unâ transire vadum tot millia cymbâ,
> Nec pueri credunt, nisi qui nondum ære lavantur.

So in the magnificent speech which Lucan puts into the mouth of Cato, when he is asked to consult the oracle of Jupiter, he proclaims as follows :—

> Ille Deo plenus, tacitâ quem mente gerebat,
> Effudit dignas adytis e pectore voces.
> Quid quæri Labiene jubes ? an liber in armis
> Occubuisse velim potius, quam regna videre ?
> An sit vita nihil, sed longam differat ætas ?
> An noceat vis ulla bono ? Fortunaque perdat
> Oppositâ virtute minas ? laudandaque velle
> Sit satis, et nunquam successu crescat honestum ?
> Scimus, et hoc nobis non altius inseret Ammon.
> Hæremus cuncti Superis, temploque tacente
> Nil facimus non sponte Dei : nec vocibus ullis
> Numen eget : dixitque semel nascentibus auctor
> Quicquid scire licet : steriles nec legit arenas,
> Ut caneret paucis, mersitque hoc pulvere verum :
> Estne Dei sedes nisi terra, et pontus, et aër,
> Et cœlum, et virtus ? Superos quid quærimus ultra ?
> Jupiter est quodcunque vides, quocunque moveris.
> Sortilegis egeant dubii, semperque futuris
> Casibus ancipites : me mon oracula certum,
> Sed mors certa facit : pavido fortique cadendum est.
> Hoc satis est dixisse Jovem.   Sic ille profatur :
> Servatâque fide templi discedit ab aris,
> Non exploratum populis Ammona relinquens.[1]

It was in a society of political tranquillity, corrupted morals, and prevailing atheism, that Christ was re- vealed to the Roman world.

[1] Lucan, *Pharsalia*, lib. ix. 564 *et seq.*

8

ESSAY II.

RISE OF CHRISTIANITY.

It has appeared by the preceding chapter that in Rome liberty had been entirely lost, morality openly violated, and religion ridiculed or despised. It was in these circumstances that a new religion was revealed in the name of 'Glory to God in the highest; on earth peace, and goodwill towards men.' Jupiter and Juno, Minerva and Venus, Mars and Mercury, Apollo and Diana, were set aside as imaginary deities. The worship due from man to his Maker, and the goodwill which the creature man was bound to show to all others of the human race, were proclaimed as the sacred commandments of God.

The time when John the Baptist foretold the coming of Jesus Christ is very definitely fixed by St. Luke. 'Now in the fifteenth year of the reign of Tiberius Cæsar, Pontius Pilate being governor of Judæa, and Herod being tetrarch of Galilee, and his brother Philip tetrarch of Ituræa and of the region of Trachonitis, and Lysanias the tetrarch of Abilene, Annas and Caiaphas being the high priests, the word of God came unto John, the son of Zacharias, in the wilderness.'[1] The same chapter of St. Luke relates: 'And Jesus himself

[1] St. Luke, chap. iii.

began to be about thirty years of age, being (as was supposed) the son of Joseph.' The circumstances relating to the miraculous conception of the Virgin Mary need not be referred to here, being fully recorded in the Gospels of St. Matthew, St. Mark, and St. Luke.

It was not long before it was made manifest that the new religion was to be preached everywhere, to all, and for ever. For John the Baptist, having acknowledged the divine mission of Jesus, and Jesus knowing that the Pharisees had heard that he, together with his disciples, baptized more persons than John, went through Samaria to Galilee. Then coming to Sychar, a city of Samaria, he asked a woman of Samaria to give him to drink ; the woman said to him, ' How is it that thou, being a Jew, askest drink of me, which am a woman of Samaria? for the Jews have no dealings with the Samaritans.' Soon afterwards the woman said, ' Sir, I perceive thou art a prophet ; our fathers worshipped in this mountain, and ye say that in Jerusalem is the place where men ought to worship.' Jesus saith unto her, ' Woman, believe me, that the hour cometh when ye shall neither in this mountain, nor at Jerusalem, worship the Father. Ye worship ye know not what; we know what we worship, for salvation is of the Jews. But the hour cometh, and now is, when the true worshippers shall worship the Father in spirit and in truth : for the Father seeketh such to worship Him. God is a Spirit, and they that worship Him must worship Him in spirit and in truth.' The woman saith unto Him, ' I know that Messias cometh, which is called Christ : when He is come, He will tell us all things.' Jesus saith unto her, 'I that speak unto thee am He.'[1]

Having thus announced his divine mission, He preached to all, as well as everywhere, faith in God and in Christ. This word *faith*, as enjoined and required by Christ, has been often repeated, but little understood.

In order to understand the meaning of the word, let us take some instances. Jesus, after a discourse of wonderful truth and power, entered into Capernaum. A Roman centurion at this time had a servant, whom he loved, very ill and like to die. The Jews represented to Jesus that this centurion had been very kind to their nation, and had built them a synagogue. Jesus proceeded towards the house in which the servant lay, when He was stopped by a message from the centurion, saying that he was not worthy that the Lord should enter into his house, and that, if He would but speak a word, his servant would be cured. Jesus spoke that word, and the servant began to mend from that hour. Then Jesus turned round to the people who were following Him, and said, 'I say unto you, I have not found such great FAITH, no, not in Israel.'[2]

Now who was the centurion who showed such admirable faith? He was clearly not a Jew. The Jews of Capernaum said, 'He loves our nation,' but they never said that he belonged to their nation. He might love the Jews, and admire their worship of one God; but he was probably a pagan, frequenting the temples of Jupiter, and worshipping the image of the

[1] St. John, chap. iv.   [2] St. Luke, chap. vii.

reigning Emperor. What he acknowledged in Jesus was a power derived from God which enabled Him to cure disease and restore the dying to life and health.

Of the same kind of faith were most of those who were cured of infirmities, and even raised from the dead, by Jesus.

The mother of Peter's wife, whom Jesus cured of a fever, must have been a Jewess. The two blind men who followed Him, and who called out, 'Thou Son of David, have mercy on us,' were evidently Jews. When they were come into the house, Jesus said unto them, ' Believe ye that I am able to do this ? ' They said unto Him, ' Yea, Lord.' Then touched He their eyes, saying, 'According to your FAITH be it unto you.' And their eyes were opened. It is clear that these men, being Jews, believed that Christ was endowed by God with miraculous power. But it may be said that the power of performing miracles was exercised by Christ in order to convince men of his divine mission, and that afterwards, when his authority was established, He would reveal to them that the Father was God, the Son was God, and the Holy Spirit was God, and yet there were not three Gods, but one God. That likewise he would teach that a man must, in order to have Christian faith, neither confound the persons nor divide the substance. In fact, however, the whole teaching of Christ forbids any such supposition. Let us observe, for instance, what, according to St. Mark, He said to the scribe who asked Him, ' Which is the first commandment of all ? And Jesus answered him : The first of all the commandments is, Hear, O Israel; the Lord our God is one Lord : and thou shalt love the Lord thy God with all thy heart, and with all thy soul, and with all thy mind, and with all thy strength : this is the first commandment. And the second is like, namely, this, Thou shalt love thy neighbour as thyself. There is none other commandment greater than these. And the scribe said unto Him, Well, Master, Thou hast said the truth : for there is but one God ; and there is none other but He : and to love Him with all the heart, and with all the understanding, and with all the soul, and with all the strength, and to love his neighbour as himself, is more than all whole burnt offerings and sacrifices. And when Jesus saw that he answered discreetly, He said unto him, Thou art not far from the kingdom of God.' [1]

The same or another dialogue is related by St. Luke. ' And, behold, a certain lawyer stood up, and tempted Him, saying, Master, what shall I do to inherit eternal life ? He said unto him, What is written in the law ? how readest thou ? And he answering said, Thou shalt love the Lord thy God with all thy heart, and with all thy soul, and with all thy strength, and with all thy mind ; and thy neighbour as thyself. And He said unto him, Thou hast answered right : this do, and thou shalt live.' [2] Comparing this narrative with the relation of St. Mark, the words ' Thou shalt live ' must mean ' Thou shalt inherit eternal life.' Can we suppose that this scribe or lawyer, who held two simple articles of faith, was not far from the king-

[1] St. Mark, chap. xii.   [2] St. Luke, chap. x.

dom of God, and yet that the future disciples of Christ were to be deprived of entrance into that kingdom unless they embraced a number of difficult and almost unintelligible propositions? Is it not clear that the man to whom it was said, ' Thou art not far from the kingdom of God,' and to whom a promise was given, ' This do, and thou shalt live,' wanted only the performance of good works to inherit eternal life? Yet what was he but a Jew—a scribe? To a Jew and a scribe, therefore, was promised by Christ the kingdom of heaven. Other parts of the Gospel, although not so clearly directed to the question of salvation, tend to the same purpose, showing the immense charity, the inexhaustible benevolence, the expansive spirit of religion and humanity which pervade the teachings of Jesus.

Having thus shown to pagans and Jews the meaning of faith, Jesus confessed that He was Christ, the Son of God, sent by Him on a mission to mankind, and as such empowered and commissioned to teach a new religion. For although God had made Himself known by his creation of the world, and all the wisest men of Athens and of Rome had recognised the supreme and omnipotent God, the Maker of heaven and earth, there was more to be done. Let us consider, then, what was that work which deserved and required a special revelation.

There are two passions implanted by God in his human creatures, which are necessary to the continuance and preservation of the species. The one of these is the love between the sexes. Without this

passion, the species would expire. The other passion
is resentment. Without this passion, a man would not
defend his person, his wife, his children, the hut in
which he dwells, and the spot of ground he culti-
vates.

But, essential as these two passions are, it is of the
nature of man to misuse all the gifts of God, to pervert
them to wrong purposes, to employ them for the
destruction instead of the preservation of the human
race.

From the first of these passions arise jealousy,
adultery, community of women, divorce, the disuse of
marriage, and the prevalence of prostitution.

From the second arise quarrels, feuds, hatreds,
continued from generation to generation, war and
desolation, conquest and slavery.

It was apparently the aim of Jesus Christ, armed
with the authority of God the Father, to restrain
these passions in the human bosom, rebuking the
unholy desires which lead to infringement of the commandments, to adultery and to murder.

There can be no doubt that if these precepts were
followed—if men were to check the indulgence of
these passions, to live in purity and chastity till their
marriage, and then to be faithful to the partners they
have chosen,[1] to give an enlarged sense to the precept,
'Those whom God hath joined together, let not man
put asunder,' to avoid act or conversation which

---

[1] Felices ter et amplius
Quos irrupta tenet copula.
.   Hor. Odes, lib. i. 13.

might break or weaken or tend to the violation of the
marriage tie—much crime would be spared to mankind,
the *casta domus* would be sanctified, and the legitimacy
of offspring assured, while the harmony of private life
would tend to the peace and happiness of the whole
community. In like manner, if men would imbibe the
qualities of meekness, gentleness, and brotherly love,
and perform such acts as peacemaking and forgiveness, which are recommended so emphatically in the
Sermon on the Mount—if they would refrain from
trespassing against others, and forgive those who
trespass against them, quarrels and ill-will would
either not arise, or would die out for want of aliment.
A man who has injured his neighbour, and finds that
injury returned, nourishes his resentment, and finally
yields his whole soul to the pursuit of hatred and
revenge. If, on the contrary, the trespass he has
committed is forgiven, he cannot but feel that he is in
the wrong, and though he may never repair the injury
there is something within him which makes him seek
by peaceable conduct to put an end to strife. Such,
then, was the scope and end of the teaching of Christ ;
the burden of the repeated precepts in the Sermon
on the Mount ; the moral of the parable of the unforgiving servant, and the whole purport of the prayer
to God to forgive us our trespasses as we forgive them
that trespass against us.

It will be observed that Christ never taught that all
men are equally sinners, and that all are involved
in condemnation until some conspicuous act, some
remarkable conversion, some heart-rending moment

of contrition and repentance, shall seal their entrance
into the community of Christians. On the contrary
Jesus proclaimed, 'I come not to call the righteous,
but sinners to repentance.' Thus also when he contrasted His own association with publicans and sinners,
with the preaching of John in the desert, He added,
'But wisdom is justified of all her children.' In
describing the joy with which the shepherd welcomed
his lost sheep, He says nothing to stigmatise the
ninety-nine which had not gone astray. But still
more emphatically, when the elder brother of the
prodigal son feels some natural soreness at the sight
of the fatted calf prepared for his penitent brother,
the father does not tell him that he also has sinned,
and that he also must fall at his father's feet, and
confess his offences ; on the contrary, he says to the
son who has been always clear of offence, and had
not transgressed any of his commandments, 'Son, thou
art always with me, and all that I have is thine.' [1]

Nothing in Christ's teaching shows more clearly
that, while sinners could by repentance obtain forgiveness, the righteous needed no repentance, than the
words, ' All that I have is thine.'

Thus we have recorded, not without comment,
that the revelation of Jesus—which held out such
glorious hopes to the righteous, and which promised
to the Jew who loved God with all his soul, and
who loved his neighbour as himself, immortal life—
opened a way of safety even to the fallen from virtue,
in the harbour of repentance. Thus to the woman

[1] St. Luke, chap. xv.

taken in adultery, of whose guilt there could be no doubt, Christ said, when her judges had slunk away, 'Neither do I condemn thee; go and sin no more.'

Still more striking is the foregoing parable, of which the circumstances were feigned by Jesus Himself, as an example of the boundless forgiveness of God. The prodigal son was not a thoughtless youth, who in a moment of weakness had fallen into sin. Being one of two sons, he had said to his father, 'Father! give me the portion of goods that falleth to me;' and when he had got his portion he went into a far country, and spent his substance in riotous living and among harlots. It was on this man, thus deliberately dissolute and wilfully depraved, that, when he returned and said to his father, 'Father, I have sinned against heaven, and in thy sight, and am no more worthy to be called thy son,' the crown of repentance was bestowed. The lord and father said to his servants, 'My son was dead, and is alive again.' He declared to his elder and faultless son, 'Thy brother was dead, and is alive again.'

When the gate was thus opened to the repentant sinner, it was made an essential condition that sin should be renounced, that the sinner should sin no more, and that the subsequent life of the forgiven should justify the act of forgiveness. The sinful woman, the prodigal son, were still liable to temptation, and resistance to that temptation was necessary, in order to the validity of the pardon.

In the same spirit those against whom a trespass was committed, were ordered to forgive those who

C

trespassed against them. The parable on this subject describes a debtor, to whom a debt of ten thousand talents is forgiven, and who refuses to forgive a debt of a hundred pence. In this proportion are arrayed the magnitude of human offences against God, and the trifling amount of man's offences against his neighbour. Thus the duty of forgiveness is inculcated, and in the punishment of the unforgiving is held out a warning to those who, seeking pardon from God, refuse to pardon the offences of their neighbours towards themselves.

Repeatedly is inculcated the doctrine of forgiveness of injuries. It is stated in the emphatic and striking manner of the East; in the Sermon on the Mount, giving a picture instead of a precept, and conveying the spirit, rather than prescribing the limit, of the Divine command—'Ye have heard that it hath been said, an eye for an eye, and a tooth for a tooth ; but I say unto you, that ye resist not evil, but whosoever shall smite thee on thy right cheek, turn to him the other also. And if any man will sue thee at the law, and take away thy coat, let him have thy cloak also.'

Here we see the example and the warning. The return we are told to make is not sacrifice, or the blood of oxen or of goats; not praise, for God has no need of our sacrifices or our homage ; but that we should show the same merciful spirit, the same forgiving and loving temper, which God has manifested towards us. The same lesson is repeated in the Lord's Prayer, 'Forgive us our trespasses (or our debts), as we forgive them who trespass towards us (or are our

debtors).' Yet more emphatically in the Gospel of
St. Matthew it is recorded, that, after teaching the
Lord's Prayer, Christ added, 'For if ye forgive men
their trespasses, your heavenly Father will also forgive
you; but if ye forgive men not their trespasses, *neither
will your Father forgive your trespasses.*'

Eternal life is thus placed before us as the recompense of forgiveness. But the reward is in fact
for this world, as well as for the next. Resentment
begets resentment; he who has exacted the utmost
farthing excites the enmity he displays; thus ill-will,
quarrels, disputes, wars are generated. A meek and
merciful spirit, on the other hand, turns away wrath,
and in this mode a blood feud may be staunched in
the beginning, and peace and good-will upon earth
prevail, as the song of the angels had foretold.

It remains that we should try to gather from the
Scriptures the nature and extent of the authority from
which the religion of Christ claimed its sacred sanction.

The Gospel of St. John furnishes us with the best
evidence on this subject. John was the disciple whom
Jesus loved; he was a witness of his conversations
with the Jews who hated Him, and with the followers
who believed in Him; to him Jesus confided the care of
his mother; to him was granted a long life, and leisure
to write both the narrative of the life of Christ, and
epistles to explain the doctrines of his Great Master.

In the tenth chapter of the Gospel of St. John it is
written: 'And it was at Jerusalem, the feast of the
dedication, and it was winter, and Jesus walked in the
temple in Solomon's porch. Then came the Jews

round about him, and said, How long dost Thou make us to doubt? If Thou be the Christ, tell us plainly. Jesus answered them, I told you and ye believed not; the works that I do in my Father's name, they bear witness of me. But ye believe not, because ye are not of my sheep, as I said unto you. My sheep hear my voice, I know them and they follow Me; and I give unto them eternal life: and they shall never perish, neither shall any man pluck them out of my Father's hand. I and my Father are one. Then the Jews took up stones again, to stone Him. Jesus answered them, Many good works have I showed you from my Father; for which of those works do ye stone Me? The Jews answered Him, saying, For a good work we stone Thee not, but for blasphemy, and because that Thou being a man, makest Thyself God. Jesus answered them, Is it not written in your law, I said, Ye are gods? If he called them gods, unto whom the word of God came, and the Scripture cannot be broken; say ye of Him, whom the Father hath sanctified, and sent into the world, Thou blasphemest; because I said, I am the Son of God? If I do not the works of my Father, believe Me not. But if I do, though ye believe not Me, believe the works; that ye may know, and believe, that the Father is in Me, and I in Him.'[1]

In the fourteenth chapter of St. John, when He knew that his hour was come, Judas said unto Him, not Iscariot, but the faithful Judas, 'Lord, how is it that Thou wilt manifest Thyself unto us, and not unto the

[1] St. John, chap. x.

world.' After some words of comfort, Jesus said, 'Peace I leave with you, my peace I give unto you; not as the world giveth, give I unto you. Let not your heart be troubled, neither let it be afraid. Ye have heard how I said unto you, I go away and come again unto you. If ye loved Me, ye would rejoice, because I said, I go unto the Father: *for my Father is greater than I.* And now I have told you, before it come to pass, that when it is come to pass, ye might believe. Hereafter, I will not talk much with you; for the prince of this world cometh, and hath nothing in Me. But that the world may know that I love the Father; and as the Father gave Me commandment, even so I do. Arise, let us go hence.'[1]

In the sixteenth chapter of the same gospel it is recorded that Jesus, when his disciples, talking among themselves, said, 'What is this that He saith unto us, A little while and ye shall not see Me; and again a little while and ye shall see Me; and because I go to my Father?' Jesus then openly declared his meaning: 'These things have I spoken to you in proverbs; but the time cometh when I shall no more speak to you in proverbs, but I shall show you plainly of the Father. At that day ye shall ask in my name, and I say not unto you, that I will pray the Father for you; for the Father Himself loveth you, because ye have loved Me, and have believed that I came out from God. I came forth from the Father, and am come into the world; again I leave the world, and go to the Father.' His disciples said unto Him, 'Lo, now Thou speakest

[1] St. John, chap. xiv. ver. 31.

plainly, and speakest no proverb. Now are we sure that Thou knowest all things, and needest not that any man should ask Thee; by this we believe that Thou comest forth from God.'[1] The peculiar merit, therefore, of St. John's Gospel is that he discards the imperfect teaching of Peter, and gives the very words of Christ, brought to his remembrance by the Holy Ghost.

The first thing we should wish to learn, in consulting the Gospel of John, is the character assumed by Christ Himself, whether in addressing the Jews, or in pouring out his last thoughts to his intimate disciples. To this end was the declaration of Christ. We cannot but be struck with the consistency of this declaration, whether made to the Jews his enemies, or to his faithful and intimate disciples—the unity of God, declared by Moses, 'I am the. Lord thy God, thou shalt have none other Gods but Me;' a doctrine embraced by Socrates, by Plato, by Cicero, and by the most enlightened of the Pagans; this doctrine was combined with faith in Jesus as the Christ, uttering the commands of God, the Son of God, but always acknowledging 'the Father is greater than I.' The religion thus revealed taught worship of one God, love of man, purity of life, forgiveness of sins upon repentance and amendment, rejection of ceremonial observances, the doctrine that the sabbath was made for man, and not man for the sabbath, that not the meat which goeth into the mouth defileth a man, but the word which cometh out of the mouth.

. This religion, thus simple and thus sublime, was

[1] St. John, chap. xvi.

sealed and attested by the death of Christ. Not that He showed in his behaviour when about to die the philosophic equanimity of Socrates, the patriotic serenity of Regulus, or the proud defiance of Algernon Sidney. His nature was gentle, loving, bursting with affection for the human kind. When the fact of the death of Lazarus was told Him, 'Jesus wept.' Now his prayer showed the depth of a heart touched with human emotions, but resigned to the decrees of God. 'And he was withdrawn from them about a stone's cast, and kneeled down and prayed, Father, if Thou be willing, remove this cup from Me; nevertheless, not my will, but thine be done.'[1]

The beginning of this prayer showed that in Christ the human nature still had so much power that, if the redemption of the world could have been gained without his death upon the cross, He would have been rejoiced at such a consummation. The end of the prayer, 'Nevertheless, not my will, but thine be done,' is beyond all admiration; and was recorded, no doubt, as an example of humility and submission to all the Christian brotherhood. For this purpose also He sent the Comforter: 'But when the Comforter is come, whom I will send unto you from the Father, even the Spirit of truth, which proceedeth from the Father, He shall testify of Me, and ye also shall bear witness, because ye have been with Me from the beginning.'[2]

This was, in effect, a promise that the inspiration of the Holy Spirit should guide those who had been with Christ from the beginning, and should dictate to them

---

[1] St. Luke, chap. xxii.   [2] Ib. chap. xv.

the lessons He had taught, and the words He had used.

The crucifixion completed the sacrifice of Christ for the welfare of mankind. After that event, when the eleven Apostles were gathered together, and spake with those who had seen Jesus, He Himself 'stood in the midst of them, and saith unto them, Peace be unto you. But they were terrified and affrighted, and supposed that they had seen a spirit. And He said unto them, Why are ye troubled? And why do thoughts arise in your hearts? Behold my hands and my feet, that it is I Myself; handle Me and see ; for a spirit hath not flesh and bones as ye see me have. And when He had thus spoken, He showed them his hands and his feet.'[1]

The eleven after this preached Christ crucified, and repeated in Asia, and in Europe, the story of his resurrection from the dead.

The religion of Christ has three main foundations :— 1. God is a Spirit, the Maker of heaven and earth. 2. Christ was sent from God, and revealed to men the message of God. When John the Baptist sent to Christ two of his disciples to ask of Him, ' Art thou He that should come, or do we look for another ? ' Christ answered and said unto them, ' Go and show John again those things that ye do hear and see ; the blind receive their sight, and the lame walk, the lepers are cleansed, and the deaf hear, the dead are raised up, and the poor have the gospel preached to them.'[2] 3. Christ died for mankind. The miracles of Christ were per-

---

[1] St. Luke, chap. xxiv.   [2] St. Matthew, chap. xi.

formed by Him, and ended with his life. The gift of miracles was continued to his Apostles, as we are informed in the Acts of the Apostles. This power, however, ceased altogether after the third century. 'But the poor have the gospel preached to them' to this day.

ESSAY III.

ST. PETER. ST. JOHN. ST. PAUL.

WHEN Jesus was about to be dragged away to prison
and to death, Peter was the one of his disciples who
protested most strongly that he would not desert his
Master. But the Lord said to him, ' Before the cock
crow twice, thou shalt deny me thrice.' It happened
as the Lord had said. On the third time, when they
that stood by said to Peter, 'Surely thou art one of
them, for thou art a Galilean, and thy speech agreeth
thereto,' he began to curse and to swear, saying, 'I
know not this man of whom ye speak.'[1] But when the
cock crowed a second time, and he thought thereon, he
wept bitterly.

It might be supposed that a man so infirm of purpose, and so unstable in his attachment to his Divine
Master, would be the most unfit person to assume the
headship of the Apostles. But ' Wisdom is justified of
all her children.' Our Saviour perceived in Simon Peter
a spirit of conciliation, and of humility in his estimate
of his own abilities, as well as a capacity to adopt the
better reason of others, when his own reason would
prefer the worse, which made him worthy of the Lord's
immortal words, ' Thou art Peter, and upon this rock
will I build my Church.' This, be it observed, was an

[1] St. Matthew, chap. xxvi.

authority given to Peter alone. It was not said or implied that his successors should have like powers, or even that he should have any successors. He was not even the first Bishop of Jerusalem ; James the brother of John had that title and authority. Yet he was during his life revered, and followed as the Apostle chosen by Jesus to be the founder of his Church.

St. John says in the second chapter of his First Epistle General, ' And if any man sin, we have an advocate with the Father, Jesus Christ, the righteous, and He is the propitiation for our sins ; and not for ours only, but also for the sins of the whole world. And hereby do we know that we know Him, if we keep his commandments. He that saith, I know Him, and keepeth not his commandments, is a liar, and the truth is not in him.' [1]

Again : ' And this is his commandment, that we should believe on the name of his son Jesus Christ, and love one another, as He gave us commandment.' [2] So also, ' Beloved, if God so loved us, we ought also to love one another ; no man hath seen God at any time. If we love one another, God dwelleth in us, and his love is perfected in us.'

This commandment ' that we should love one another ' John is never weary of repeating. ' If a man say, I love God, and hateth his brother, he is a liar, for he that loveth not his brother whom he hath seen, how can he love God whom he hath not seen ? And this commandment have we from Him, That he who loveth God, loveth his brother also.' [3]

[1] St. John, 1 Ep. Gen. chap. ii,   [2] Ib. chap. iii.   [3] Ib. chap. iv.

We may here admit 'the pleasing tradition that when he (St. John) grew so feeble from age as to be unable to utter any long discourse, his last (if we may borrow the expression), his cycnean voice dwelt on a brief exhortation to mutual charity. His whole sermon consisted in these words: "Little children, love one another;" and when his audience remonstrated at the wearisome iteration of the same words, he declared that in these words was contained the whole substance of Christianity.'[1]

Yet as Peter was unequal to a work requiring great energy and indefatigable labour, and as John retired early to Ephesus, some other instrument was required to accomplish the mighty task of changing the religion of the Roman empire. That which Divine Wisdom proposed to be done, Divine Foresight prepared the means to do.

Paul was a Jew of Tarsus, circumcised on the eighth day, a Pharisee of the strictest sect, impassioned in all he undertook, a man gifted with energy, with sincerity, with indefatigable powers of work, and with unconquerable eloquence. He had persecuted the Christians, and when certain Jews stoned Stephen he kept their clothes. The story of Paul's conversion may best be told in the words of Paul himself pronounced on a solemn occasion. Festus, the Roman governor, being at Cæsarea, Paul was brought before him on the accusation of the Jews. He appealed to Cæsar. Shortly afterwards King Agrippa and Queen Bernice went to Cæsarea to salute Festus. Festus

---

[1] Milman's *History of Christianity.*

thought it right that Paul should be heard, and speaking to King Agrippa said, ' There is a certain man left in bonds by Felix, about whom, when I was at Jerusalem, the chief priests and elders of the Jews informed me, desiring to have judgment against him, to whom I answered, It is not the manner of the Romans to give up any man before that he which is accused have the accuser face to face, and have licence to answer for himself concerning the crime laid against him. Therefore, when they were come hither, without any delay, on the morrow I sat on the judgment-seat, and commanded the man to be brought forth, against whom, when the accusers stood up, they brought none accusation of such things as I supposed, but had certain questions against him of their own religion, and of one Jesus, which was dead, whom Paul affirmed to be alive.' Agrippa said to Festus, ' I would also hear the man myself.' On the morrow Agrippa, in open court, said unto Paul, ' Thou art permitted to speak for thyself.' Then Paul stretched forth the hand, and answered for himself: 'I think myself happy, King Agrippa, because I shall answer for myself this day before thee touching all the things whereof I am accused of the Jews, especially because thou art expert in all customs and questions which are among the Jews ; wherefore I beseech thee to hear me patiently. My manner of life from my youth, which was from the first among my own nation at Jerusalem, know all the' Jews ; which knew me from the beginning, if they would testify, that after the most strictest sect of our religion, I lived a Pharisee. And now I stand and am

judged for the hope of the promise made of God unto
our fathers, unto which *promise* our twelve tribes, instantly serving *God* night and day, hope to come. For
which hope's sake, O king, I am accused of the Jews.
Why should it be thought a thing incredible of you that
God should raise the dead ? I verily thought with myself that I ought to do many things contrary to the name
of Jesus of Nazareth, which thing I did also in Jerusalem ; and many of the saints did I shut up in prison,
having received authority from the chief priests ; and
when they were put to death, I gave my vote against
them. And I punished them oft in every synagogue,
and compelled them to blaspheme ; and, being exceedingly mad against them, I persecuted them even unto
strange cities. Wherefore, as I went to Damascus
with authority and commission from the chief priests,
at midday, O king, I saw in the way a light from
heaven, above the brightness of the sun, shining round
about me, and them which journeyed with me. And
when we were all fallen to the earth, I heard a voice
saying unto me, in the Hebrew tongue, Saul, Saul,
why persecutest thou Me? It is hard for thee to
kick against the pricks. And I said, Who art Thou,
Lord? And he said, I am Jesus, whom thou persecutest; but rise, stand upon thy feet, for I have appeared unto thee for this purpose, to make thee a
minister and a witness, both of these things which
thou hast seen, and of those things which will appear
unto thee, delivering thee from the people and from
the Gentiles, unto whom I send thee, to open their
eyes, that they may turn from darkness to light, and

from the power of Satan unto God, that they may receive forgiveness of sins, and inheritance among them
which are sanctified by faith that is in me. Wherefore, King Agrippa, I was not disobedient unto the
heavenly vision, but showed first unto them of Damascus, and Jerusalem, and throughout all the country of
Judæa, and to the Gentiles, that they should repent
and turn to God, and do works worthy of their repentance. For these causes the Jews caught me in the
temple, and endeavoured to kill me. Having, therefore, obtained help of God, I continue unto this day,
witnessing both to small and great, saying none other
things than those which the prophets and Moses did
say should come; if at least Christ was liable to suffering and first rising from the dead, was to show light
unto the people, and to the Gentiles.'[1]

This striking narrative has in it many things remarkable. First, the justice of the Roman law, which
would not allow any man to be condemned unless his
accusers were brought face to face before him, and
unless he were allowed to make his own defence in
person. Secondly, the art of Paul in praising the
learning of King Agrippa, and in appealing to the
Pharisees, as if the only accusation against him were
that, like the Pharisees, he believed that the dead
should rise again. Thirdly, the wonderful clearness
and precision of the narrative. The words, ' it is hard
for thee to kick against the pricks,' taken from a common Greek and Roman proverb, alluding to oxen
kicking against a goad, or horses kicking against a

[1] Acts, chap. xxvi.

spur, seems to imply that Paul had already felt some pricking of his conscience at sight of the martyrdom of the good and pious men whom he had persecuted. This pricking of his conscience has always struck me as the fit prelude to the heavenly vision which he saw at mid-day. A sermon which I once heard from Sydney Smith in the cathedral of St. Paul's enumerated powerfully the circumstances of this miraculous conversion.

We know that from this time Paul became the most effective preacher of the Christian faith in Central Asia. Here, as he recounts in his Epistle to the Galatians—' But when Peter was come to Antioch, I withstood him to the face, because he was to be blamed. For before that certain came from James he did eat with the Gentiles; but when they were come he withdrew and separated himself, fearing them which were of the circumcision.[1]

Seeing how Peter turned and shrank from asserting his independent action, when James, the brother of Jesus Christ, sent certain to him, it is clear that a man of so weak a character, brought up in the scanty learning of a fisherman, afraid to own his Master and Saviour, when he was in danger of his life, would never have had the spirit to vindicate the faith of Jesus. Had he been left uncontradicted, Peter would, in all probability, have sunk into a Jewish sectary, sometimes professing that Christ had risen from the dead, but never asserting his faith manfully or becoming the Apostle of the Gentiles. But when Paul, learned in

[1] Galatians, chap. ii.

all the law of Moses, who had sat at the feet of
Gamaliel, and who combined with accurate and extensive learning a bold and intrepid spirit, was chosen
to preach Christ crucified, then indeed a new religion
was spread over the world, and the Cross was triumphant. It cannot be denied, however, that the arguments
by which the Christian religion was perverted from a
revealed law of love, given by God to man, into
a subtle metaphysical theory respecting the nature of
the Trinity and Christ's substance, were partly derived
from the epistles of St. Paul. But although St. Paul
has said things 'hard to be understood,' there is no
one of the Apostles who has insisted more strongly on
the necessity of righteousness, and of the fruits of the
Spirit, 'love, joy, peace, long-suffering, kindness, goodness, faith, mildness, self-control.' A short account of
his teaching will prove that this is a just view of the
character of St. Paul. If any one wishes to study
farther this question, I would refer him to the excellent work of Mr. Matthew Arnold, entitled 'St.
Paul and Protestantism.'

It should be observed that in teaching various
bodies of Christians assembled at Ephesus, in Galatia,
at Corinth, at Philippi, at Colossæ, and at Rome, Paul
found it necessary to repeat the same doctrines, and
often in the same words. But to us these repetitions
are most useful, as they not only make the meaning
of Paul clearer, but point out to us the parts of
Christian doctrine on which he thought it essential
most frequently and most earnestly to insist.

The doctrine taught by St. Paul, though often in-

volved in unnecessary obscurity and lengthened by
innumerable parentheses, may be deduced clearly from
the epistles he has written. He maintains :—1. That
the Gentiles, refusing to know the supreme God, became subject to sin. Thus in the first chapter of the
Epistle to the Romans he says, 'And even as they
did not choose to retain God in their knowledge, God
gave them up to a reprobate mind, to do the things
which are not fit to be done, being filled with all
unrighteousness, wickedness, covetousness, malicious-
ness, full of envy, murder, strife, malignity, whisperers,
slanderers, haters of God, insolent, proud, boasters,
desirers of evil things, disobedient to parents, without
understanding, covenant breakers, without natural
affection, unmerciful, men who, knowing well the
righteous judgment of God, that they which do such
things are worthy of death, not only commit the same,
but also consent to them that do them.'[1]

Then describing the result of Christ's passion and
resurrection, Paul says, 'Know ye not that to whom-
soever ye yield yourselves servants to obey, his servants ye are whom ye obey; whether it be of sin
unto death, or of obedience unto righteousness? But
thanks be to God that ye were [once] servants of
sin, but ye obeyed from the heart the form of doctrine,
whereunto ye were delivered; and being made free
from sin, ye were made servants to righteousness. I
speak after the manner of men, because of the infirmity of your flesh ; for as ye yielded your members
servants to uncleanness, and to iniquity unto iniquity ;

[1] Alford's New Testament.

so now yield your members servants to righteousness unto sanctification. For when ye were servants of sin, ye were free in regard to righteousness. . . . But now being made free from sin and made servants to God, ye have your fruit unto sanctification, and the end everlasting life.'[1] Indeed there is no one of the Apostles of Christ who dwells so frequently, so repeatedly, so strongly. on the duties of morality as St. Paul. Could he believe that the greater part of his hearers were unable to perform those duties? that they were banished before their birth from all hope of seeing God? that his lessons would be to them utterly vain and useless? It would be absurd to indulge such a supposition.

These passages contain the whole of the doctrines of Paul. He never speaks of the old Pagan times without coupling with them disbelief in God ; he never speaks of the Christian dispensation without its fruit, righteousness, love, joy, peace, everlasting life.

The error of those who have wrested the words of Paul to their own condemnation is, that they have separated the two things, faith and righteousness, which Paul kept in all his teachings united and inseparable. They have erected an idol of faith without its fruits, and have disjoined righteousness and everlasting life. A greater or more fatal perversion of the Apostle's doctrine could not be. On the subject of foreknowledge and predestination St. Paul says, ' Moreover we know that to them that love God all things work together for good, to them who are called according to

[1] Alford's New Testament, Romans, chap. i. vol. ii. part 1, pp. 51, 52.

[his] purpose. Because whom He foreknew them He also pre-ordained to bear the likeness of the image of his Son, that He might be the firstborn among many brethren ; and whom He pre-ordained, them He also called ; and whom He called, them He also justified ; and whom He justified, them He also glorified.'[1]

This text has been the cause of much difference of opinion. 'Those He foreknew would believe' is the sense accepted by Origen, Chrysostom, and Augustine. The sense of adopted, 'whereby God has ever distinguished his sons from the wicked,' is the meaning according to Calvin, who teaches that the words imply not mere prescience, as some persons ignorantly suppose. What seems certain is, that mere prescience is the only sense consistent with the free will of man. Yet to reconcile logically free will and foreknowledge, is a task above human faculties.

What St. Paul meant precisely it is difficult to discover, but we cannot imagine or infer that he meant to differ from the declaration of our Lord Jesus Christ, who in the Sermon on the Mount proclaimed, 'Not every one that saith unto me Lord, Lord, shall enter into the kingdom of heaven, but he that doeth the will of my Father which is in heaven.'[2] These words evidently suppose that men can, by the exercise of their own free will, do the will of God. Thus the whole doctrine of predestination, in the sense that some men are born to be eternally punished, whatever

[1] Alford's New Testament, Paul's Epistle to the Romans, chap. viii. The quotations from St. Paul are all from Alford's Revised Version in his New Testament.

[2] St. Matthew, chap. vii.

they may do, is explicitly and by anticipation condemned by Christ.

From this summary, however brief and imperfect,
it appears that the religion taught by Christ and
by his Evangelists, Matthew, Mark, Luke, and John,
agreed with the religion taught by Paul, an apostle
joined by revelation to the Apostles of Christ.

It appears, moreover, that the religion thus taught
to the Roman world conveyed to mankind the great
truth, that there is one God, the Maker of heaven and
earth. It taught, moreover, that Christ was the only
Son of God, sent by God upon the earth, and crucified
at Jerusalem in the reign of Tiberius. By the lessons
revealed to mankind, by natural and revealed religion,
men were taught to love God with all their hearts,
and their brethren as themselves. To the righteous
was promised eternal life, and to the penitent who
led a new life, admission to the happiness promised to
the righteous.

It has been said that, as St. Paul was the Apostle
of Faith, St. John was the Apostle of Love. But this
is not the true distinction. St. Paul said that all the
commandments were condensed in this, ' Love one
another ;' and when he said, ' These three, Faith, Hope,
and Love,' he added not, the greatest of these is Faith,
but ' the greatest of these is Love.'[1]

We may now proceed to some of the most remarkable of St. Paul's Epistles.

The Epistle of St. Paul to the Galatians, as it is one of

[1] See Dean Stanley's *St. Paul*; Epistles to the Corinthians, chap.
xiii. ; and the *Commentary*, p. 239.

the earliest, so also it is one of the most important of the epistles of that great Apostle of the Gentiles.

Galatia, as it is described by historians, was a district in the northern part of Asia Minor, occupied by a mingled population. The descendants of the Gaulish invaders, from whom the region derived its name, retained to a late period vestiges of their original race in the Celtic dialect, and evidently great numbers of Jews had settled in those quarters. Paul twice visited the country; and his epistle was written, probably, at no long period after his second visit. There are no more authentic works, in all the literature of Greece and Rome, than the greater part of the epistles of Paul.[1] The Epistle to the Galatians begins with some account of the gospel which Paul preached, and the manner in which he had received it.

' I certify you, brethren, that the gospel which was preached of me is not after man. For I neither received it of man, neither was I taught it, but by the revelation of Jesus Christ. For ye have heard of my conversation in time past in the Jews' religion, how that, beyond measure, I persecuted the Church of God and wasted it; and profited of the Jews' religion above many mine equals in mine own nation, being more exceedingly zealous of the traditions of my fathers. But when it pleased God, who separated me from my mother's womb, and called me by his grace to reveal his Son in me, that I might preach Him among the heathen; immediately I conformed not with flesh

[1] Alford's New Testament; Paley; Milman's *Christianity.* Dean Stanley's Apostolical Sermons.

and blood, neither went I up to Jerusalem to them
which were Apostles before me; but I went into
Arabia, and returned again to Damascus. Then, after
three years, I went up to Jerusalem to see Peter, and
abode with him fifteen days. But other of the Apostles
saw I none, save James the Lord's brother.'
Again, in the second chapter, he relates as follows :
' Then fourteen years after, I went up again to Jerusalem with Barnabas, and took Titus with me also.
. . . But neither Titus, who was with me, being
a Greek, was compelled to be circumcised . . .
they who seemed to be somewhat in conference added
nothing to me ; but contrariwise, when they saw that
the gospel of the uncircumcision was committed to me,
as the gospel of the circumcision was unto Peter (for
He that wrought effectually in Peter to the apostle-
ship of the circumcision, the same was mighty in me
towards the Gentiles), and when James, Cephas, and
John, who seemed to be pillars, perceived the grace
that was given unto me, they gave to me and Barnabas
the right hand of fellowship ; that we should go unto
the heathen, and they unto the circumcision.'[1]
Having thus established his title to be the Apostle of
the Gentiles, he shows in a subsequent passage how he
asserted that title, and how he sought to unite the converts of the circumcision and the converts of the Gentiles in one body of the Church. ' But when Peter
was come to Antioch, I withstood him to the face, because he was to be blamed. For before that certain
came from James, he did eat with the Gentiles ; but,

[1] Galatians, chap. ii.

when they were come, he withdrew and separated himself, fearing them which were of the circumcision. And the other Jews dissembled likewise with him ; insomuch that Barnabas also was carried away with their dissimulation.   But when I saw that they walked not uprightly, according to the truth of the gospel, I said unto Peter before them all, " If thou, being a Jew, livest after the manner of Gentiles, and not as do the Jews, why compellest thou the Gentiles to live as do the Jews? "'   Following up this bold remonstrance, he prevailed over the timid and hesitating disposition of Peter, and affirmed with irresistible force, 'I do not frustrate the grace of God, for if righteousness come by the law, then Christ is dead in vain.'[1]

What then was the doctrine which Paul sought to commend to Jews and Gentiles, and thereby to fulfil the commands of Christ, and teach the nations to be Christian?   It is displayed in the remaining chapters of the Epistle to the Galatians.   It was simply that the just should live by faith, and that faith should work by love.   Thus he declares, 'For in Jesus Christ neither circumcision availeth anything, nor uncircumcision, but faith which worketh by love.'[2]

Observe Paul does not say, 'neither circumcision nor uncircumcision, but faith.'   No.   He says, 'faith which worketh by love; ' and he presently explains what love is.   'But the fruit of the Spirit is love, joy, peace, long-suffering, gentleness, goodness, faith, meekness, temperance ; against such there is no law.   And they that are Christ's have crucified the flesh with the affections

---

[1] Galatians, chap. ii.   [2] Ib. chap. v.

and lust.'[1] So, also, in that powerful exhortation to
brotherly love, in the thirteenth chapter of the First
Epistle to the Corinthians, he declares, separating the
common practice of almsgiving from the divine virtue
of brotherly love, that though he were to bestow all
his goods to feed the poor, and give his body to be
burned, and have not brotherly love, it profiteth him
nothing.   Finally, he sums up his exhortation in the
words, 'And now abideth faith, hope, love, these
three; but the greatest of these is love!'[2] It is
astonishing that any one reading these words should
represent to himself Paul as an Apostle who exalts
faith exclusively, above all other Christian virtues.

Again, in that admirable fourteenth chapter of the
Epistle to the Romans we are told, 'the kingdom of
God is not meat and drink, but righteousness, peace,
and joy in the Holy Ghost.' 'Let us, therefore, follow
after things which make for peace, and things where-
with one may edify another.   For meat destroy not
the work of God.'

The religion of which Paul was the Apostle was the
whole religion of Christ; a religion of purity and of
love. 'I seek,' he said, 'to apprehend that for which
also I am apprehended by Christ.' 'As many as are
led by the Spirit of God are the sons of God.' What
he especially taught was the righteousness of God, the
non-fulfilment of it by man, the fulfilment of it by

[1] Galatians, chap. v.
[2] Stanley translates the Greek word, 'love;' Liddell and Scott,
'brotherly love.'   Charity does not now convey the meaning of the
original.

Christ [1]—Christ's life and death. The importance for
us, according to Paul, is that, 'denying ungodliness and
worldly lusts, we should live soberly, righteously, and
godly,' and that we should be able to 'bear fruit to
God,' 'in love, joy, peace, long-suffering, kindness,
goodness, faith, mildness, self-control.' Of Christ's life
and death, the scope was 'to redeem us from all
iniquity, and make us purely zealous for good works.'
What for Paul was life? and what was death? Not
the ordinary physical life and death ; death for him is
living after the flesh, obedience to sin ; life is mortifi-
cation by the Spirit of the deeds of the flesh, obedience
to righteousness. Thus he says to the Colossians, 'If
ye then be risen with Christ, seek the things which are
above.' Elsewhere he says, 'I see a law in my members fighting against the law of my mind, and bringing
me into captivity.'

The complaint of Horace :

> Video meliora proboque
> Deteriora sequor,

is almost literally repeated by St. Paul. But the result
for Horace was to sink into vice ; for Paul to rise into
righteousness.

St. Paul taught that God by his outward works, by
the mechanism of the world, by all things which He
had created, had declared his existence to men without
a special revelation. When he saw an altar at Athens
with the inscription 'To the unknown God,' he burst
upon that vain and superstitious city with the words

---

[1] *St. Paul and Protestantism*, by Matthew Arnold.

echoing from Mars' Hill, 'Whom ye ignorantly worship, Him reveal I unto you.' In his teachings at
Athens, in his Epistle to the Romans, in his Epistles to
the Corinthians, he taught the existence of one God,
the mission of Christ, and the nature of his commandments. Blaming the Romans for living in sin when
Christ had not yet appeared on earth, he said, 'For
the wrath of God is revealed from heaven, against all
ungodliness and unrighteousness of men, who hold the
truth in unrighteousness ; because that which may be
known of God is manifest in them, for God hath
shewed it unto them. For the invisible things of him
from the creation of the world are clearly seen, being
understood by the things that are made, even his
eternal power and Godhead, so that they are without
excuse, because that when they knew God, they glorified him not as God, neither were thankful, but became
vain in their imaginations, and their foolish heart was
darkened. Professing themselves to be wise they became fools, and changed the glory of the uncorruptible
God into an image made like to corruptible men, and
to birds, and to four-footed beasts, and creeping things.'[1]
In this discourse Paul clearly signifies that the things
which are made cause the invisible things of Him to
be clearly seen ; that is to say, that the things that are
made are the proofs of a maker ; that is, a watch signifies a watchmaker ; a palace, a builder; a ship, a
shipwright ; so, by every analogy, by even the most
simple inductive process, the invisible things of God
are clearly seen. Thus have inferred the intelligent ;

[1] Romans, chap. i.

thus have argued the simple, from the things that are made to his eternal power and Godhead.

Having thus shortly stated the inductive proof of the eternal power of God, proving the invisible from the visible, without a special revelation, St. Paul proceeds to show the lamentable state of immorality, corruption, and wickedness, into which men, deceived by their vain imaginations and foolish hearts, had fallen. Having opened to the Romans the designs of God and the atonement of Christ, he sums up the duties of Christians in these words: 'Owe no man, but to love one another; for he that loveth another hath fulfilled the law. For this, Thou shalt not commit adultery; Thou shalt not kill; Thou shalt not steal; Thou shalt not bear false witness; Thou shalt not covet; and if there be any other commandment, it is briefly comprehended in this saying, Thou shalt love thy neighbour as thyself: Love worketh no ill to his neighbour; therefore love is the fulfilling of the law.'[1]

Thus also to the Galatians, after recounting the evil things done by the wicked, he says: 'I forewarn you, as I also forewarned you before, that they which do such things shall not inherit the kingdom of God. But the fruit of the Spirit is love, joy, peace, long-suffering, kindness, goodness, faithfulness, meekness, temperance.'[2]

The most powerful preacher of Christ and of his moral lessons was undoubtedly St. Paul.

Followers of Paul's word, but not of his meaning,

[1] Romans, chap. xiii.   [2] Galatians, chap. v.

have imagined that he taught the doctrine, of a God so angry with man that nothing but the death of his Son could appease his fury. But such is not the doctrine of the Apostle. He taught, indeed, that the death of Christ was a propitiation for the sins of man. But this death was a proof not of the anger, but of the love of God. When the nations were sunk in ease and luxury, overcome by vice, and wrapt in sloth, what could arouse them so powerfully as to hear that the Son of God had appeared on earth, that He had been sent by God to live as a man, but without sin, and that, after a life of blameless purity, He had suffered a death of shame and agony in order to redeem mankind? If the condition of this redemption was love of God and love of man, what motive could be offered to the heathen so powerful, so persuasive, so effective, so certain to carry with it the minds and hearts of the millions of the Roman empire? When Paul preached this doctrine at Derbe, his eloquence induced the people to believe that the god Mercury had appeared among them. We are told by Gibbon of certain prevailing causes of the spread of the Christian religion. But what cause so compelling belief, what doctrine so directly leading to martyrdom as the infusion into men's minds, the invasion into men's hearts of the thought that the Son of God had appeared upon earth, and had suffered death upon the cross for their sakes? It was not then to satisfy the anger or stern justice of God that the GREAT SACRIFICE was made, but that by this offering of a divine life, once given for mankind, the world might be restored from its depth of evil, and Paradise

be regained for the race of Adam. It was therefore
a part of the perversion of the teaching of Christ and
his Apostles, to separate in St. Paul's doctrine faith
from love, and to represent an Apostle who wrote
against all ceremonial observances, all keeping of new
moons, all precise definitions, as the author of a
doctrine which placed in faith alone the perfection
of Christian life. The very words, 'The just shall
live by faith,' expressed very clearly that not all who
had faith should live, but only those who were just
and had faith. Otherwise Paul would have said 'All
who have faith shall live.'

Thus the Christian religion as taught by Christ himself, by Peter, by John, by Paul, is one and the same,
prescribing love to God and love to man. To accept
half this religion is, in the words of Paul, to introduce
'hatred, variance, emulations, wrath, strife, seditions,
heresies, envyings, murders, drunkenness, revellings, and
such like.' Such have been the effects of the corruptions of Christianity, whether introduced by the fanciful
theories of the Fathers, or the inordinate ambition of
the Church of Rome, or the learned errors of Duns
Scotus, of Thomas Aquinas, of Luther, or of Calvin.

It must be noted here, before we leave the first
steps of the Apostles of Christ, that much of the
success obtained in the teaching of all nations, which
He commanded in his last words to his disciples, was
due to the signal abilities and rare faculties of Paul.
He had the vehemence and the fire, and was largely
endowed with the art of an orator, watching the
temper of his audience, and captivating the favour of

his judges. As a moral teacher, he was earnest, strict, and persuasive, but also amply furnished with wisdom and discretion. At Corinth a difficult instance of immorality awaited him. A young man of his congregation had formed a scandalous connexion with his father's wife. Paul pointed out the heinous guilt of such conduct, and at the same time acted with consummate prudence. When he was assured of repentance of the sin, and had obtained the promise of a good life, he did not insist on the expulsion of the sinner from the Christian community. A member of the Order of Jesus could not have shown more tact and discretion in the treatment of a young congregation than was displayed by the eloquent Apostle of the Gentiles.

To the persuasive power which caused him to be taken for the god Mercury; to the sincerity which imbued others with the conviction by which he was himself animated; to the prudence which combined in fellowship and attachment the disciples of Corinth, and of Athens, of Galatia, of Philippi, and of Thessalonia, the rapid progress of the Christian belief in the early days of its propagation, must be in great part attributed.

ESSAY IV.

PROGRESS OF CHRISTIAN RELIGION, TILL THE REIGN OF CONSTANTINE.

A GREAT historian has enumerated and dilated upon what he affirms to be the secondary causes of the prevalence of the Christian religion. But he has nowhere enumerated the primary cause of the belief in a new and startling religion. There can be no doubt that men adopted the belief that, 'In the beginning was the Word, and the Word was with God, and the Word was God.'[1] They believed also that ' the Word was made flesh, and dwelt among us, full of grace and truth.' They likewise believed that Christ was crucified, and that He had power to open the gates of immortal life, to all who should believe on Him, and should obey his commandments. Such a belief was sufficient of itself to spread the Christian faith over the world.

The present essay will contain a rapid sketch of the growth of the Christian Church from the reign of Tiberius to that of Constantine.

The religion of Rome had always been more political

---

[1] The Greek word *logos* means the word by which the inward thought was expressed, and also the inward thought itself. Neither the Latin nor the English language has a word which comprehends both senses. See Liddell and Scott's *Lexicon*.

than religious, and in the time of the empire it became altogether an engine of the state. Persecution was employed, therefore, for the purpose, not of setting up Jupiter, or Mars, or Diana, but in order to deify the reigning emperor, and give him thereby additional influence and authority. When the mob of Ephesus called out, ' Great is Diana of the Ephesians,' the civil magistrate did not support the worship of Diana, or arrest those who contemned her divine character, but rebuked the multitude for the disorder they had caused. The offence of the Christians in the eyes of the Roman governors was not heresy or blasphemy, but sedition ; not an act of disrespect to the gods, but of contempt and irreverence to the emperor. It was in this spirit that Festus, caring little for the name of Christ, or the immortality of the soul, called out to Paul that much learning had made him mad. The carelessness of Gallio has been a favourite subject of reproach on the part of many pious Christians ; but it was owing to men of the stamp of Gallio on the throne of the Cæsars, or on the seats of justice, that Christianity, when not obtruded on the attention of Cæsar, or his organs, grew up in the shade, till it overtopped the Palatine Hill, and surmounted the Capitol. A good instance of the zeal for martyrdom on the part of the Christians, and of the reluctance with which the Roman authorities yielded to the popular thirst for persecution, is exhibited in the story of the death of Polycarp.

Polycarp was the most distinguished Christian of the East ; he had heard the Apostle St. John ; he had preached the doctrines of St. Paul ; he had presided

E

with dignity over the see of Smyrna. When the persecution under Aurelius commenced, it raged with
extreme fury in Asia Minor. Polycarp concealed himself in a village, but two slaves, under the influence of
a bribe, betrayed the place of his retirement. He
exclaimed, 'The will of God be done.' He then
ordered food to be prepared for the officers of justice,
and requested time for prayer, in which he spent two
hours. He was conducted on a day of great public
concourse towards Smyrna. On his way he was met
by Herod the Irenarch, and his father Nicetas, who
with much respect took him into their own carriage.
The Christians imagined they heard a voice from
heaven saying, 'Polycarp, be firm.' On his refusal
to salute the Emperor by the title of Lord, and to
sacrifice to the heathen gods, he was thrust out of the
carriage, and conducted to the stadium. The people
shouted aloud that Polycarp had been taken. The
Proconsul entreated him, in regard to his age, to disguise his name. He refused, and proclaimed aloud
that he was Polycarp. ' Swear,' it was said, ' by the
genius of Cæsar ; retract and say, Away with the godless.' The godless was the term by which the Pagans,
with the usual injustice of bigotry and ignorance, desig-
nated the Christians. The old man, with his eyes
turned upwards, said, ' Away with the godless !' The
Proconsul urged him further, ' Swear, and I release
thee ; blaspheme Christ.' Polycarp replied, ' Eighty
and six years have I served Christ, and He has never
done me wrong ; how can I blaspheme my King and
my Saviour ? ' The Proconsul threatened to expose

him to the wild beasts. ' It is well for me,' said Polycarp, ' to be speedily released from this life of misery.'
The Proconsul threatened to burn him. ' I fear not
the fire that burns for a moment; thou knowest not
that which burns for ever and ever.' The Jews and
Heathens heaped up fuel for a pile ; Polycarp in a
prayer to God exclaimed, ' I thank Thee that Thou
hast graciously thought me worthy of this day and this
hour, that I may receive a portion in the number of
thy martyrs, and drink of Christ's cup for the resurrection to eternal life, both of body and soul, in the
incorruptibleness of the Holy Spirit, among whom may
I be admitted this day.' The fire was kindled, but
would not burn, and an executioner was at once sent
to dispatch the aged martyr.

Such were the Christians in their days of trial.

We have in the memorable correspondence between
Trajan and Pliny, a record of the treatment of the
early Christians by a wise emperor and an enlightened
governor.

It was about the 111th or 112th year of the Christian era that Pliny informed the Emperor that certain
Christians had been denounced to him. He had spared
no pains to ascertain the nature and acts of this new
sect; he had not scrupled to put to the torture two
maid servants who ministered at their worship, and
attended their meals. But all his investigations only
enabled him to report, that they had a custom of meeting before daylight, and singing a hymn to Christ, as
to a god. They met again in the day and partook of
food, but of a perfectly innocent kind. They had no

unlawful bond of union, but were under obligation to each other, not to commit theft, robbery, adultery, or fraud. They held it a point of duty to restore to the depositors any goods committed to their custody. Upon this information Pliny, acting upon some law to us unknown, or perhaps in accordance with the general maxims of the empire, required them to worship the bust of the Emperor, and to curse Christ. Those who did so were permitted to depart; those who refused were led away to execution.

Trajan approved what Pliny had done, but desired him not to search for persons who had adopted the new sect, which he seems, like his delegate, to consider as a harmless, though superstitious community, and above all not to encourage spies, which he says is a thing of the worst example, and not suitable to the spirit of the age.

Hadrian in a similar spirit, but with more toleration, decreed that Christians should not be condemned, except upon full evidence, and according to the forms used in other criminal trials. Philip II. of Spain and Louis XIV. of France were not so merciful.

Here perhaps it may be well to remark, that the language of Paul's epistles, in which he orders obedience to the temporal power of the Cæsars, and declares that the powers that be are ordained of God, should be understood to have reference not to the occasional acts of tyranny and cruelty of Nero or Domitian, which extended to no great distance from Rome, but to the regular course of jurisprudence, and the legal tribunals of the vast Roman empire. We may read in the Old

Testament the abundant proofs of caprice, self-will, and inhumanity of the Eastern kings. In the book of Esther for instance, when the Jews were denounced, an edict went forth that all the Jews were to be killed. When the influence of Esther obtained the revocation of this bloody edict, it was ordered, not that the Jews should be let alone, but that they should be at liberty to kill their persecutors. In the same spirit was the order, under pain of death, to worship the image which Nebuchadnezzar the king had set up. Far different and far better was the administration of justice under the laws and influence of Rome. A man accused was entitled to be heard, and to be brought before his accusers face to face. It was to this open trial and fair hearing of an accused person, that Paul desired respect to be paid; it was in accordance with this regular course of justice that Hadrian decreed that Christians should receive protection and safety.

It has often been repeated that the morality of the Gospel was not different from, or superior to, that taught by the best heathen philosophers, and that precepts to do unto others as we would wish others to do unto us, might be learnt from the doctrines of Zeno or Epicurus. But much depends on the trust placed in the teacher. Compare the authority of Seneca, rolling in wealth, living in the lap of luxury, and suspected not unjustly of being an accomplice in the murder of Agrippina, with the affection and reverence inspired by Christ, who, after a life of purity, without a house wherein to lay his head, was content to suffer death, calling to God, ' Not my will

but thine be done;' suffering ignominy for the sake of
mankind, going to his God and to our God, with·a
humble submission to the 'dishonour of Golgotha,' in
the faith that his commandments, honestly obeyed,
would tend to the happiness of mankind, and open the
gates of immortality.   It was under this influence that
the little congregation in Bithynia, sang hymns to
Christ before daylight; it was in obedience to his commandments that they abstained from theft, from embezzlement, from adultery.   It was under the powerful
exhortations of St. John, of St. Paul, of Polycarp, and
their followers, that the Christian community spread
and grew throughout the Roman empire.   Nor was
this teaching uniformly or even generally persecuted.
The writings of Justin Martyr and Tertullian, the
apostolical letters of Clement of Rome to his colleague of Corinth ; the invectives against pagan idolatry,
and the proofs afforded of the Divine mission of
Christ, were circulated throughout the empire.   The
glorious result is thus briefly but impressively related by Gibbon.   Referring to the gradual decline
and growing weakness of the Roman empire he writes,
' While that great body was invaded by open violence,
or undermined by slow decay, a pure and humble
religion slowly insinuated itself into the minds of men,
grew up in silence and obscurity, derived new vigour
from opposition, and finally erected the triumphant
banner of the Cross on the ruins of the Capitol.'[1]

   The great author who wrote these words has
himself assigned the virtues of the first Christians as

[1] Gibbon, chap. xv. vol. ii. p. 265.

one of the causes of the dffuision of Christianity over the world. While confessing and admiring these virtues, he does not forget his characteristic talent for irony and sarcasm. Sitting in the seat of the scorner he observes 'the abstinence from pleasure, and the aversion to active life, of the unfeeling candidate for heaven.' He enjoys the wit of Lucian who, in describing the life of Peregrinus, relates the hypocritical frauds by which a pretended convert took advantage of the simplicity of the honest and credulous Christians. He is amused by the guards and restrictions placed by the early fathers on the institution of marriage, and he has his jest at the expense of Origen, who avoided temptation by mutilation. He remarks with justice that the merit of the sinners, who endeavoured to expiate their youth of license by a mature life of unheard-of purity, was somewhat lessened by their fear of a malignant world, ever ready to mark the failings of those who claim credit for superior sanctity. But, in spite of all his sneers, Gibbon is obliged to admit that, with many errors, some arising from a desire to attain a perfection not given to mortals, and some from a sullen desire to restrain, by minute rules, the social enjoyments of life, the early Christians gave the example of an improved morality to the Roman world. While Ignatius, Polycarp, and others furnished mankind with sublime models of a heroism equal to the patriotic devotion of Coccles, Curtius, and Regulus, there were multitudes who, without the ambition of martyrdom, pursued their way in the sequestered vale of life, stained with no guilt, and seeking no fame. In order to depre-

ciate the moral precepts of Christ, it has been said that
no one obeys the command—'If anyone take thy coat,
give him thy cloak also.' This is a metaphorical and
Eastern mode of saying, Return good for evil. Yet
Joseph went far beyond giving his cloak to those who
had taken his coat. When his brethren saw him coming
they said, 'Here cometh the dreamer, let us slay him.'
When diverted from this needless crime, they sold him
as a slave to merchants. Yet when he ruled in Egypt,
he not only rescued his brethren from famine, but settled them in peace and prosperity in the heart of Goshen.
Such was the Christian spirit of Joseph the Jew.

After a time, however, the more gifted among the
Christian community were ready to avow that, although
they did not wish to intrude in the councils of princes,
and while they had observed faithfully the lessons and
example of their master, they were aware that, in the
business of life, they were as well fitted to take their
part as their less scrupulous pagan brethren. Wisdom
is justified of all her children ; no less in the hero than
in the hermit ; no less in Gustavus Adolphus and
William of Orange than in St. Jerome and St. Ambrose.
I will here insert the account of the objects of Natural
and Revealed Religion given by Dr. Samuel Clarke in
his work on the Catechism. His Arian heresies may
as well be omitted. His Christian faith is the doctrine
of an enlightened man well-read in the Holy Scriptures.

'I believe in God the Father Almighty Maker of
heaven and earth.

'To believe in God is to believe that there is a Being,
eternal and infinite, perfect and self-sufficient, all power-

ful and all wise, just and righteous, holy, merciful and good, a Being whose duration no time can exhaust, from whose presence no swiftness can flee, whose power no force can resist, from whose knowledge no secret can be concealed, from whose justice no art can escape, by whose goodness all things are sustained; a Being who is everywhere present, whose power causes and directs everything, and his kingdom ruleth over all. This is the God of Nature ; and Nature itself (of which ignorant men often speak as of a real being or agent) is nothing else but the perpetual efficaciousness of his will and laws.

'The grounds upon which we believe in such a Being are numberless. For indeed everything proves the being of God. The imperfection of all other things, and their absolute incapacity to be the cause or necessary reason of their own being; the natural conscience and universal apprehensions of all mankind; the strictest searches and inquiries of the learned, and the most obvious and unavoidable observations of the unlearned. The greatness, the variety, the motions, the beauty, the order and harmony of the world; the fitness of everything to its proper end ; the growth of plants, the sagacity of animals; the structure of the body, and the faculties and the soul of man. Whatever we observe in nature, in the heavens, and upon the earth ; and whatever is supernatural, as miracles and prophecies— all these things conspire to prove to us that there is a God.' . . . .

Farther 'to believe in God' signifies moreover, to believe there is but one God. For so the ancient Greek

creeds always expressed it : ' I believe in one God.' And
this is also a fundamental truth of natural religion. For
as it is sufficiently apparent, even to ordinary capacities, from the universal harmony of nature, that all
things both in the heavens and in the earth are under
one direction, under the uniform direction of one
Supreme Will, so to men of science and ability it is
moreover strictly demonstrable, from the nature of necessary immensity and eternity, that there can be but
one God, supreme over all. And what natural reason
thus teaches, revelation abundantly confirms. ' The
Lord, he is God, there is none else beside Him.' ' Thou
shalt have no other gods but Me.' ' Hear, O Israel
the Lord our God is one Lord.' ' To us there is but
one God, the Father, of whom are all things.' ' One
God and Father of all, who is above all, and through
all, and in you all.' [1]

Passing to the incarnation, our author, speaking of
the propitiation for sins offered by Christ, rebukes those
who say, that God could not absolutely have forgiven
sinners without such a complete satisfaction, and cen-
sures those, who undertaking to explain beyond what
is written, have taken upon them to affirm that the sufferings of Christ were exactly equal to those which the
damned were to undergo. Whereas Dr. Clarke says,
' But since God is supreme Lord of all, and may do
that He will with his own and (without wrong to any)
may remit of his own right what He pleases, and give
no account of his doings, and may punish or forgive

[1] Deut. chap. iv. 35; Exod. chap. xx. 3; Deut. chap. vi. 4;
1 Cor. chap. viii. 6 ; Eph. chap. iv. 6.

sinners upon what terms and conditions He himself judges fit; it seems much more reasonable to remit this whole method of man's redemption not into any absolute necessity in the nature of the thing, as if God could not have found out any other means, which it becomes not us to presume to judge of; it seems much more reasonable to resolve this whole method into the wisdom and good pleasure of God, who chose to vindicate the honour of his laws and government in this way rather than any other.'[1]

Nor is it difficult to imagine why God chose to vindicate the honour of his laws and government in this way rather than any other. For what teaching of Socrates or Plato, of Cicero or Seneca, what causes enumerated by Gibbon, what authority enforced by Trajan or Marcus Aurelius, could have inspired all nations with a reverence for the commandments and laws of God in a manner equal to the love and obedience instilled by the death of the Son of God upon the cross?

In speaking of those who may hope to obtain resurrection from the dead, Clarke says:

' If the Holy Catholic Church be understood to signify all good men, under all the different dispensations of religion, from the beginning to the end of the world, then the communion of saints consists in this, that they are all servants of the same God; all guided and sanctified after divers manners, by the same Spirit; all live in hope of the same divine promises, made known at sundry times, and in different ways and

---

[1] *Catechism*, by Dr. Clarke, p. 78.

degrees, and shall all finally be made partakers of the same glory, according to their different capacities and deserts, in the eternal kingdom of God.'

Restraining again the term Holy Catholic Church to the Christian Church, Dr. Clarke says : ' Consequently 'tis the duty of all Christians, living together at the same time, to endeavour to keep this unity of the spirit in the bond of peace, by uniting in a visible and eternal fellowship of love and charity, joining publicly in the same worship of God ; mutually assisting, comforting, instructing each other ; with all lowliness and meek- ness, with long-suffering forbearing one another in love. In a word, doing all the good offices that it becomes members of one and the same body to do for each other.' [1]

Such was the belief entertained by a learned and pious member of the Church of England. But the world had to go through many ages of superstition, many ages of bloodshed, and has still to go through a period of discord, of malice, and ill-will, before it reaches the period of unity of the spirit in the bond of peace and in righteousness of life, for which the Church of Eng- land supplicates the Almighty in her prayer for ' all sorts and conditions of men.'

[1] *Catechism*, pp. 124, 125.

ESSAY V.

COUNCIL OF NICE.

It is of the nature of man to corrupt and to pervert every good gift of God. Thus, the pure religion of Christ became very soon corrupted with superstitions, was then perverted into a source of bitter hatred and ill-will ; was degraded by the usurpation of the Bishop of Rome ; and, lastly, transformed into a school of vice and immorality resembling the picture which St. Paul has left to us of Roman society under the empire.

I proceed to speak of each of these signs of degeneracy. From the earliest days of Christianity began the habit of canonising the martyrs and pious men and women, who were objects of reverence to their contemporaries. It has been strangely argued, that because these practices and habits began in the first ages after the death of Christ, they are, therefore, to be deemed parts of the true Church. Unhappily from the very beginning of the Christian community we must date the abuses which cling round everything that is human. The sanctification of the so-called saints and martyrs did not shock the moral sense of the early Christians. It was at first a natural effect of the reverence and affection felt for those devout men and pious women who had devoted their lives to the observance of a pure religion, and, in many instances, had testified by their deaths the sincerity and constancy of their faith. What more consolatory to the feelings of the survivors : what more conducive to the success of this ' new way ' than prayers for the happiness of the dead, and lasting monuments to the memory of the indefatigable apostles and of the fearless martyrs of the religion of Christ ? But that which is natural and apparently harmless in the flower, may be poisonous and fatal in the fruit. As the Christian sect grew from a retired and humble society to a large and rich community, the temptation to pass easily from the old worn-out polytheism to the new religion became more prevalent. The Letter from Rome of a celebrated author shows us how general, how fascinating, how exact was the adoption of pagan worship and pagan ceremonies by the Christian pro-selytes. The saints and martyrs of the Christians were enthroned in the place of the gods, demi-gods, and heroes of the Roman world. St. Peter of Rome, St. John the Baptist of Genoa, St. James of Compostella in Spain, St. Januarius of Naples, attracted the worship of the new Christians, who felt little regret for their old idols. An archbishop of Canterbury who had contended with his king for supremacy, had fallen by the hands of assassins. His martyrdom was readily consecrated by the Church. Bishop Burnet has contrasted the value of the gifts offered in one year to God, to Jesus Christ, and to St. Thomas in the cathedral of Canterbury. In the same manner, the offerings to St. James, in the cathedral of Santiago in Spain, far surpassed any gifts placed on the altar of Christ.

But above and beyond all other objects of worship, the converts to Christianity embraced with ardour and zeal the worship of the Virgin Mary. The Greek and Roman Pagans had worshipped their goddesses—Juno at Mycenæ and Argos, Minerva at Athens, Venus at Cyprus and at Paphos, Diana at Ephesus. But the proud majesty of Juno, the stately wisdom of Minerva and the lascivious loves of Venus were not to be compared with the divine purity of Mary holding her child in her arms, and combining the chastity of the parturient virgin with the sorrows of the desolate mother. In all parts of Europe, Asia, and Africa the images of the Holy Mary, blessed among women, were adored with passionate devotion, made famous by miracles attributed to the image or the portrait, and invoked as the Queen of Heaven, to whose influence over her Son all blessings were to be attributed, and to whose displeasure every calamity might be traced.

It was to no purpose that it was recorded in the Scriptures, that when a devout woman had said, ' Blessed is the womb that bare Thee, and the paps that gave Thee suck,' Jesus Christ had replied, ' Yea, rather blessed are they that hear the word of God and do it.' The Father who created heaven and earth, the Son who redeemed mankind, were named for the sake of honour; but their divinity was neglected and passed by, while the Virgin Mary was appealed to in every emergency, and was believed to rule all things that happened in the world.

The teaching of Christ, the Sermon on the Mount, the conversation with the woman of Samaria, the parables taught to his disciples and followers, had enforced the love of one God the Father Almighty, and had explained, by many examples and many precepts, the duty of man to his neighbour. But there had been throughout a remarkable reserve on the mysterious subjects of the nature of God and of Christ's relation to the Father; of the qualities and functions of the Holy Spirit; of the objects and the nature of future reward and punishment.

Hence the opportunity for man to indulge his pride of intellect, his superiority over his contemporary Christians, his skill in argument, and his triumph over weaker opponents. There is no great fame to be acquired by pardoning those who trespass against us, or by standing up to say humbly, 'Lord, be merciful to me a sinner.' But if a man can persuade his generation that he has found doctrines in Scripture regarding the Eternal and the Invisible which no one else has been able to discover; if he can by logical subtlety prove to their minds that the substance of the Spirit of Christ is the same as the substance of the Spirit of God the Father, all men will admire his ingenuity; he will be applauded as a great apostle and a mighty leader; he will gain honour, distinction, and power.

On these subjects, therefore, the weakness of human nature fastened, and a field full of noxious weeds grew from the cultivation which the learned bestowed on the unpromising soil. If instead of making the love of God and our neighbour the test of faith, metaphysical doctrines could be inculcated by sophistry, and defended by unintelligible argument, it was clear that men might find in Christianity a fertile source of dispute instead of a certain rule of life. If the relations and the attributes of God, of Christ, and of the Holy Spirit were to be ascertained and defined, it was clear that human reasoning, and not Divine Wisdom, would be the arbiter and the standard of Christianity. For the command that all men were to be loved would be substituted the precept that men who were mistaken in their arguments and wrong in their conclusions according to the prevailing opinion were to be hated, proscribed, and punished. The first disputes of Christians which caused bitter and lasting divisions were not indeed directly mixed with theological controversy. They arose from the worldly ambition of Donatus to become bishop of Carthage, and the preference given to Cæcilian by the majority of the electors. It is true that the appellation of heretic, and the reproach of deserting the standard of Christ, were freely hurled from one party to the other, and separated the African Church into two bitter factions, so long as Christianity prevailed in Africa. But the contest was not properly a question as to the meaning of texts or the possession of theological truth.

It was from Alexander, Bishop of Alexandria, Athanasius his supporter, and Arius his opponent, that the great controversy arose, which, springing from a metaphysical difficulty, became the fertile source of war and bloodshed, the abundant fountain of theological hatred.

It will readily be perceived how tempting was the prospect of leaving the beaten roads of the early

F

Christians to wander through the pathless forests of controversy and ascend the heights of a new heaven. The early Christian seeking to imitate the benevolent Samaritan who ministered to the wounded traveller, or to follow the example of the merciful lord who forgave his debtor, or like the loving father to receive with joy a penitent son, followed plain precepts, and practised unobtrusive virtues. But the doctor of theology, who displayed acuteness in pointing out inferences which Christ had never revealed to his disciples, came victor out of conflicts with his learned rivals. He defined what Jesus had left obscure, and explained relations to the Godhead which Christ had left to the conclusions of private judgment. Thus Athanasius, followed by crowds of admiring pupils, radiant with flashes of rhetoric, and exulting over the opponents whom he had crushed, stood at last on the narrow summit of orthodoxy, neither lost in the fog of the Sabellian nor stopped by the stumbling-block of the Arian, and waved his triumphant banner over Europe, Asia, and Africa. It is to be lamented, however, that in this difficult struggle the spirit of Christianity was lost—that man was taught to hate his neighbour and to exalt himself.

The existence of a Messiah with two natures—the one that of a man liable to the infirmities, the sorrows, the failings of a human being ; the other that of a Divine Being who lived with God before Abraham was, whose thought and word were those of Divine wisdom and Divine benevolence—was not easy of comprehension. Speedily there arose two sects, one of which regarded

Christ merely as a prophet, a being like Isaiah or John the Baptist, divinely inspired, but with all the weakness of our mortal nature; the other, which looked upon Him as a being altogether spiritual, who had neither been born of woman nor suffered death upon the cross, but had condescended for a time to wear the human form, and had returned to heaven before Judas betrayed or Pilate condemned Him. The first were called Ebionites; the second Gnostics.

In process of time these two parties gave rise to views of the nature of Christ which, without being utterly opposed to each other, yet differed so much as to be the foundation of contrary doctrines, of adverse parties, of violent animosities.

It appears from Fleury, the ecclesiastical historian, who gives the fairest account of this controversy, that Arius maintained that God the Father was really and not metaphorically a Father, and that Christ was really and not metaphorically a Son. From these premises he contended that God the Father, by whom Christ was begotten, must have existed before his Son, and that a being who was begotten must have had a beginning. Thence, he contended, there must have been a time when God the Father, being perfect God, contained in Himself all the plenitude of the Divinity. By his own free will, said Arius, He called into existence his Son, who is therefore a creature, and, as such, inferior to his Creator. But He was called into existence before the world was created, and was designed by his Father to be his instrument in creating the world. All the creatures (according to Arius) of the Father are his sons, as is distinctly stated in Isaiah i. 2; and this instance shows that the begotten need not be of the same substance as the begetter, which is also proved by Job xxxviii., where dew is supposed to be spoken of as begotten by God. Christ, who existed before the foundation of the world, received from his Father an immutable and Divine nature.

Athanasius, on the other hand, contended that Christ existed from all eternity, that He had equal power with the Father, and was, like Him, to live to all eternity. He seems to have misapplied the term 'begotten,' in attributing to the Man Christ, the Son of Mary, while He lived upon earth, a term which belonged only to the Divine Being who at the command of God created heaven and earth. But the apparent contradiction of applying to Christ as God a word only applicable to Christ as Man was obviously a temptation to Alexander and Athanasius. They wished above all things to make men believe what to common sense appeared incredible.

The real difficulty arose from the presumption of man in pretending to judge, without any authority from Scripture, of the nature of Divine Beings.

It was therefore with great wisdom that Constantine wrote both to Alexander and to Arius, exhorting them to drop the matter in dispute, and to live in peace with one another. Jeremy Taylor says of this letter: 'The epistle of Constantine to Alexander and Arius tells the truth, and chides them both for commencing the question—Alexander for broaching it, and Arius for taking it up. And although this be true, that it had been better for the Church it had never begun, yet being begun, what is to be done with it? Of this also, in that admirable epistle, we have the Emperor's judgment (I suppose not without the advice and privity of Hosius) . . . . for first he calls it a vain piece of a question, ill begun, and more unadvisedly published ; a question which no law or ecclesiastical canon defineth ; a fruitless contention ; the product of idle brains ; a matter so nice, so obscure, so intricate, that it was neither to be explicated by the clergy, nor understood by the people ; a dispute of words, a doctrine inexplicable, but most dangerous when taught, lest it introduce discord or blasphemy, and therefore the objector was rash and the answer unadvised, for it concerned not the substance of faith or the worship of God, nor the chief commandment of Scripture, and therefore why should it be the matter of discord ? For though the matter be grave, yet, because neither necessary nor explicable, the contention is trifling and toyish. . . . So that, the matter being of no great importance, but vain, and a toy in respect of the excellent blessings of peace and charity, it were good that Alexander and Arius should leave contending, keep their opinions to themselves, ask each other's forgiveness, and give mutual toleration.'[1]

But this advice to leave contending was advice which neither Arius nor Athanasius was prepared to take. What each desired was a contest, a victory, a triumph for himself—the humiliation or, if necessary, the death of his opponent. In fact, the Spirit of

[1] *Liberty of Prophesying*, 1, 2. Taylor's *Works*, vol. viii. *p.* 61.

Christ had departed from Christ's Church; and as the subtle intellects of Alexandria were bent on a dispute, there was no subject on which it was easier to hang one than the nature of the Father, the Son, and the Holy Ghost.

It was thought expedient to hold a council to solve the difficulty. A council was therefore summoned to meet at Nice, in Bithynia. This council was attended by 318 bishops. Constantine himself attended the council, seated on a low stool, and leaving outside his guards. The emperor being deeply intent on promoting peace and Christianity on each side, and his bishops still more intent on war and victory, the difficulty was to find a question upon which the parties could differ. Alexander maintained that Christ had been begotten from all eternity; Arius, that He had been begotten millions of years before the creation of the world. The point was so abstruse, and the ground so slippery, that an apprehension prevailed that it would be impossible to make a quarrel. The tyrant majority stood aghast. Eusebius of Cæsarea, with the approbation of the emperor, proposed the following creed :—

' I believe in one God, the Father Almighty, Maker of all things both visible and invisible, and in one Lord Jesus Christ, the Word of God, Light of Light, Life of Life, the only begotten Son, the Firstborn of every creature, begotten of the Father before all worlds, by whom also all things were made. Who for our salvation was incarnate, and lived amongst men, and suffered, and rose again on the third day, and ascended to the Father, and shall come in glory to judge the quick and dead. And we believe in one Holy Ghost. Believing each of them to be and to have existed, the Father, only the Father, and the Son, only the Son, and the Holy Ghost, only the Holy Ghost : As also our Lord, sending forth his own disciples to preach, said, " Go and teach all nations, baptizing them into the name of the Father, and of the Son, and of the Holy Ghost ; " concerning which things we affirm that this is so, and that we so think, and that it has long so been held, and that we remain steadfast to death for this faith, anathematising every godless heresy. That we have thought these things from our heart and soul, from the time that we have known ourselves, and that we now think and say thus in truth, we testify in the name of Almighty God, and of our Lord Jesus Christ, being able to prove even by demonstration, and to persuade you that in past times also thus we believed and preached.' [1]

To this creed neither Athanasians nor Arians could object. There was evident danger that there might be no quarrel, and that the wish of Constantine for peace and harmony might be fulfilled. At this prospect of agreement, of peace, and mutual charity, the bishops were confounded. At length an Arian bishop uttered a word which he said the Arians could not admit into their creed. That word, unknown to Scripture, unknown to the early Christians, was ' Homoousion,' or consubstantial. The Arians, said the Arian bishop, declined to say that Christ the Son was of the same substance as God the Father. The Athanasian

[1] Stanley's *Eastern Church*, pp. 155, 156, edit. 1861, 8vo.

party, not much caring about the word, were too happy to find any way of fastening a quarrel upon their opponents.

Ambrose, one of the orthodox, has truly said that an Arian had drawn from the scabbard the sword by which the head of the Arian heresy was cut off. The joy was great, all chance of peace was over, war was declared, the quarrel was found, and, as an historian has said, the contending parties fought in the dark about terms which no one understood. The words, '*only begotten, that is to say, of the substance of the Father, God of God,*' were inserted in the creed. The emperor assented, and the symbol of faith was complete. It is not to be supposed, however, that there were not some men of calm minds and charitable tempers who knew that the beginning of strife was like the letting out of water, and who deplored the miseries to which Christendom was about to be exposed.

An incident, illustrating the simplicity of one person at least among the members of the council, is related by Socrates, its historian. He says that, at a moment when disputes were running so high that there seemed likely to be no end of controversy, a layman, whose person bore marks of having suffered mutilation for his Christian faith, suddenly stepped from among the combatants, and exclaimed, ' Christ and the Apostles left us not a system of logic, but a naked truth, to be guarded by faith and good works.' [1]

But neither then nor in any subsequent age has the world profited by this simple and truly Christian doc-

---

[1] Stanley's *Eastern Church*, p. 131.

trine. The attempt of every church has been to prove itself right, and every other sect wrong, not to show a true belief by ' faith and good works.'

The character of Athanasius has been portrayed with a vigorous hand and a masterly command by Gibbon. What has been said of Archbishop Laud may be applied to Athanasius. He was ' a melancholy exemplification of the appalling fact that some of the nobler qualities of the churchman may co-exist with the total want of the purest Christian virtues, and blend with some of the worst, most unchristian vices.'[1] Athanasius was bold, fearless, ready to contend in argument and to lay down his life for that which he believed to be the truth. But he abounded in theological hatred ; he excelled in vituperative invective ; he was always forward in private and in public to nurse dissension, to excite to bloodshed, and to make Christianity consist not of love, not of charity, but of metaphysical definitions, which might give him an opportunity of cursing and crushing his opponents.

Yet the Nicene creed itself, as it is still called, has been much altered from the form adopted in the council. Instead of the words ' only begotten, that is, of the substance of the Father, God of God,' we have in our Prayer Book ' the only begotten Son of God, begotten of his Father before all worlds, God of God,' thus adopting very nearly the doctrine of Arius, who had no objection to say that Christ was begotten before all worlds. Likewise the anathema, or curse, at the end of the creed signed at Nice is omitted, and in this

[1] *Annals of St. Paul's*, by Milman, p. 331.

respect the creed is become more Christian. The words 'of the same substance with the Father,' which are not scriptural, alone demonstrate the triumph of Athanasius over Christian charity. Upon the whole matter we should do well to listen to the opinion of Hilary, Bishop of Poitiers, who, in a letter to the Emperor Constantius, thus expresses his sentiments:— 'It is a thing equally deplorable and dangerous that there are as many creeds as opinions among men, as many doctrines as inclinations, and as many sources of blasphemy as there are faults among us, because we make creeds arbitrarily, and explain them as arbitrarily. The Homoousion is rejected and received, and explained away by successive synods. The partial or total resemblance of the Father and of the Son is a subject of dispute for these unhappy times. Every year, nay every morn, we make new creeds to describe invisible mysteries. We repent of what we have done, we defend those who repent, we anathematise those whom we defended. We condemn either the doctrine of others in ourselves, or our own in that of others, and, reciprocally tearing one another to pieces, we have been the cause of each other's ruin.' [1]

Dr. Jortin, speaking in his 'Remarks on Ecclesiastical History' of the slight provocation upon which Christians anathematised one another, says, in that caustic style which belonged to him, 'It is really a wonder that they did not at last insert in their litanies,

---

[1] *Hilarius ad Constantium*, lib. ii. c. iv. v. p. 1229.

" We beseech Thee to curse and confound the Pelagians, Semi-Pelagians, Nestorians, Eutychians, Monothelites, Jacobites, Iconoclasts, and all heretics and schismatics."'[1] ' The eternal generation of the Word is not found in Scripture, nor is He called the Son of God upon any account antecedent to the incarnation.' So says Dr. Bennet, and so say some other writers on both sides of the controversy.[2] Surely those writers had much to say for themselves.

Dr. Jortin conveys his own sentiments in the following passage:—' Scripture, say the Protestants, is the only rule of faith in matters pertaining to revealed religion, and they say well. Whatsoever is not clearly delivered there may be true, but cannot be important. Hæc mea est sententia, neque me ex eâ ullius unquam aut docti, aut indocti movebit oratio.'[3]

It has been said very truly by a Roman Catholic writer of the doctrine of Trinity in Unity, that in attempting to combine them ' you gain nothing but a mystery, which you can describe as a notion, but cannot depict as an imagination. . . . And hence, perhaps, it is that the latter doctrine is never spoken of as a mystery in the New Testament, which is addressèd far more to the imagination and affections than to the intellect.'[4] Rightly so addressed, because Christ and his Apostles wished to teach a religion ; Athanasius to

[1] Jortin's *Remarks on Ecclesiastical History,* vol. i. p. 376 (Trollope's edit.).
[2] Ibid. p. 367.   [3] Ibid. pp. 364, 365.
[4] *The Grammar of Assent.*

found and maintain a church. We shall see how far he succeeded in this purpose.

One thing is certain. The unhappy decision of the Council of Nice was the signal for centuries of bloodshed. Thousands of human beings died to confirm or contradict a doctrine which none of them understood.

ESSAY VI.

RISE OF THE CHURCH OF ROME.

THE day which saw the support of the Roman Emperor given openly and avowedly to the Christian religion ought, many Christians will think, to have inaugurated peace and good-will upon earth. That the consequences were so far from fulfilling this expectation may be attributed to several causes, which I will endeavour to enumerate.

The personal character of Constantine abounded in pride and ostentation, but was entirely wanting in humanity, and was disgraced by enormous crimes.

Constantine had many natural advantages, and he improved them by care and cultivation. He was tall, handsome, with a manly countenance and an agreeable voice; he studied war so successfully as to become a victorious general; and he preached sermons so effectively as to induce a bishop to declare that he was inspired. On the other hand, he imitated the worst emperors among his predecessors in listening to spies, in giving faith to their monstrous inventions, and in putting to death without pity the objects of their calumnious charges. It was at the instigation of spies, or prompted by their reports, that he sacrificed the

life of his son Crispus, and that, a few years afterwards, he put to death his wife, the Empress Fausta.
The grounds of accusation and the names of the accusers have, in both instances, been hidden in mystery;
and so far was this secrecy carried that the historian
of his life, the Bishop Eusebius, does not even relate
or allude to the fact of these cruel and unnatural
executions. The Christian profession of Constantine
was delayed till near the moment of his death, apparently from the belief, common in the Church at
that age, that the rite of baptism washed away all
crimes and all sins, whether of commission or omission,
for which the baptized person was answerable previous
to the reception of that holy sacrament.

It was another misfortune for the Roman Empire,
and indeed for Christians all over the world, that instead of embracing consistently the doctrines whether
of Athanasius or of Arius, Constantine fluctuated from
one to the other, and thus encouraged a bloody conflict, which, having its rise not only in his own in-
consistencies, but in the opinions and conduct of
his sons and nephews, spread massacre, revolution,
and war over the world for many generations. It
was no wonder, therefore, that the subjects of Constantine, witnesses of the pomp of their emperor,
gazing at his newly invented diadem . covered with
precious stones, his silken garments, his oriental magnificence, and beholding at the same time the crimes
perpetrated within the walls of his palace, should
brand by a scathing epigram the blaze of jewels
which recalled Diocletian, and the murders which

repeated the memory of Nero. Hence an inscription
was found one day over the gates of the Palatine:

> Saturni aurea sæcula quis requirat?
> Sunt hæc gemmea, sed Neroniana.[1]

In the twentieth year of Constantine's reign, the
Council of Nice had been held; the Arian doctrine
had been condemned as heresy; Arius himself had
been proscribed by the pen of the emperor, and for-
bidden to return to Alexandria. At a later period
Constantine gave an audience to his favourite sister
Constantia, whose husband and whose son he had put
to death. At her prayer he agreed to restore Arius
and the Arian party. In the thirtieth year of his
reign a fresh council was held at Tyre; at this council
Eusebius of Cæsarea, the Arian, presided; the church
of the Holy Sepulchre was dedicated, and it was
ordered, at the bidding of Constantine, that Arius
should be received in triumph at Constantinople. On
the very day of the expected triumph, Arius died in a
sudden and horrible manner.

The various revolutions in the life of Athanasius,
his triumph at Nice, his defeat at Tyre, his wonderful
influence at Rome, his popular ovation at Alexandria,
his vast energy and ability, are recorded by Gibbon,
and expatiated upon by the historians of the Church. Yet
Arianism, nourished by the vacillation of Constantine,
upheld by the plausibility of its doctrine and by the
protection of great princes, stood its ground in the
world for several centuries. The first conqueror of

---

[1] *Sidon. Apollinar.* Gibbon, vol. iii., 8vo, chap. xviii.

Rome, Alaric, the first conqueror of Africa, Genseric, were Arians. The Vandals embraced the opinions of Arius. Theodoric the Great, who became king of Italy, was an Arian. The Lombards were Arians for many generations. The kingdoms of Southern France and Northern Spain were Arian till Clovis, the orthodox barbarian, crushed their hosts on the plains of Poitiers. It was not till the sixth century that Arianism was renounced by King Recared in the Basilica of Toledo.

A more permanent and important change caused by an act of Constantine—the transfer of the seat of empire from Rome to Constantinople—was the growth to greatness and supremacy of the Roman Catholic Church. But that event, so singular in its causes and so wonderful in its effects, was gradual in its approach. For we have now arrived at the period when the Church of Rome, which had alternately crept humbly under the negligence and indifference or been tormented by the persecution and cruelty of the pagan emperors, was to rise slowly from the ground, trying her wings cautiously, till she perched on the roofs of palaces, and crowed from the pinnacles of temples her loud note of triumph. A scheme more artfully devised, embracing the proudest courts, and stooping to the lowest peasants, defying sovereigns with her spiritual menaces, and nourishing multitudes with her indiscriminate charity, could not well be. The secrets of families were laid open to her penetrating insight, armies were moved to war at her imperious commands, emperors held the stirrup for her infallible head, the proudest kings of Europe were bidden to lay down their crowns by her peremptory·decrees.

It must be our business to fix the moment of this great crisis ; to shew what the Pope had hitherto been, and to explain how, at the commencement of the fourth century, a Power which under the name of religion included morals, and which under the name of morals included all the social and political relations of states, internal and external, laid broadly and deeply the foundations of its spiritual and temporal dominion.

1. The first position of the bishops of Rome was not very dignified. The rumoured journey of St. Peter to Rome, and his establishment there as the first bishop, rests on no authentic document, and is probably one of the many fictions which were invented in other times to adorn and elevate the greatness of the Roman pontiffs. In the early history of the Church, it appears that when a council was held at Rome, the bishop of Rome presided ; when at any other episcopal city, the local bishop was the president. When Constantine united the Church with the State, he took upon himself the office of summoning and, if he chose it, of presiding, over all councils of the clergy. After Constantine had removed the capital of the empire to Constantinople, the emperors ceased altogether to reside at Rome, and when a Roman emperor was to be found in Italy, it was at Milan or Ravenna, rather than at Rome, that he chose to hold his court. But the name of Rome had not perished ; the authority, which was not inherited by a viceroy or senate, was quietly assumed by the

G

bishop, and men willingly resorted to a Christian prelate who did not attempt to assert by violence a supremacy which seemed due to learning, to age, and to the virtues of conciliation and mildness.

2. Another circumstance which contributed greatly to induce men to fix their trust on the bishop of Rome was the course pursued by successive prelates in relation to the Athanasian and Arian controversy. There are no words in the New Testament which declare that Christ is of the same substance as God the Father, in the sense of the Athanasians, or that there was a time before all worlds, when Christ had a beginning, as the Arians were pleased to maintain. The Athanasians fixed upon the word *Omoousion*, because it was repugnant to the Arians, and the Arians declared that there was a time when Christ began to exist, in order to obey the arbitrary dictum of Arius. But the more vague and undefined the matter of controversy, and the less either had a foundation in Scripture, the more desirable it appeared to the Church that one of the two doctrines should be firmly embraced, and consistently upheld. By following Athanasius they found a flag and a bond of connection. With the support of the Pope they called themselves the Orthodox, and they had succeeded at the Council of Nice, by the help of the Arians themselves, in fixing the stigma of Heterodoxy on their opponents.

The indolent love of pleasure of Constans, and the intolerance of Constantius, gave these two rival emperors alternate success. But the real palm of victory remained with the Church of Rome, which, by its consistent adherence to what was called the orthodox cause, marshalled under its standard the most eminent of the bishops.

3. Another promising advantage for the Church of Rome was the translation of the whole Bible into Latin by St. Jerome. In performing this task, he not only evinced wonderful industry and unparalleled application, but he made language itself bow to his authority, and melted the hard iron of the Roman tongue into a compound breathing the airy fancy of the Eastern genius, and fraught with the lofty imagination of Isaiah, the Hebrew prophet.

The Vulgate, as it was called, became the book of the Catholic Church ; was stored in all her libraries ; diffused among all her clergy; strengthened the bond of union among her converts of all nations, and gave to the Papal system harmony as well as force.

4. Amid the corruption and degradation of the ancient capital of the world, there was still existing a Roman spirit which now was on fire for religion as it had once been for patriotism. Paula and her daughter were to Jerome what Volumnia had been for Coriolanus, and Cornelia for the Gracchi. Followed by these heroic women the great writers of the third and fourth centuries spoke the language of statesmen and rulers, while the most eloquent of the Greek fathers aspired only to the literary glory of accomplished historians and skilful orators. It still might be said of the Greek authors,

Orabunt causas melius;

while the Roman could still exclaim

> Tu regere imperio populos, Romane, memento:
> Hæ tibi erunt artes; pacisque imponere morem,

Jerome could persuade and govern alike the noble women of Rome and the hermits of the Thebaid.

Augustine, bishop of Hippo, could frame a whole body of divinity and steer his course safely as a great orthodox father on a sea where Calvin was wrecked as a hopeless heretic.

The career of St. Ambrose is, perhaps, still more extraordinary.

In considering the rise of the Church of Rome, we must regard four men as the main authors and contrivers of that Roman supremacy which in the name of the Pope and the Church succeeded to an empire as potent over minds and consciences as the rule of Sylla and of Pompey, of Cæsar and of Nero had been over their bodies and their loyal obedience. The four men to whom I allude were Athanasius, Jerome, Augustine, and Ambrose.

Athanasius, by the energy of his nature, and his practical logic, which partook more of the vigour and acuteness of the West than of the speculative subtlety of the East, was well fitted to obtain control over the vacant minds of the Roman people. The attention of Constantine was absorbed in constructing, organising, and ruling a new capital city. Men like Athanasius, Jerome, Augustine, and Ambrose disposed of Rome and Italy very much as they pleased. Athanasius taught himself the language and imbibed the literature

of Rome. He thus became fitted to assume the lead
of the orthodox party; to preach and to write in Latin
with the vehemence and the power which distinguished
his Greek productions. Gibbon has prided himself on
his character and narrative of the life of Athanasius, as
the most masterly part of his history of the Decline
and Fall of the Roman Empire. It seems to me that
the thirty pages in which the career, triumphs and
sufferings of Athanasius are described by Gibbon
well deserve this eulogium. It would be useless to
attempt to abridge or condense the admirable narration,
and the powerful portrait which these pages contain;
they may be read as Tacitus is read, with admiration
and homage to the mighty author. The Arian fancy,
which never was anything more than an arbitrary
assumption without a basis in Scripture, gave way
before the positive creed of the school of Athanasius,
calculated to furnish Christians with new motives for
adoring their Divine Master, and new reasons for attachment to the Church, which used his name and
framed a system of government well fitted to overthrow
the last remnants of pagan worship, and to destroy the
temples which still adhered to the worship of Jupiter,
of Juno, of Mars, of Venus, of Apollo. The Romans,
as I have elsewhere said, carried into their new religion
much of the same spirit of faith and loyalty which,
according to Polybius, enabled the Roman people to
march with irresistible discipline to the conquest of the
world. Thus, when Constantius proclaimed that two
rival bishops, Liberius and Felix, should govern each
his own congregation, the people assembled in the

lines of Rome, and as if they were celebrating the
victor in an animating race, shouted with the voice of
thousands, 'One God, one Christ, one Bishop.'[1]   The
qualities of Jerome, which gave him so much influence
over the new establishment, was not so much to be
attributed to vigour in dispute, and a skilful management of the weapons of controversy, as to his social
influence and powers of conversation.   Marcella a rich
widow, Paula a noble matron, and her daughter Eu-
stochium, yielded without a struggle to the voice which
bade them devote themselves to a life which they
deemed the most pleasing to Christ.   He inspired
their efforts and blessed their unremitting labour ;
their abstinence from all pleasure, and their activity
in propagating the new faith.   By the advice and
in the company of her spiritual guide, Paula abandoned Rome and her infant son, retired to the holy
village of Bethlehem, founded an hospital and four
monasteries, and acquired, by her alms and penance,
an eminent and conspicuous station in the Catholic
Church.

Augustine was the son of a wealthy family at Carthage.   His mother Monica was famed for her piety
and humility.   She bore without complaint the in-
fidelities of her husband, and submitted without anger
or reply to the outbursts of his violent temper.

The youth of Augustine was deformed by the extreme license of his conduct, and the wild errors of
his religious belief.   For many years, indeed until he
was nearly thirty years old, he was a Manichæan,

[1] Milman; Jortin; Gibbon.

and followed the teachings of the most renowned professors of that heresy. At length he seems to have been converted by the discovery, that while the Christian professors could tell truly the position of the planets at a particular time, and the days when an eclipse would occur, the Manichæan sages shewed a total ignorance on these subjects.

Augustine, when he was about thirty years of age, embraced the faith of Christ; he left off his licentious life, reformed his morals, dismissed his concubine, and became one of the greatest leaders of the Christian hierarchy. In the early days of his conversion he went to Milan, where he attended constantly and with earnest devotion the sermons of Ambrose. His attention was caught by the frequency and earnestness with which Ambrose repeated the text, 'The letter killeth, the Spirit giveth life.' It was the peculiar talent of Augustine to organise the Christian Church in every part of Europe, in Asia, and in Africa. Devout men, placing themselves in correspondence with Jerome and with Augustine, made long journeys. They passed the Alps to and fro, and carried epistles of advice and doctrine to the remotest parts of the known world. In this respect he has been compared to St. Paul. I will copy an account of some of the characteristics of Augustine from a celebrated work:—'He displayed an ardent zeal like that of Paul; a sleepless vigilance like that of Paul for the spiritual needs of the church; like Paul, also, a vigorous power of argumentation, a perception of the force of heretical objections, and an energy of rapid retort. Like the

Apostle again, he had been the ardent devotee of a
hostile system of religious opinion.   The Manichæism
of his early life had nourished the fire of enthusiasm in
him ; as in the youthful bosom of St. Paul the prejudices of a Pharisee had glowed into the flames of a
persecutor.   Neither of them could take a passive
subordinate part in any course in which they might be
engaged.   The parallel only fails when we think of
the frankness and simplicity of the Apostle, compared
with the shrewdness and versatility of the Saint.'   We
see the strength of Augustine in his organisation of
the Church itself, a work of greater difficulty, than
the dexterous use of the civil power.   The Church
of the West during the period when he flourished—
the latter half, that is, of the fourth century and the
commencement of the fifth, was daily becoming a more
complex machine, more unwieldy to ordinary hands,
demanding talents of the first order to grasp its various
relations, and a commanding moral power to direct
and control the whole system.   Such occasions, it has
been observed, are often found to call forth the spirits
that alone are meet to cope with them.   Jerome was
a spirit of this mould ; still more so was Augustine.
He had not the learning, or the eloquence, or the
depth of character which Jerome possessed ; but he
had the advantage of a more pliant temper, a more
social taste, a more personal influence—an influence,
not merely from his station, and talents, and moral
power, but evidently from affection for the man.   In
Jerome there was a strong tinge of Oriental enthusiasm.   Augustine was throughout the Latin Church-

man. It is the care of the churches which he evinces through his whole career. We never lose sight of him as the chief pastor of the flock, as the head of a vast spiritual community, for which he appears to hold himself responsible. His very writings, in fact, are so many actions. Our opinion of them as compositions is lost in the impression which they give of the design of the writer to produce some practical effect. We do him injustice, when we contemplate him simply as the writer, or the literary debater. In this respect we are apt to pronounce him inconsistent, or even contradictory to himself, but this very inconsistency is a strong evidence of the really practical design of the writer. He was too acute a logician not to see the speculative consequences of his own statements ; too skilful a rhetorician not to suspect that his own positions might be urged against him. But, at the same time, he had too deep an acquaintance with the practical course of things not to be aware that the skill of the logician is not omnipotent over the affairs of life, and that he who would rightly avail himself of men and things, must sometimes be content to wear that guise of paradox, which the actual constitution of the world often exhibits in itself. A feeling of surprise, indeed, must arise in our minds, when we look back to the fourth century, and contemplate that restless activity by which the leading members of the Latin Church were distinguished. An active communication subsisted at this epoch throughout the church at large. Athanasius or Jerome, from his retreat in the solitudes of the Thebaid, could make his counsels felt in the heart

of the empire; and Chrysostom, from his exile on
Mount Taurus, could keep up incessant intercourse with
the Faithful at the most remote places. But in the
Western Church more especially the correspondence of
feelings and designs was vigorously sustained by the
leaders of the Church, evidently as the great instrument
of unity in doctrine and government. No point of
heterodoxy was touched in one part of the empire, but
it regularly spread in widening circle until it reached
the opposite extreme. The bishops and rulers of the
Church had the deacons and presbyters at their command, to bear their various communications of intelligence, and their replies to the questions sent to them
from the distant provinces of their communion. Sa-
gacious, practical men, at different important stations,
formed a chain of communication which was kept in
constant tension, and vibrated throughout civilised
Europe and Christian Asia.

The prudence and sagacity of Athanasius were shown
by his transfer of his influence to the Western world,
and thus planting in the ancient capital the centre of
a great Church. Remarkable events took place at
Alexandria about the year A.D. 428, when Cyril was
bishop. Ammonius, a fierce and savage monk, threw a
large stone at Orestes, the prefect of the city, which
hit him on the head, and to the alarm of the crowd,
blood gushed forth. Ammonius was seized, tortured,
and put to death. Cyril caused the body to be buried
and the honours of a Christian martyr prostituted on
this ruffian. Worse events followed. Hypatia was a
maiden honoured for her learning, admired for her

beauty, and respected for the modesty of her manners and purity of her conduct. She gave lectures, largely attended, which were founded on the Platonic doctrines of Plotinus. The success of these lectures is said to have excited the envy of Cyril,whose sermons did not attract an equal concourse. Some of the ferocious partisans of this Christian bishop seized Hypatia, dragged her from her chariot, with revolting indecency tore off her clothes, and with atrocious cruelty rent her limb from limb. The Christians of Alexandria did this, professing to be actuated by Christian zeal in the cause of a Christian prelate,[1] and monks consecrated to God became the worst of murderers.

The character of Ambrose was one of the most striking in these very critical times. He was proceeding to Milan, where he was prefect, when the see fell vacant. He summoned the people to a meeting for the purpose of proceeding to the election of their future bishop. Unexpectedly to him, when he consulted the electors, a cry arose, which seemed to pervade the whole assembly, of 'Ambrose for our bishop.' He accepted the new honour, and determined to do his duty without fear or partiality. An occasion arose which required the utmost exertion of firmness and courage. Botheric was the general of the troops assembled at Thessalonica ; he had among his slaves a boy whose beauty excited the desire of one of the charioteers of the circus. Botheric imprisoned the charioteer, and rejected the clamours of the multitude. On the day

---

[1] Milman's *History of Latin Christianity*, vol. i. p. 149. See also the brilliant romance of Hypatia.

of the public games, the mob lamented the absence
of their favourite; finding that their supplications were
not listened to, they attacked the unhappy general,
who fell a victim to their fury. He and several of
his principal officers were inhumanly murdered, and
their mangled bodies were dragged about the streets.
The fiery temper of Theodosius could not bear the
delay of a judicial enquiry, and he resolved upon the
surrender of the population of a great city, the metropolis of Illyria, to the fury of his barbarian soldiers.
The people of Thessalonica were invited, in the name
of their sovereign, to the games of the circus. As soon
as the crowd were assembled, the soldiers, who had
been secretly posted round the circus, received the
signal for a massacre.

For three hours the carnage continued without dis-
crimination of age or sex, of innocence or guilt. The
most moderate accounts state the number of the slain
at seven thousand ; some writers affirm that the
total amounted to more than fifteen thousand.

The mind of Ambrose, on receiving the news, was
filled with horror and anguish ; he retired into the
country to indulge his grief, and in a letter to Theodosius represented strongly the enormity of the crime,
which could only be effaced by years of penitence. He
therefore advised Theodosius to confine himself to the
use of prayer, and not to presume to approach the altar
of Christ, or hope to receive the Holy Eucharist, with
hands which were still polluted with blood. In conformity with this warning, when Theodosius, after be-
wailing in private his rashness and his fury, proceeded

to perform his devotions in the great church of Milan, he was stopped in the porch by the archbishop, who declared to his sovereign that private contrition was not sufficient to atone for the massacre, or appease the justice, of his offended God. Theodosius humbly represented that David, the man after God's own heart, had been guilty, not only of murder, but of adultery. The Archbishop fearlessly replied, ' You have imitated David in his crime, imitate then his repentance.' In conformity with the order of Ambrose, the Emperor of the Romans, stripped of the ensigns of royalty, appeared in a mournful and suppliant posture in the midst of the multitude assembled in the church at Milan, and humbly solicited, with sighs and tears, the pardon of his sins. After a delay of about eight months, Theodosius was restored to the communion of the Faithful. Posterity has applauded the firmness of the archbishop, and the example of Theodosius proves the value of those principles which, in this instance at least, forced a monarch, exalted above the apprehension of human punishment, to obey the laws and respect the ministers of an invisible Judge. While the authority of a spiritual sovereign was a conspicuous proof of the influence of Athanasius, of Jerome, of Augustine, and of Ambrose, rising to supremacy and dominion, the temporal power of the Roman emperor was weakened by rivalry and conflict, or sunk into weakness and imbecility.

In the time of Gratian, the Roman legions were commanded or permitted to lay aside their armour. The Goths and the Vandals, Alaric and Attila, divided

among them the kingdoms over which the sway of
Rome had been so long acknowledged. The eternity
of the Roman empire, which had been so confidently
predicted by Virgil and succeeding poets, faded to
a shadow. At the end of the fifth century, Clovis,
king of the Franks, fought a great battle, called the
battle of Tolbiac. He married Clothilda, the niece of
the King of Burgundy, who was a Christian, and
earnestly entreated her husband to embrace the same
faith. In the stress of the battle, Clovis invoked
the God of Clothilda. The same king established
Christianity in his dominions, and saw the end of the
long contest between the Orthodox and the Arian,
which had given rise to so much alternate persecution and such rivers of blood. The Christian religion
everywhere triumphed. Paganism disappeared by
voluntary or forced conversion, and the Christian
worship was established in all the Western countries
of Europe.

ESSAY VII.

*HISTORY OF THE CHURCH OF ROME TILL THE
RISE OF THE MONASTIC ORDERS.*

THE history of the Church of Rome bears, in some
respects, a curious resemblance to the history of Rome
under the rule of the republic and the empire; both
the civil and the ecclesiastical government have been
distinguished by the eminence of men of great virtue;
the purity of Paulus Æmilius and Marcus Aurelius may
vie with the charity and benevolence of Gregory the
Great. So, likewise, with the female characters of
republican and imperial Rome on the one hand, and
of spiritual and ecclesiastical Rome on the other, Volumnia and Cornelia may be matched by Paula and
her daughter. The sublime phrase of Arria, 'It does
not hurt Pœtus,' will find its parallel in the fortitude
of Agatha and other female martyrs of the Christian
Church. So, likewise, in the extreme of vice, Clodia
and Messalina have their match in Theodora and
her daughter. In other respects, likewise, heathen
and Christian Rome have their simliarity, Republican
Rome was at the lowest degree of depression after
the battle of Cannæ, when the Roman ensign bade
his troops fix his standard in the ground in the hearing of the senate, and a confident patriot did not

hesitate to purchase the ground on which Hannibal
was encamped. Sacred Rome, both in ancient and in
modern times, has had its reverses and its revivals ;
Charles V. and his legions made a prisoner of the pope;
Napoleon I. ordered one of his generals to enter the
Vatican, and send pope Pius VII. a prisoner to France.
Yet all the experience of humiliation has hitherto been
succeeded by the hallelujah and triumphant shouts of
the faithful clergy of the holy pontiff, echoed by millions
of spiritual subjects throughout the civilised world.

I am about to touch briefly on some of these revolutions, to join in the admiration which is inspired
by temperance and sobriety, by disinterested care for
the welfare of the Roman people, and to fix the
stigma of reprobation on those popes who made their
palaces the scenes of libidinous excess and infamous
usurpation.

To begin with a bright example. Gregory the Great
was of a senatorial family, his father bore the name of
Gordian ; his mother that of Sylvia. He inherited considerable estates in Sicily, the produce of which he
used to supply from his own resources the poor of the
Roman people, who in previous centuries had obtained from the bounty or policy of the emperor a
supply from the annual fleet from Egypt. The whole
time of Gregory was passed in prayer, reading, writing,
and dictation. Fabulous legends commemorated the
boundless extent of his charity. The successive visits of
a shipwrecked sailor exhausted all he had, except a
silver vessel set apart for the use of his mother ; this
he likewise gave, and the mendicant sailor at length

revealed himself to be an angel. Gregory became an abbot, and his severity was not less conspicuous than his benevolence. His brother Justus, who became a monk, had concealed, against the law of the monastery, three pieces of gold; when he was dying he confessed his crime. Gregory prohibited all approach to the bed of his brother, and when he was dead commanded his body to be cast out upon the dunghill. It was not till the end of sixty days that Gregory proclaimed that his prayers had been successful in releasing his brother from the flames of hell.

I need not repeat the story of the fair-haired boys who were exposed for sale in the slave-market of Rome, and of whom Gregory said, when told that they were Angli, ' Non Angli sed Angeli.'

In a time of the deepest calamity, when the Tiber had overflowed its banks and a dreadful pestilence was added to the miseries caused by the inundation, Gregory was called upon by the public voice, which he could not permanently resist, to ascend the papal throne. In performing the duties and elevating the reputation of the Holy See, Gregory surpassed all who had gone before him. The ritual of the Church assumed more perfect form and magnificence ; the chant, which took its name from the pontiff, was more full and more rich than that of Ambrose at Milan, and the Pope condescended himself to instruct whole schools of singers.

The revenues of the Papal See were greatly increased and enlarged. When collected they were distributed for the relief of the poor, and for abundant

*H

charities and endowments. The administration of
the Pope was unimpeachably just and humane. While
intent on relieving the peasantry and all the subjects of the Roman See from oppressive exactions and
illegal demands, Gregory kept up a correspondence
with the most distant regions. He converted the Lombards from the Arian heresy, and sent Augustine to
convert the English to Christianity. Gregory died in
the fulness of his fame, leaving the reputation of a
rigid adherent to the ecclesiastical rules of which he
was in great part the founder, of a wise administrator
of the power and the influence to which the Roman
See had already attained, of a ruler who denied himself every sinful indulgence, of a sovereign more powerful than the Emperor of the East, of an author whose
writings would have enabled him in a private station
to guide the opinions of the world.

We have now to lament the change which disgraced
the end of the ninth and the beginning of the tenth
century.   .

The immorality of the Holy See during the middle
ages is well painted by the Cardinal Baronius :—' What
was the appearance of the Holy Roman Church when
powerful and base prostitutes governed Rome ? by
whose will sees were changed, bishops were assigned,
and, what is shocking and horrible to relate, their
lovers were introduced pontiffs into the seat of
Peter, and who are by no means to be counted in
the number of the popes of Rome, unless as marking
the succession. For who can call those legitimate
Roman pontiffs who were thus introduced by harlots

without the sanction of law? For there is no mention of the clergy in the election, or even as consenting to the confirmation of them. All the canons suppressed in silence, the decrees of the popes strangled, the ancient traditions and the old customs for the election of popes proscribed, the sacred rites and former usages nearly extinct. This lust of ambition, trusting to the secular power, insane with the passion of reigning, drew everything to itself.'

The late Dean of St. Paul's appears to doubt the representation of Baronius, and to think that the rigour of a puritanical sect has mixed itself with the fidelity of the historian. Yet the names of Theodora and Marozia remain, and no one seems to doubt that the one was the mistress and the other the mother of a pope. Indeed the titles of John X. and John XI. remain in the roll of the holy pontiffs, and they were as much entitled to the worship of the cardinals and the claim of infallibility as Gregory the Great and Pius VI.

The whole stream of history has been rendered foul and turbid by a crime, which is perhaps of more importance to the world than the vices or illegitimacy of two or three of the popes, however flagrant and however notorious.

In the year 867, Nicholas I., a very able and distinguished pope, died. During the time he filled the papal throne appeared the record of the gift of the sovereignty of Italy by Constantine the Great to Pope Sylvester. This gift is now acknowledged to have been a forgery. By the time of Ariosto it had become

the object of open satire, even in Italy. Astolpho finds
it among the chimæras of earth in the moon :

> Or puzza forte.
> Questo era il don (se però dir lice)
> Che Constantino al buon Silvestro fece.
>
> *Orl. Fur.* xxxiv. 80.

At the same time appeared the False Decretals, pre-
tending to be a collection made by Isidore of Seville,
containing a vast number of decrees relating to the
forms of public worship, to the administration of
the Roman See, to the powers and prerogatives of
the popes from the time of Clement I., through many
successive centuries. These decrees, regulations, and
directions are drawn up in a tone of the most profound
piety and the most sincere desire for the advancement
of the Christian religion. Yet no one now doubts that
Isidore of Seville had nothing to say to their editor-
ship, that they are not only very impudent, but very
clumsy forgeries, to which Pope Nicholas I. must
have been a consenting party, if not an actual con-
triver. It is now alleged that as many of the provisions and regulations thus forged have been acknowledged as genuine by a long succession of Popes, and
were allowed to pass by Hincmar, the opponent of
Nicholas, it little matters whether they were authentic
documents or awkward forgeries. The forgery of
what are called the False Decretals has been exposed, together with the famous donation of Constantine, in 'the Pope and the Council,' by Janus, supposed to have been written by two learned Germans,

and in many other learned works, some of them written by adherents of the infallibility of the pope. Whether the acknowledgment of a whole train of forgeries in the ninth and tenth centuries be of great or little consequence to the judgment of the pope's infallibility by the Council of the Vatican, does not appear to me to be a matter of much moment. The Protestants rely upon the words of the New Testament, and as the Pope's infallibility can derive no support from Holy Writ, it is not for Protestants to trouble themselves with the dispute.

Yet there is one aspect in which the various forgeries, interpolations, and misrepresentations of the popes, the cardinals, and the Curia of Rome are of great importance. We may neglect the encroachments and the usurpations of Hildebrand, of Gregory IX., of Innocent IV., and others, invested with the authority or the influence of the Roman See. But we cannot forbear to 'mark and inwardly digest' the system which these encroachments tended to erect, the corruptions by which they were disgraced, and the catastrophe in which they terminated.

By various steps, sometimes audacious and hasty, sometimes artful and slow, the whole patronage of naming the archbishops and bishops of Europe, of appointing them in the first place, and disposing of their influence in the second place, was vested in Rome. A candidate, who wished to be a bishop, borrowed an enormous sum from the usurers and jobbers of Rome, and afterwards discharged his debt by selling all the clerical patronage within his gift. If the sale of his spiritual patronage should be stopped by reform, the bishop or the usurer would be ruined. Hence it was found impossible in the days of Leo X. and of Adrian, to reform the gross abuses of the Papal See. Those abuses were so obstinately upheld and so scandalously enlarged, that no resource remained but the Reformation.

Soon after the beginning of the twelfth century, the pope ceased for half a century to be the centre round whom the public opinion of the most educated classes revolved, and who influenced the more enlightened nations of Europe.

Yet, before the rise of St. Bernard and the monastic orders, there occurred that great contest between Hildebrand and the secular princes of Europe, which covered all Europe with blood, and might have established, for a time at least, a theocracy fatal to the government of kings and of parliaments, and destructive of social happiness, the ties of marriage, and the peace of every state. It is necessary upon this occasion to mark who were the chiefs that led the opposing forces and what were the principles for which they contended. The contending chiefs were not equally matched ; Hildebrand, who rose from a family of the middle classes at Rome, was a man of extraordinary energy and immense ambition. In some few cases he met with his match : for instance, the papal influence had been used in favour of the Norman Conquest of England. The banner of St. Peter floated in the van of William's army at the battle of Hastings ; but when Hildebrand, who had become pope, and had assumed the title of Gregory VII., demanded the fealty of the King of England, the Conqueror returned this short and haughty answer, 'I have not, nor will I swear fealty, which was never sworn by any of my predecessors to yours.' But to kings of a less determined character, the pope's language was imperious and insulting: to Philip I., king of France, he wrote in these terms, 'No king has reached such a height of detestable guilt in opposing the churches of his kingdom as Philip of France.'

The subjects upon which Hildebrand was determined to have his own will were two: the first was the suppression of simony, the second the prohibition of the marriage of the clergy. On the first of these subjects the pope was not likely to obtain his own will; every transaction, involving the appointment of a bishop, a canon, or a priest, was stained by bribery, in which the giver and the receiver were equally guilty and equally secret. Rome was becoming more and more a spiritual market, where those who had taken an oath against simony were deeply implicated throughout their whole lives in simoniacal practices. These practices continued for at least four centuries, and were the proximate cause of the Reformation. The other question, that of the marriage of the clergy, still more excited the anger of Gregory, and gave rise in every country to the most violent quarrels, and disturbed the peace of every community. Those who followed Hildebrand in his invectives against the marriage of priests were obliged to confess that in almost every priest's house concubinage prevailed;

but this name was often calumniously affixed to connections which had received the sanction of religion.
In Normandy, in France, in England, in Spain, and
in Germany, the sons and daughters of priests were
acknowledged, and lived in the home of their fathers;
but the adherents of Hildebrand affixed every sort
of opprobrious name to these connections: incest and
unnatural crime were usually imputed to the married
priests; and it is impossible to ascertain how much
truth there might be in these passionate imputations.
It is certain, however, that the celibacy of the clergy
was productive of a far worse state of morals than
their concubinage. The peace of families was invaded, the secrets of married life became the property
of the priests, and a way was thus opened to the extension of the priestly power over every relation of
life. Of this Hildebrand must have been well aware,
but while he denied himself every gratification that
exceeded the most rigid rules of abstinence from
any sensual indulgence, his ambition seems to have
counselled him to create an order of men wholly
subject to sacerdotal rule, who might govern the
laity with an iron rod, and obey the slightest wish
of the one tyrant, who commanded their separation
from all human and social affections. In this object,
Hildebrand was to a great degree successful; the
celibacy of the clergy became, after the eleventh
century, the prevailing usage; and the concubinage
of the priest, if known to exist, was not allowed by
the priests, who obtained in confession the secrets
hidden from the husband and the father.

Yet although, in the long struggle which took place on this subject, Gregory was triumphant, and the Roman clergy were content to sacrifice married happiness and all the kindly relations which subsist between the parent and the child, the victory of ambition was not obtained without many a painful contest, and the general prevalence of hypocrisy and of falsehood.

The great contest which took place was between Gregory, a man of unconquerable will and the most self-denying habits, of mature age, bold and resolute in the wars which he undertook, artful and designing in the negotiations which he directed, and his rival, Henry IV., emperor of Germany, a young man, ill-educated, whose camp was followed by troops of concubines, and whose chief advisers were men whose characters inspired little respect. · In the year 1006, Gregory prepared to make war against Henry. Henry, on his side, summoned the prelates of Germany to Worms, and wrote thus bitterly of his own position and that of the pope : 'Henry, not by usurpation, but by God's ordinance, king, to Hildebrand, no longer pope, but the false monk ; ' and again, 'I Henry, by the grace of God king, with all the bishops of my realm, say unto thee, "Down, down ! " ' This war ended calamitously for Henry. In the year 1077, Gregory appeared at Canosa in the character of an imperious and haughty conqueror, Henry as a defeated and humble penitent. On January 25, on a dreary winter morning, Henry was permitted to enter within the two outer of the three walls which guarded the castle of Canosa ; he was clad in the thin, white linen dress of the penitent. A first, second, and a third day he stood fasting, awaiting the merciless decree of the pope. Even on the third day he would not have been admitted to the pope's presence had he not implored the mediating influence of the Countess Matilda. This scene has been narrated by one of the most accurate of monkish annalists, Lambert of Hertzfeldt. From his account it appears that when Henry implored humbly the assistance of the Abbot of Clugny, the godfather of the Emperor, the Abbot turned to the Countess and said, 'Thou alone canst accomplish this.' To female entreaties Gregory at length yielded, and permitted Henry, still in the garb of penitence, with bare feet, to stand before his priestly throne. The Emperor, a man of a singularly tall and noble person, after falling on his knees before the Countess, was admitted to stand before the Pope, a grey-haired man of unimposing stature, bowed with years and fasting. The Pope insisted, before he would grant absolution, that if Henry should recover his kingdom, he should rule according to the counsel of the Pope, and correct whatever was contrary to the ecclesiastical laws. Henry having sworn to fulfil these conditions, absolution was granted him. But Gregory had not yet done with his victim. Having ordered the Eucharist to be prepared, he called the King towards the altar, lifted in his hands the consecrated host, and said, 'I have been accused by thee, and by thy partisans, of having usurped the Apostolical See by simoniacal practices, of having been guilty, both before and after my election to the episcopate, of crimes which would disqualify me for my sacred office. I might justify myself by proof, and by the witness of those who have known me from my youth, whose suffrages have raised me to the Apostolic See. But to remove every shadow of suspicion, I appeal from human testimony to divine. Behold the Lord's body; be this the test of my innocence. May God acquit me by his judgment this day of the crimes with which I am charged; if guilty, strike me dead at once.' He took and ate the consecrated bread. A burst of admiration thrilled the congregation.

Henry was appalled. Gregory exclaimed, ' Do thou, my son, as I have done.' The King hesitated. He retired to a short distance to consult his followers. He then said, that, before he accepted this challenge, he ' must appeal to the princes who adhered to his cause. · The Pope, who had already granted absolution, granted his request for time, received the King at a banquet, and treated him with courtesy.

There seems to have been much reluctance on the part of the haughty and severe Gregory to push the quarrel to extremities. He might, no doubt, have deposed Henry, who would hardly have recovered from such a blow. Why did he pause? Was the compassion of Matilda roused by the humiliation of a handsome sovereign kneeling at her feet? Was the Pope, doubtful of the policy of provoking the nobles of Germany and the chiefs of Lombardy into a bloody and dangerous resistance? Were the ashes still burning and prepared for a new conflagration?

Be the causes what they might, from this time

Henry was allowed to recover his strength, and the object of Hildebrand, that of reducing the sceptres of Europe to subjection under the triple tiara of Rome and the mitres of the sacerdotal order, was never attained. Far other was the event of the struggle.

A bloody war was carried on for many years between Gregory as the assertor of the sacerdotal, and Henry as the champion of the secular power. A rival to Henry was set up in the person of Rudolph of Suabia, but in a great battle on the Elster, Rudolph was mortally wounded.   In his dying words he seemed to express his doubts of the justice of the cause in which he had fought. Gazing upon his hand, which had been cut off by a sabre, he said, 'With this hand I ratified my oath of fealty to my sovereign Henry ; I have now lost life and kingdom. Bethink ye, ye who have led me on, in obedience to whose counsels I have ascended the throne, whether ye have guided me right.' [1]

After this event Henry, though defeated in battle, advanced into Italy. The Italians were generally for Henry.

For three years Henry besieged Rome, withdrawing his army during the heats of summer. At length Guiscard the Norman relieved Gregory, and captured Rome in the guise of a barbarous enemy. The Romans rose in insurrection. Guiscard gave the order to fire the houses. The inhabitants were hewed down by hundreds, nuns were defiled, matrons forced, the rings cut from their fingers. The vengeance of the

[1] Milman, vol. iii. p. 190.

Holy See was yet not satisfied. Thousands of Romans were sold as slaves. The ancient part of the city was destroyed. The old city was deserted, and new streets built over the Campus Martius. Such was the triumph of the cause of God, as it was represented by Gregory the pope, by Guiscard the Norman, and his followers the Saracens.

Gregory retired from the castle of St. Angelo to Salerno, where he soon after died by a lingering disease. Persuaded to the last of the justice of his cause and the piety of his conduct, he exclaimed, 'I have loved justice and hated iniquity; and therefore I die in exile.' Such was his haughty mind to the last.

ESSAY VIII

TRANSUBSTANTIATION. MONASTIC ORDERS.

AMONG the consequences which flowed from the growing superstition of the Christian schools, was the doctrine of Transubstantiation, which, beginning with an excess of devotion and awe at the commemoration of the Lord's Supper, had at length, at the instigation of Paschasius Radbert, a monk of Corvey, become a perpetual miracle. According to this monk, the elements ceased entirely to be what they still seemed to be to the outward senses. The bread and wine, it was affirmed, were annihilated, being changed into the body and blood of the Redeemer. The bread and wine used in the sacrament, it is true, were to the researches of chemical science not different from any other bread and wine placed on a table for food or refreshment, but in the minds of Christians, the real body and blood of Christ. This doctrine gave rise to bitter controversy, sometimes assuming the shape of the free exercise of thought and enquiry upon subjects of large discourse to the free exercise of the human understanding, at other times opening the way to wild flights of imagination. Speculators sank often, when dwelling upon this dogma, into a materialism founded solely upon a very gross theory. Among those who took part in these controversies were—Berenger of Tours, John Scotus or Erigena, and Lanfranc of Pavia. The following lines of Dryden contain that poet's argument in favour of transubstantiation :—

Good life be now my task; my doubts are done:
What more could fright my faith than Three in One?
Can I believe eternal God could lie
Disguised in mortal mould and infancy?
That the great Maker of the world could die?
And after that trust my imperfect sense,
Which calls in question His Omnipotence?
Can I my reason to my faith compel,
And shall my sight and touch and taste rebel?
Superior faculties are set aside :
Shall their subservient organs be my guide?

The weakness of this argument, eloquently as it is expressed, arises from the fact, that the conversion of the bread and wine of the sacrament into the body and blood of Christ, is not affirmed in the New Testament. The Church of England has therefore justly declared, ' Transubstantiation (or the change of the substance of bread and wine) in the supper of the Lord cannot be proved by Holy Writ; but is repugnant to the plain words of Scripture, overthroweth the nature of a sacrament, and hath given occasion to many superstitions.' Such is the belief of Protestants ; yet, although incredible to all but Roman Catholics, it would not be proper to speak, in the coarse manner of Swift in the ' Tale of a Tub,' of a doctrine which is deeply rooted in the minds of so great a portion of the Christian world.

This is properly the place to insert some account of the Monastic Orders. Bingham has divided the monastic age into three periods. In the first, there

were men and women who abstained from marriage,
refused amusements, and practised severe fasts, but in
the midst of society. In the second, hermits fled from
the Decian persecutions, and led a life of solitary priva-
tion. The third commenced with monastic institutions,
and led to life in the deserts of Africa, and to the great
monasteries and convents of Europe in the West. St.
Pachomius, who is said to have been the founder of
these institutions, is reported to have enlisted 9,000
monks. In the days of St. Jerome they had increased
to 50,000; an Egyptian city, named Oxyrinchus, is
said to have contained 20,000 nuns and 10,000 monks.
Egypt had become the possession of monks; there
the monastic system attained its extreme development, and practised its most severe austerity. St.
Jerome was at once its leader and its panegyrist.
St. Jerome was a man of much learning, of great
virtue, and considerable abilities; yet his admiration for the life of the Egyptian hermits is revolting and almost incredible. He declares, with a
fervour of approbation, that he had seen a monk who
for thirty years had lived on a small daily portion of
barley bread and muddy water; another, who lived in
a hole, and never ate more in a day than five figs; a
third, who cut his hair only on Easter Sunday, never
washed his clothes, wore his tunic till it fell to pieces,
and stared till his eyes grew dim.[1] His skin was like a
pumice stone. St. Macarius carried about him eighty
pounds of iron; he exposed his body naked to the

[1] Lecky's *History of European Morals from Constantine to
Charlemagne*, vol. ii. p. 424 et seq.

stings of venomous flies. St. Eusebius carried one hundred and fifty pounds of iron, and lived for three years
in a dried-up well. St. Sabinus would only eat corn
that had become rotten by remaining for a month in
water. St. Marcian and others confined themselves to
one meal a day, so small that they constantly suffered
the pains of hunger. St. Besarion for forty years never
lay down when he slept. The cleanliness of the body
was regarded by these fanatics as a pollution of the
soul. St. Athanasius relates how St. Antony, the
patriarch of monachism, who lived to extreme old age,
had never washed his feet.[1]

But enough of these monstrous practices. Tertullian, writing in the second century, to confute some
charges made by pagans, declared that, unlike the
hermits of India, Christians did not fly from the world,
but mixed with pagans in the forum, in the public
baths, and in the ordinary business of life.

With these social customs, the Christians of the West
had persuaded the world to change its religion, and
when monastic institutions travelled into Europe,
bringing habits of intercourse and familiarity with
business, they governed the world. In the twelfth
century there were two roads to eminence and to fame.
A young man of high birth and lively talents might
shine in arms at tournaments, or rise to distinction
in the polemical contests of theological display. St.
Bernard was born of noble parentage in Burgundy.
His father, Tecelin, was a man of high honour and

[1] Lecky, vol. ii. p. 117.

I

courage ; his mother Alith was famed for her piety and charity. Bernard might have aspired to high military distinction or to the most eminent post in the Church. He enquired instead for the poorest, the most severe, the most inaccessible of monasteries. He found it at Citeaux, and the force of his example drew into monastic life his brothers, his sister, and even his father. From Citeaux he marched with a colony of monks to a valley in Champagne, where he led a life of harsh labour, hardly eating enough to keep him alive, and so mortifying his senses that they lost all perception of things within his sight, hearing, and taste. He suffered the direst extremity of famine, till the neighbouring peasants with reverential piety brought to him and his companions supplies of food. He called his monastery by the melodious name of Clairvaux. His miracles became famous, his name spread through France, Italy, Germany, England, and Spain.

The papal tiara was in dispute between Innocent II. and Anacletus II. Innocent appealed to France, and the king of France, by the advice of Bernard, decided in his favour. Henry I. of England hesitated. ' Thou fearest the sin of acknowledging Innocent,' said Bernard ; ' answer thou for thy other sins ; be that one upon my head.' Henry submitted ; Germany and Spain followed the example of France and England. Innocent entered Italy ; the Emperor Lothair and Bernard accompanied him to Rome, where Innocent rewarded the Emperor and his Empress by crowning them with solemn pomp in the Lateran church.

Bernard, while constantly sighing for the shades of

Clairvaux and seclusion, could not resist the orders of the Pope and neglect the interests of the Church. He employed the Emperor Lothair against the King of Sicily. Anacletus died in the fortress of St. Angelo, and on April 4, 1139, a council of a thousand bishops and numerous abbots was held in the palace of the Lateran.

Innocent and Bernard were alike unforgiving. After inveighing against his rival, the Pope gave forth his decree:—' We degrade all whom he has promoted; we expel from holy orders and depose all whom he has consecrated.'[1]

Not content with thus raising his client the Pope, Bernard animated the King of France and the Emperor of Germany to undertake a new crusade. Popular enthusiasm was roused; the crusade was undertaken by the two most powerful sovereigns in Europe. But the issue was unfortunate; crusades were out of date, and the sovereigns returned baffled and inglorious, with the loss of thirty thousand lives in battle and by disease.

The triumphs of Bernard the recluse in the world and over the world were not yet complete. After the death of Innocent II. and three short-lived successors, Eugenius III. was elected pope, because he was a Cistercian, the friend of Bernard, and the foe of Abelard. 'People say,' wrote Bernard to Eugenius, 'that you are not pope, but that I am.' ('Aiunt non vos esse papam sed me.') Of the Pope he wrote in the spirit of the Puritans, 'Is this a man to gird on the

[1] Milman.

sword, and to execute vengeance on the people, to
bind their kings with chains, and their nobles with
links of iron?' Eugenius, however, became a more
powerful pope than had been expected. · He recovered
Rome, and forced the republic of Arnold of Brescia
to capitulate. Bernard died in the year 1153.

I wish only to notice the most prominent revolutions
in the history of the Church. One of these is the
influence of Abelard. The life of Abelard furnishes
a curious proof of the prevalence of logical forms
in substitution of the loving spirit of Christianity,
and is in another respect an interesting episode in
the great epic of the Christian Church. When
Abelard was not more than twenty years old, he travelled through France, arguing, discussing, and com-
bating with his unbending logic the most famous
doctors of divinity. He met William of Champeaux,
and other men of brilliant reputation, with an acuteness which showed him a thorough master of the
thrust and parry of theology. His quick perception
and bold advance against the strongest positions of
the Christian dogma made him an adept in spiritual
fence. When he was more than forty he fell under
the sway of another passion. He coolly meditated
the seduction of a young girl, the daughter of a canon
of the name of Fulbert. The canon, tempted by
the learning and cheapness of the tutor, admitted
Abelard into his house, and even told him that
if his daughter were disobedient he might use corporal chastisement to correct her. Heloise was enthusiastic, full of admiration of Abelard's talents;

the canon credulous and unsuspicious. It was soon rumoured that the preceptor had seduced his pupil; and the matter became so notorious that the lovers were obliged to fly, and Heloise soon after gave birth to a male child. The canon awakened from his dream, was furious, and as a just reparation insisted upon Abelard's marrying his daughter. This condition Abelard readily accepted, though, as a priest, his worldly prospects would be much injured, if not totally overclouded by his marriage. But a woman is not to be outdone in generosity, and Heloise, though she reluctantly consented to marry, loudly protested that she was not the wife, but the mistress of Abelard.

> Not Cæsar's empress would I deign to prove,
> But make me mistress to the man I love.[1]

The enraged canon, with his relations and friends, determined by one act of signal vengeance to incapacitate the priest. By the laws of the Church the mutilation of Abelard would ensure his exclusion from its honours. This vengeance was inflicted. But the tender, loving, noble nature of Heloise was not thus to be overcome; she urged Abelard to pursue his distinguished career as a theologian, and retired herself into a convent. She inhabited, for a time, the Paraclete, a building erected by Abelard himself. She then became an abbess, and saw Abelard in secret interviews.

Abelard had endeavoured, with piercing and unsparing logic, to point out the various differences

---

[1] Pope's *Eloisa to Abelard.*

which had disturbed the unity of the Church, and to mark the variations of the most revered fathers in defining the mysterious doctrines of Christian theology. He had tested by reason and by analysis the doctrine of the Trinity and the sacraments of the Church. Bernard, inflamed with holy zeal, panted for the condemnation of so bold a reasoner. In a letter to the Pope he complained, 'These works of Abelard are flying about all over the world; they no longer shun the light, they find their way into castles and cities; they jump from land to land, from one people to another. A new gospel is promulgated, a new faith is preached. Disputations are held on virtue and sin not according to Christian morality; on the sacraments of the Church not according to the rule of faith; on the mystery of the Trinity not with simplicity and soberness.' Abelard, in an evil hour for himself, challenged Bernard to allow him to make good his charges. A council had been summoned at Sens to approve the translation of the body of the patron saint; the second day of this council was fixed for the theological duel between Bernard and Abelard. But when the hour arrived, Abelard, foreseeing the result, refused to argue the question, and appealed to Rome. But the growing anger of Bernard was not to be thus appeased. After taunting his adversary with his silence, he proceeded, after the withdrawal of Abelard, to send for his books, and desired one of the persons present to read out the objectionable parts. The bishops grew weary, and sent for wine to relieve their fatigue. The wine

made them still more sleepy, and they sat, some
leaning on their elbows, some with cushions under
their heads, some with heads dropping on their knees.
Still they had voice enough to cry, whenever the
reader paused, ' damnamus,' till at length, overcome
by sleep, they could only faintly breathe ' namus.'

Abelard's chance before the Pope was still more
hopeless. The report of the Council of Sens declared, ' Abelard makes void the whole Christian
faith by attempting to comprehend the nature of God
through human reason.' Before the charge was fully
known at Rome, Abelard, absent and unheard, was
condemned by the supreme pontiff. Abelard had set
out for Rome, but was delayed by severe illness, and
took refuge in the hospitable abbey of Clugny.
There Peter the Venerable received him, and thus
testifies of · his pious behaviour, ' I never saw his
equal for humility of manners and habits ; St. Ger-
manus was not more modest, St. Martin poorer. He
allowed no moment to escape unoccupied by prayer,
reading, writing, or dictation. The heavenly visitor
surprised him in the midst of these holy works.' [1]
After two years of ill-health he died, and the words
just quoted were written by Peter the Venerable to
Heloise, who still took an affectionate interest in
his welfare. His remains were conveyed to the Paraclete, where for twenty-one years Heloise mourned, with
all a woman's fondness, her teacher, her lover, and
her husband.[2] For him she had sacrificed her virgin
honour and her worldly fame.

[1] Milman, vol. iii. p. 377.   [2] Ibid.

Arnold of Brescia was the foremost of the disciples of Abelard ; indeed the only one who has left a great reputation behind him. Declining the study of abstruse theology, he was in doctrine strictly orthodox ; but his ardent temperament, and his indignation at the grasping ambition and boundless avarice of the priesthood, led him to denounce the wealth of the clergy, and to proclaim austerity of life, and abstinence from all carnal gratifications, as the only mode of following the precepts of Christ. With his religious severity he combined a love of republican democracy ; his political zeal enabled him to establish in Brescia, and even in Rome for a short time, a social republic, where power was elective, and the Church was deprived of her palaces, her lands, her luxury, and her wealth.

After a troubled career of alternate victory and defeat, he was at length slain by order of the Pope. But his name still survives in the memory of Italian reformers, and of late years a large subscription has been commenced to erect a statue to his honour in his native place.

Another remarkable illustration of the manner in which the Western monasteries gave a practical bias to monastic life, and sought to influence, animate, and govern the world, is afforded by the life of St. Dominic.

While lecturers and orators of all kinds declaimed against the scandalous lives of the clergy, Dominic instituted an order of men whose whole business was to preach and to teach on behalf of the orthodox Church. His success was prodigious. Dean Milman says of him :

'By him Christendom was at once overspread with a host of zealous, active, devoted men, whose function was popular instruction. They were gathered from every country, and spake therefore every language and dialect. In a few years, from the sierras of Spain to the steppes of Russia, from the Tiber to the Thames, the Trent and the Baltic Sea, the old faith, in its fullest mediæval, imaginative, inflexible vigour, was preached in every town and hamlet. The Dominicans did not confine themselves to popular teaching ; the more dan- gerous, if as yet not absolutely disloyal seats of the new learning, of enquiry and of intellectual movement, the universities of Bologna, Paris, and Oxford, are invaded and compelled to admit these stern apostles of unswerving orthodoxy.' [1]

St. Dominic was born in the year 1170, in the vil- lage of Calaroga, between Aranda and Osma, in old Castile. He bore the noble name of Guzman. His disciples asserted that he was born without original sin, having been sanctified in his mother's womb. Mingling classical fable with sacred history, they af- firmed that bees settled on his lips. He early showed devout enthusiasm and profound sagacity. During a famine he sold his clothes to feed the poor. He joined, as a canon, a chapter of extreme austerity ; but it was observed that he preferred the conversation of young girls to the garrulity of old women. He remained in the chapter of Osma from his twenty- fifth to his thirty-fourth year.

In the year 1203, the Bishop of Osma, a prelate of

[1] Milman's *Latin Christianity*, vol. iv. p. 248.

great ability and acknowledged piety, was sent on a mission to Denmark, to negotiate the marriage of Alfonso VIII. with a princess of that kingdom. He took Dominic with him, and they crossed the Pyrenees together. The intent of the mission was frustrated by the death of the princess, but the journey into Languedoc brought the prelate and his companion to the region where the Albigensian heresy flourished, and papal authorities were observed to be employed in its suppression. On their return the bishop and his companion went to Montpellier, where they encountered the three papal legates, Peter of Castelnau, the Abbé Arnold, and Brother Raoul. Seeing the pomp of the legates, their large retinue and vast expense, Dominic gave them a severe reproof: ' It is not by the display of power and pomp,' he said, ' cavalcades of retainers, and richly houseled palfreys, by gorgeous apparel, that the heretics win proselytes; it is by zealous preaching, by apostolic humility, by austerity, by seeming, it is true, but yet by seeming holiness. Zeal must be met by zeal, humility by humility, false sanctity by real sanctity, preaching falsehood by preaching truth.' By this bold remonstrance the legates were, for a time, shamed; they dismissed their splendid equipages, and pursued their way with bare feet. But whatever effect their preaching might have had was marred by the murder of Peter of Castelnau, when crossing a river, by a retainer of Count Raymond.

From that time the slaughter of the Albigenses was the only object pursued. The Bishop of Osma retired to his diocese. Dominic remained, and while Simon de Montfort defeated and dispersed the heretics at the great battle of Muret, the saint was in a neighbouring church praying for the success of the orthodox army.

What St. Dominic's panegyrists have said of his assisting at the tribunals where heretics were condemned to the flames may be mistaken, and what the pope of a subsequent age has celebrated, that he was the founder of that admirable institution, the Inquisition, may be exaggeration; but it is certain that, in taking leave of the Albigensian provinces, he appealed to force as the remedy for erroneous opinions. After high mass at the convent of Prouille, he thus spoke : 'For many years I have spoken to you with tenderness, with prayers, and tears ; but according to the proverb of my country, where the benediction has no effect the rod may have much. Behold now we rouse up against you princes and prelates, nations and kingdoms ! Many shall perish by the sword. The land shall be ravaged, walls thrown down, and you, alas ! reduced to slavery. So shall chastisement do that which blessing and mildness could not do.'[1] Dominic now took up his residence at Rome. He was made by the Pope, Honorius III., master of the sacred palace. His success as a preacher was unrivalled. No wonder that when he founded an order of preachers and teachers, those young men who hoped to emulate his eloquence and to exercise a lasting influence over their age, flocked to his sacred

[1] *Latin Christianity*, vol. iv. p. 256.

standard. But his power did not stop there. He associated with his order lay persons of both sexes and of all ages; they attended the churches where a Dominican was expected to preach, and propagated his doctrines in every rank and order of society. St. Dominic himself confided to an intimate colleague the secret that he had never asked anything in prayer to God which God had not granted. This secret, discreetly divulged, vastly augmented the influence of the Dominican brotherhood. Dominic died at Bologna on August 6, 1221.

Francis, the son of a merchant or shopkeeper of Assisi, a romantic town situated between Rome and Florence, was born in 1182. When young he squandered his father's property in procuring rich dresses and giving costly banquets. Being attacked by a dangerous illness, he became on his recovery fanatical in his religious devotion. But his piety was not less costly to his prudent father than his prodigality. Being trusted with a horse and a bale of goods to be sold, he gave the price of the goods and the money obtained by the sale of his horse to a priest, for the purpose of rebuilding the church of St. Damian. He dressed himself as a beggar, and solicited alms in the streets. Having proposed to Pope Innocent III. to found a new order, the Pope, repelled by the dirty and sordid appearance of this devout beggar, rejected him with contempt. But on better information he received the mendicant in public, and authorised the foundation of the Order of St. Francis. The result of the foundation of the Dominican and Franciscan orders did not fully appear till the thirteenth century. Then flourished the five famous schoolmen, Albert the Great and Thomas Aquinas, Dominicans; Bonaventura, Duns Scotus, and William of Ockham, Franciscans. Of these, the most known, at least by name, is Thomas Aquinas. But they all laboured in the field of controversy, and all aimed at the great and apparently difficult task of converting the pure and simple religion of Christ, breathing love and charity, into a hard, logical, and voluminous science, requiring scholastic learning, but dispensing with, or at least passing by, or laying light stress upon, moral virtues.

But if the task was difficult, the way had been carefully prepared by men of acute intellect, immense power, and prodigious influence over their age. Athanasius, Jerome, and Augustine had taught theories of the nature of God and Christ, which the sons and successors of Constantine enforced by the sword.

ESSAY IX

THE SCHOOLMEN.

DEAN Milman has compared the works of the Schoolmen to the pyramids of Egypt, constructed with
immense labour, prodigious in the extent and variety
of their passages and divisions, and totally useless
to all succeeding generations. But the learned Bishop
Hampden has well remarked,—' The existence alone
of that system in the very heart of the Christian
Church for so many centuries—for more than a thousand years, if we comprise the period of its formation antecedent to its perfect maturity—for more
than five centuries if we look only to its perfect development—is a most striking fact.' Dr. Hampden
goes on to state, that although we meet with some
incidental remarks on the theoretic character of the
system in works of philosophy or theology, yet ' with
these remarks it is usually dismissed as a method
long gone by, which had its day and is now extinct.'
But the age of the Schoolmen is an age in which the
struggle of Christian scholars to impart to religion the
light of advancing knowledge ; to borrow from ancient
philosophy its highest lessons, and to spread the light so
borrowed over the whole religious world, occupied the
greatest minds and embraced the labours, the leisure,

the deliberation of an intelligent and active age. The sublime abstractions of Plato at first dazzled the scholars of the time; the dialectical skill and logical precision of Aristotle afterwards entranced and conquered the minds of Albert the Great, of Thomas Aquinas, and of all the leaders of intellectual progress for centuries. Athanasius, Augustine, Jerome, and Ambrose had sought in the Christian Scriptures the knowledge of God and the true sense of the lessons which Christ Himself had given to mankind. The Schoolmen expanded their studies by profound research into Greek philosophy, into the classical works on ethics of Latin authors, and the ingenious and extensive productions of Arabian scholars. Unhappily in this research they converted the simple and sublime theology of Christ and his moral teachings into a metaphysical doctrine fenced with subtle definitions, hedged with dialectical armour, but totally unfit to replace a religion in which God spoke to mankind and taught them with authority what to believe and what to do.

It would be entirely incorrect, however, to say that the Scholastic method is a method long gone by, with which we have nothing to do. On the contrary, upon the arguments of the Schoolmen were founded the tenets of the Roman Catholic Church as contained in the decrees of the Council of Trent, and the articles of the Reformed Church of England as agreed to by Convocation and approved by Queen Elizabeth and by Parliament.

The materials from which the Schoolmen framed

their system of theology were various, and to many minds might have appeared irreconcilable.

There was first the theology of Plato, according to which God was the supreme Creator, and the universe his only begotten son.

Then came the theology of Aristotle, which materialised the universe, and, having converted the ideas of Plato into real material substances, argued upon them with all the force and subtlety of that admirable logic of which he was the prime founder and teacher.

After these, and to be combined with these, were the words of Christ and the doctrines of St. Paul.

Christ had said, ' I am in God.' But He had also said that He was inferior to the Father.

Albertus Magnus, the great Schoolman, said ' that what was in God was God,' and proved dialectically that God the Son was equal to God the Father.

It is true that the Schoolmen thus laid down a dogma in direct contradiction to the words of Christ. But it will be found that the Schoolmen always preferred the logic of Aristotle to the word of Christ. Indeed, their object was not so much to follow Christ as to build a new edifice of theology with the materials which they borrowed from the Greek philosophers.

The consequence was the Athanasian creed, of which the author is unknown. It has been adopted by the Church of Rome and the Church of England, and has been made the condition of salvation by the ingenious

Schoolmen who preferred logic and metaphysics to the sublime simplicity of the Gospel.

The religion of Christ, as expounded by Himself and taught by his Apostles, was extremely simple. Men were taught to love one another; to forgive injuries; to abstain from murder, adultery, theft, and the appropriation of goods deposited with one of their community. The Apostles were to teach this religion in the name of the Father, the Son, and the Holy Ghost; of the nature of the invisible Beings who created and ruled the world but little was said. Christ had taught the woman of Samaria that God is a Spirit, and that those who worship Him must worship Him in spirit and in truth.

So likewise, in speaking to the scribe, He did not define the nature or the substance of the Spirit of God; He contented Himself with the words conveyed to mankind by Moses—'I am the Lord thy God: thou shalt have none other gods but Me.' Borrowing these words from the law of Moses, Christ taught from the same law the duty of man to love God with all his heart and soul, and to love his neighbour as himself. Christ, and his latest Apostle St. Paul, illustrated and enforced these Divine commands.

In other places and in earlier times a different religion had prevailed. Plato had taught that God had created the world, and he even used the phrase, 'The only begotten son of God;' but, in the idea of Plato, 'the only begotten son of God' was the universe. Aristotle reduced his vague notions to order and logical precision. About the twelfth and thirteenth

K

centuries there arose a set of very learned men who conceived the idea of uniting the religion of Christ with that of the Greek philosophers; but as the ideas of Plato were exceedingly intangible and indefinite, they founded this part of their religion rather on the teaching of Aristotle than on the dialogues of Plato. Paolo Sarpi, well versed in the theology of Rome, has said, 'If it were not for Aristotle, we should want many articles of faith : 'In che aveva una gran parte Aristotele coll' aver distinto esattamente tutti i generi di cause, a che, se egli non si fosse adoperato, noi mancaremo di molti articoli di fede.'[1]   Christ taught men to love God with all their heart and soul, without defining his attributes, or describing in detail his operations.

The religion of the Schoolmen, taking a totally different course, began with the existence and the functions of the Supreme Being, and was profuse in discussions upon the hierarchy of Heaven, the relation of the Holy Ghost to the Father and the Son, and the rank and position of the legions of angels which surrounded the throne and obeyed the commands of God.

It is no wonder, therefore, that these learned men should have left to posterity a religion totally transformed from the ancient forms of Christianity.   An accomplished Jesuit has said that there are no doctrines worth mentioning to be gathered from the writings of the first four centuries of the Christian era.   In fact, a new body of divinity sprang up which has largely influenced the opinions of modern times; and opinions,

[1] Paolo Sarpi, *Istoria del Concilio di Trento*, year 1547.

falsely supposed to have been those of Athanasius, have been recommended as of more authority than the words used by Christ Himself, or the weighty declarations which have been sanctified by the pen of St. Paul. I have said that the nature of Christ, as declared by Himself, was seldom defined. But towards the end of his life he declared, both to the Jews his enemies and to his followers and friends, the character He bore and the power He assumed. He said to the Jews, ' Is it not written in your law, I said, Ye are gods? If he called them gods, unto whom the word of God came, and the scripture cannot be broken ; say ye of Him whom the Father hath sanctified and sent into the world, Thou blasphemest, because I said, I am the Son of God? If I do not the works of my Father, believe Me not. But if I do, though ye believe not Me, believe the works : that ye may know, and believe, that the Father is in Me, and I in Him.' [1]

To his disciples He revealed Himself more fully. When He was about to die, and knew his doom, He said, ' If ye loved Me, ye would rejoice, because I said, *I go unto the Father: for my Father is greater than I.'* [2] Thus, having always addressed God Almighty as ' Our Father' and 'My Father,' and having said, when He was about to die, ' I go to my Father and your Father,' He revealed to the Jews that God was in Him, and He was in God. He also revealed more specially to his disciples, ' My Father is greater than I.' Such were the express and positive words of Christ. But the Schoolmen, being skilful dialecticians,

---

[1] St. John, chap. x.   [2] Ibid. chap. xiv.

concluded that because Christ declared He was in the Father, and the Father in Him, He was a separate Person, equal to God the Father. They asserted in the Athanasian Creed, as it is called :

'For there is one Person of the Father, another of the Son, and another of the Holy Ghost.

'But the Godhead of the Father, of the Son, and of the Holy Ghost is all one: the glory equal, the majesty coeternal.   .   .   .

'So the Father is God, the Son is God, and the Holy Ghost is God. And yet they are not three Gods, but one God.   .   .   .

'And in this Trinity none is afore or after other: none is greater or less than another. But the whole three Persons are coeternal together, and coequal.'

The words of Christ, 'My Father is greater than I,' and the words of the anonymous author of the so-called Athanasian Creed, that the three Persons, Father, Son, and Holy Ghost, are 'coeternal together and coequal,'[1] are evidently inconsistent with each other. Either the words of Christ must be accepted, and those of the Aristotelian or so-called Athanasian Creed rejected ; or the creed of Aristotle must be accepted, and the words of Christ rejected.

It would not be correct to attribute what is called the Athanasian Creed to the authorship prevalence of the great Schoolmen of the thirteenth century. Still, failing any authority which would enable me to fix the date of the introduction of that creed, or to name any

---

[1] The Confession of our Christian Faith, commonly called the Creed of St. Athanasius, Book of Common Prayer.

person who did not shrink from avowing its authorship, I will insert here what I have to say upon that head. In speaking of the harmony in thought, as well as of the deep impression left by the character of St. Athanasius in Western Christendom, Dean Stanley remarks that the most remarkable testimony is the ancient hymn, ' Quicunque vult,' which, throughout the middle ages and by our own Reformers, was believed to be the Creed of St. Athanasius. The learned world is now fully aware that it is of French or Spanish origin. It not only contains words and phrases which to Athanasius were unknown, but it distinctly and from the first asserted the doctrine of the double procession of the Spirit, which never occurs in the writings of Athanasius, and which, in all probability, he would have repudiated with his Oriental brethren of later times. But its partial resemblance to his style, and the assumption of his name, have given it an immense support.

Gibbon remarks in his famous history : ' The three following truths, however surprising they may seem, are now universally acknowledged. 1. Athanasius is not the author of the creed which is so frequently read in our churches. 2. It does not appear to have existed within a century after his death. 3. It was originally composed in the Latin tongue, and consequently in the Western provinces.' [1]

In later times, Archbishop Tillotson was unwilling to retain what is called the Athanasian Creed as part of our Articles of Religion. He writes to Bishop

[1] Gibbon, vol. vi. 8vo, note, p. 291.

Burnet in reference to Burnet's 'Exposition of the Thirty-nine Articles:' 'The account of Athanasius's Creed is in no way satisfactory; I wish we were well rid of it.' [1]   So do I.

What is called commonly the Creed of St. Athanasius is the work of an unknown author.   It is certain that the terms 'person' and 'substance,' 'consubstantial,' *hypostasis*, and other terms do not belong to the age of Athanasius.   The term *omoousion*, which is defined 'consubstantial, being of the same substance,' appears in the proceedings of the Council of Nice, but the creed called Athanasian appeared first in the Latin language.[2]   It was attributed at one time to Vigilius, Bishop of Tapsus, commonly called Vigilius Tapsensis. But subsequent enquiry has proved that the faith declared in the Athanasian Creed, was by no means the faith of Vigilius.   It has been said that the fact of the creed being anonymous gives value to its authority.   But that the words of an anonymous author ought to be preferred to the revealed words of Christ Himself I must firmly deny.   It is for all Christians to choose which authority they prefer.   They cannot accept a contradiction in terms for their sincere faith. They must accept the words of Christ and abandon the anonymous author, or adhere to the anonymous author and abandon the words of Christ.

---

[1] *Life of Tillotson.*

[2] ὁμοούσιος, ον (οὐσία), consubstantial, Plotin. Eccl.; τὸ ὁμοούσιον, sameness of essence or substance, opp. to τὸ ὁμοιούσιον, Eccl.: so, ὑμοουσιότης, ητος, ἡ; and ὑμοουσιαστής, οῦ, ὁ, one who maintains the doctrine of τὸ ὁμοούσιον.—Liddell and Scott's *Greek Lexicon*, p. 993.

But there is more to be said on this great subject. It was not the assertion of a single doctrine by Christ which was contradicted by this anonymous creed; but the whole theory of the author of the creed, and afterwards of the Schoolmen, amounted to the substitution of a religion founded upon Plato and Aristotle for the Church founded by Christ. Christ had declared more than once that he who embraced 'in spirit and in truth' two commandments was not far from the kingdom of God. One of these commandments was, 'Thou shalt love the Lord thy God with all thy heart and with all thy soul;' the other was, 'Thou shalt love thy neighbour as thyself.' One thing is quite apparent in these commandments: they were not injunctions to believe any definition of the nature of God. The existence of a Supreme Being, who had made heaven and earth, was taken for granted by Christ as the belief delivered by one to those to whom He spoke; his commandments were directed to the heart, and not to the understanding. The existence of God being assumed, according to the faith promulgated by Moses, man was told to love God with all his heart, and his neighbour as himself. 'God spake these words, and said, I am the Lord thy God: thou shalt have none other gods but Me.'

Thus the unity of God had been proclaimed by Moses and accepted by Christ. To the words of God, proclaimed by Moses, Christ had added, 'God is a Spirit, and they who worship Him must worship Him in SPIRIT and in TRUTH.' He had also declared that He came to fulfil the LAW.

All the teaching of Christ and his Apostles was in conformity with these commandments. Christ taught that it was not enough to say 'Lord, Lord,' but what was essential was to obey the commands of God. The disciples of Christ were told, 'If a man does not love his neighbour whom he has seen, how can he love God whom he has not seen?' The worship of the Virgin Mary was reproved in the words which told men rather to hear the commands of God and do them than to call for blessings on the mother who bore and nurtured Christ. St. Paul, in a similar spirit, had pointed out that a man who loved his neighbour would work him no ill.

The parables of Christ were all conceived in a similar spirit. The Samaritan who helped his neighbour, attended to his wounds, and left money for his support, was, in the eyes of the pharisaical Jews, a heretic. Christ, who did not share in the religious opinions of the Samaritan, held him up as an example of love to his neighbour. The priest and the Levite, who passed by on the other side, may have held doctrines of the most orthodox character, entirely free from the taint of the Samaritan errors, but they were evidently condemned as wanting in that love which is placed by his Apostle before faith and hope. The early Christians adopted these commandments for their guidance. The Christians who lived in the time of Trajan, and were condemned by Pliny, held themselves bound to return any treasure deposited with them to the person who had deposited it.

Thus the religion taught by Christ united two parts

—the one consisting of love to God and to all mankind, as the principle from which their actions should
flow ; the other, of actions derived from this fertile
and all-pervading principle.

The time had come, however, when the whole basis
of religion was to be changed. A number of able men,
deeply learned in Greek philosophy, abandoned almost
entirely the precepts of Christ, and out of the faith of
Christ, of Plato, and of Aristotle compounded a new
religion which was to give mankind a more perfect
understanding of the nature of the Supreme Being
than they had hitherto possessed. Nothing was wanting in the way of artificial, logical distinctions—or.
in definitions so subtle that the minds of the most
experienced philosophers failed to catch the precise
meaning of the terms used. The arts of Greek logic
were used in the construction of epithets so evanescent
and ambiguous that men of average understanding were
completely baffled in the attempt to affix to them the
true but hidden meaning. According to this new faith,
a man must subscribe to a number of propositions he
could not understand, but need not be very solicitous
whether the commandments, ' Thou shalt do no murder,'
' Thou shalt not steal,' and other moral laws were neglected or observed. Such was the certain, though
doubtless the unintentional, effect of the theology of
the new doctors. Accordingly, in the beginning of
the sixteenth century, when Martin Luther offered to
appear to discuss the meaning of the New Testament,
it was felt at Rome that the theologians upon whom
the cardinals relied for explaining and defending the

religion of the Roman Church were so imperfectly
acquainted with the Gospel that they could not be
expected to meet Luther on equal terms.[1] In effect,
the Roman Church from this time no longer rested on
the Bible, but was founded on the religion partly of
Christ, but partly, perhaps mainly, of Aristotle and
other pagan philosophers. One of the fairest ex-
pounders of the Scholastic philosophy, the late Bishop
Hampden, has said of it:

'Thus did the theologians of the Schools, with duti-
ful officiousness, gather up the fragments of revealed
truth; but, in the meantime, they lost the opportunity of feeding on the bread of God which came
down from heaven. Their piety became a superstition,
transubstantiating the truth of God into the verbal
elements by which it was signified.'[2] This has also
been the case with some eminent professors and theologians of the present day. But let us accompany Dr.
Hampden a little further:

'From the observations already made, it would
appear that the ethical nature of the Christian Scriptures had been insufficiently attended to by the divines
of the Schools. Eager to erect their theology into a
philosophy of the Divine Being, they were comparatively indifferent to the humbler truths which lay in
the walk of men's every-day life. But they did not at
the same time omit the consideration of human duties,
as I shall have an opportunity of showing on a future
occasion. What I would point out now is the dis-
paragement of Revelation as a code of moral discipline,

[1] Paolo Sarpi, *Istoria del Concilio di Trento.*
[2] Hampden's *Bampton Lectures.*

and the exaltation of theology, in the sense of a theoretic science, as the appropriate subject of the inspired volumes. This would follow, indeed, from the influence of that dialectical spirit with which they pursued the whole enquiry into Divine truth. *Conclusions*, and not precepts or rules of conduct, were the object of attention as they read ; and instead, therefore, of tracing the coincidence of revealed obligations with the internal laws of our moral nature, they were intent on applying the rules obtained, whether from Scripture or from the works of philosophers, to particular cases, and forming a code of casuistry rather than a theory of moral sentiments and duties. Happily for the ethical system of the Schools, the chief human authority followed was that of Aristotle.'[1] Be that as it may, it appears from the testimony and on the authority both of Paolo Sarpi and Bishop Hampden that the theology of the Schoolmen of the thirteenth and fourteenth centuries is founded not so much on the religion of Christ, as on the philosophy of Aristotle.

The boldness of Dr. Hampden in letting out so much truth raised a great outcry against him. All who joined in his opinion were called Socinians. This nickname had great effect with those who refused to read Hampden, and had never read Socinus. But no matter. ' Men are on fire in favour of falsehood ; they are cold as ice for truth.'[2]

Of all the learned Schoolmen, Thomas Aquinas has

---

[1] Hampden's *Bampton Lectures*, 3rd edit. Lecture II. p. 94.
[2] ' L'homme est de feu pour le mensonge,
Il est de glace aux vérités.'
LA FONTAINE.

of St. Bernard, the episcopal authority. Raymond,
Count of Toulouse, became the object of papal inter-
dict and rancorous enmity. He was loose in his
life; he had had five wives, three living at the same
time, and two of them of his kindred, within the
prohibited degrees. Peter of Castelnau and other
legates made pompous processions through the provinces. In crossing a river Peter de Castelnau was
killed; it is supposed by some follower of the Count
of Toulouse, but the pope, misled by false information,
or carried away by his own violent passions, declared
the Count of Toulouse himself guilty of the murder,
and heaped upon him the fiercest denunciation.

It would be tedious and disgusting to follow the
history of the persecutions ordered by the pope and
the King of France against the Albigenses. Immense
armies were collected, dreadful massacres were perpetrated, and the ferocity of the most savage tribes was
exceeded by the insane fury of those who professed
to enforce the spirit of the Gospel.

These reflections lead me to portray the origin,
progress, and history of persecution.

The treatment of heretics is thus prescribed by St.
Paul in his epistle to Titus, the first bishop of the
Cretans.

'A man that is an heretic after the first and second
admonition reject; knowing that he that is such is
subverted, and sinneth, being condemned of himself.'[1]

This peaceable rule seems to have been obeyed so
long as the Christians were not favoured by the state.

[1] Ep. to Titus, chap. iii.

The Council of Elvira in Spain, held in 303, at which Osius of Cordova and many other prelates assisted, decreed that if a heretic desired to be reconciled to the Church, he should be admitted on condition of undergoing a canonical penance of ten years. Other councils adopted the same course.

But when the emperors became Christians, and the Church was united to the state, a very different rule was adopted.

The first decree of persecution on behalf of the Christian Church was issued by the Emperor Theodosius, and the first victims were the Manichæans. Theodosius published in 382 an edict against the Manichæans, declaring that their lives should be forfeited and their goods confiscated. This decree sanctioned the employment of spies and secret accusers, and thus contained the germ of the Inquisition.[1]

The Albigensian war was connected with the establishment of the Inquisition. 'Never,' says Dean Milman, ' in the history of man, were the great eternal principles of justice, the faith of treaties, common humanity, so trampled under foot as in the Albigensian war. Never was war waged in which ambition, the consciousness of strength, rapacity, implacable hatred, and pitiless cruelty, played a greater part.'[2] Such a war was the great example followed by the Church of Rome in the war against the Lollards, in the burning of John Huss and Jerome of Prague, in the persecutions of heretics at Rome by the pope, in England by Queen

[1] Llorente, vol. i. Jortin's *Remarks*, vol. ii. p. 39.
[2] Milman's *Latin Christianity*, vol. iv. p. 408.

demons with as many elaborate distinctions and varieties as the rest of the system. Nothing can be more
logically marked out than the distinctions between these
spiritual beings; nothing more elaborate than the
attempts to avoid the errors of Arius and Sabellius.
Yet it is evident throughout that the system was
founded rather upon the doctrines of Aristotle than
upon those of Christ and Paul.

In short, nothing can more clearly prove the truth
of Bacon's remark, that there is great danger in the
attempt to mingle theological systems with philosophical
opinions—the danger of teaching a heterodox religion
on the one side, with an unsound philosophy on the
other. Aquinas was to be taken as the type of those
schools which in the fifteenth century built up a new
fabric of theology, which was henceforth to be substituted for the Christianity of the older fathers of the
Church. A learned Jesuit very truly said, according to
his own reading and his own opinions, that for the first
three centuries of the Christian era no writer worth consulting is to be found. In fact, the teachers of the fourteenth century founded a new system, which was, in effect,
an attempt to make a complete theory of the spiritual
world, founded rather upon the writings of Plato and
Aristotle than upon the simple and sublime teachings
of Christ and Paul. In order to enable them to perform
their task, they searched every avenue of learning.
One abundant source of knowledge was open to them
in the translation, by Arabic writers of celebrity, of
the classical works of Greece. The lectures upon
Aristotle were placed on the footing of orthodox

theology. The errors first disseminated were only to be corrected by searching the voluminous works of the most learned Schoolmen. The doctrines thus taught did not resemble, as Dean Milman imagined, the vast buildings erected to Cheops and other Egyptian monarchs, known by the name of the Pyramids of Egypt, and neglected as much as known, as useless products of ingenuity and labour. The doctrines of the Schoolmen were adopted by sovereigns and states as the true faith, and hundreds of thousands of bloody victims were offered in the pursuit of that unity of the faith which, in the opinion of the persecutors of Toulouse and the Inquisition of Spain, could not be purchased at too dear a price. I now turn to that progress of persecution which commenced with the Emperor Theodosius, and of which we have scarcely as yet seen the termination. Let me, however, say a few words by way of preface.

The doctrine that salvation can only be found in the Church is the fruitful source of persecution.

In examining the speculative logic of Christianity, we have to examine, according to Dr. Hampden, the principal obstacle to the union and peace of the Church of Christ. The reason is not far to seek; the Scriptures intimate to us certain facts concerning the Divine Being, and this kind of knowledge teaches us how to feel towards God. It is in truth the language which we understand, the language formed by our own experience and practice.

When, therefore, we are told to love God with all our hearts and minds, we understand very clearly that

we ought to worship Him, and to endeavour to obey
his commandments. So likewise, when we are told
to love our neighbour as ourselves, we may well understand that love worketh no harm to the object of love,
and that, as St. Paul explains it, love comprehends a
great number of duties comprised in the word love.
But when we proceed to define the nature of God,
his relation to Christ and to the Holy Ghost, it is
evident that the evil which logical theology has
imported into religion will be sufficiently apparent.
Signs have been converted into things, the combination
and analysis of words, which logical theology has
produced, have given opportunity to the passions of
men to arm themselves in defence of the phantoms
thus created. Thus, St. Augustine, the father of Latin
orthodoxy, while he directs his students to learn the
use of the weapons of disputation, especially warns
them against the passion for wrangling, and a childish
sort of ostentation of deceiving an adversary. '

Vanity mixed itself largely in these disputes. Every
teacher of theology invented some subtle distinction,
or some form of illustrating an old truth, which
had not been thought of by his contemporaries.
Thus, instead of being occupied in loving, the whole
world was given up to disputation ; and instead of
being intent on the practice of those virtues of which
Christ constantly preached the necessity, the pro-
moters of the Athanasian Creed prided themselves on
a number of logical puzzles, which seemed to throw
into a maze the most refined reasoning of the scholastic
doctors of their day.

Thus many men, who would have kept the tenor of their way piously, charitably, quietly, found themselves involved in an obligation to decide that their simple neighbours would perish everlastingly, and became partizans in one or more of these wars of perse-cution which saturated alternately with blood those towns of Languedoc, of Belgium, of Castile, of Andalusia, where they prevailed. To this history we shall presently address ourselves.

ESSAY X.

PERSECUTION.

THE increased power of the pope, the foundation of the orders of St. Francis and St. Dominic, and the lessons of scholastic philosophy, formed an immense system which showed at once the strength and the weakness of the Roman Church. The pretensions of the popes could not fail to produce a strong reaction. Accordingly, in the twelfth century, there arose in the different countries of Europe individuals of singular talents and learning, who were admired as prophets by their admirers, and arraigned as heretics by their opponents. Peter de Brueys who preached in the south of France for above twenty years, was arraigned by Peter the Venerable as denying (1) infant baptism ; (2) respect for churches ; (3) the worship of the cross ; (4) transubstantiation and the Real Presence ; (5) prayers, alms, and oblations for the dead. He was condemned, and burnt at St. Gilles, in Languedoc. To the five errors which had dimmed the fame of Peter de Brueys, his successor, Henry the Deacon, added many more. But soon these errors were not confined to individuals, or promoted solely by the eloquence or fame of individuals. Great bodies of heretics, distinguished as Manichæans or Waldenses, rose and confronted the Church in various districts of France and other countries of Europe. In the south of France, the Count of Toulouse and his vassals brought from the Crusades the gallantry of the Moors of Spain, and promoted a gay licence of manners, adverse not only to the austerities of monkish Christianity, but of pure Christian morals. The Troubadour, who was the poet laureate of his court, contributed by his poetry to spread a worship of the poetical mistress, and a neglect or contempt of the lawful wife. The cities rose in opulence and splendour, the chant in the castle chapel was silent or unheard. The pope and the King of France thought the time of repression was come. Innocent III. had hardly ascended the pontifical throne when he wrote an imperious letter to the Archbishop of Auch, followed by a papal manifesto, which broadly proclaimed the outlawry of all heretics, the right as well as the determination to banish them, to confiscate their property, and even to put them to death. The heretics on their side distinguished themselves not only by their disregard of the papal precepts, but by tenets of their own, aspiring to a perfect reformation of manners. In the year 1204 five of the most noble ladies of Provence promised to give themselves up to God and his gospel, to eat neither meat, eggs, nor cheese, to allow themselves only vegetables and fish, and to be faithful to the heretical sect, even unto death. The pope looked to the community founded by St. Bernard for the suppression of this dangerous heresy. He transferred to Peter of Castelnau and Raoul, both of the order of St. Bernard, the episcopal authority. Raymond, Count of Toulouse, became the object of papal inter- dict and rancorous enmity. He was loose in his life; he had had five wives, three living at the same time, and two of them of his kindred, within the prohibited degrees. Peter of Castelnau and other legates made pompous processions through the pro- vinces. In crossing a river Peter de Castelnau was killed; it is supposed by some follower of the Count of Toulouse, but the pope, misled by false information, or carried away by his own violent passions, declared the Count of Toulouse himself guilty of the murder, and heaped upon him the fiercest denunciation.

It would be tedious and disgusting to follow the history of the persecutions ordered by the pope and the King of France against the Albigenses. Immense armies were collected, dreadful massacres were perpe- trated, and the ferocity of the most savage tribes was exceeded by the insane fury of those who professed to enforce the spirit of the Gospel.

These reflections lead me to portray the origin, progress, and history of persecution.

The treatment of heretics is thus prescribed by St. Paul in his epistle to Titus, the first bishop of the Cretans.

' A man that is an heretic after the first and second admonition reject; knowing that he that is such is subverted, and sinneth, being condemned of himself.'[1]

This peaceable rule seems to have been obeyed so long as the Christians were not favoured by the state.

[1] Ep. to Titus, chap. iii.

The Council of Elvira in Spain, held in 303, at which Osius of Cordova and many other prelates assisted, decreed that if a heretic desired to be reconciled to the Church, he should be admitted on condition of undergoing a canonical penance of ten years. Other councils adopted the same course.

But when the emperors became Christians, and the Church was united to the state, a very different rule was adopted.

The first decree of persecution on behalf of the Christian Church was issued by the Emperor Theolosius, and the first victims were the Manichæans. Theodosius published in 382 an edict against the Manichæans, declaring that their lives should be forfeited and their goods confiscated. This decree sanctioned the employment of spies and secret accusers, and thus contained the germ of the Inquisition.[1]

The Albigensian war was connected with the establishment of the Inquisition. 'Never,' says Dean Milman, 'in the history of man, were the great eternal principles of justice, the faith of treaties, common humanity, so trampled under foot as in the Albigensian war. Never was war waged in which ambition, the consciousness of strength, rapacity, implacable hatred, and pitiless cruelty, played a greater part.'[2] Such a war was the great example followed by the Church of Rome in the war against the Lollards, in the burning of John Huss and Jerome of Prague, in the persecutions of heretics at Rome by the pope, in England by Queen

[1] Llorente, vol. i. Jortin's *Remarks*, vol. ii. p. 39.
[2] Milman's *Latin Christianity*, vol. iv. p. 408.

Mary, in the Low Countries by the Duke of Alva, and finally, in that most horrible of all tribunals, the Spanish Inquisition.

The army which moved from Lyons into Languedoc was computed to muster, besides knights and nobles, 200,000 soldiers. The young Vicomte de Berniers threw himself into his own town of Berniers, and valiantly defended it. The city was stormed; a general massacre ensued. Neither sex nor age were spared. From twenty to fifty thousand persons were slain. The cruel command was uttered, 'Slay them all, God will know his own.' The Monk of Vaux Cernay, the historian of these atrocities, says, ' Our people put to the sword all whom they could find, slaying them with fire and sword. For which blessed be the Lord, who delivers to us some of the wicked, although not all.'[1] Such was the religion of Christ, as explained by the monks. When Raymond VII. surrendered his title of Count of Toulouse, after the return of Louis IX. (St. Louis) to France, the Inquisition was instituted, with nearly all its features of horror and infamy. No advocate might appear before the tribunal, no witness was confronted with the accused, the proceedings were carried on in profound secrecy.

In 1229, at the Council of Toulouse, the tribunal of the Inquisition, under the papacy of Gregory IX., first received a regular form, and proceeded under the direction of the Dominicans to exercise its formidable powers. At the same council it was ordered that boys of fourteen, and girls of twelve years old, should take

---

[1] Coll. des Mémoires, p. 303.

an oath of fidelity to the Roman Catholic Church, attesting also their opposition to heresy. By another decree of the council, the reading of the Holy Scriptures was strictly prohibited to the laity. This was one of the measures perseveringly sanctioned by the Church of Rome with the intent to conceal from their lay followers a knowledge of the gospel. This was in fact a main cause of dispute between the pope and Wickliff, the pope and Jerome of Prague, the pope and John Huss, the pope and Martin Luther.

The grand project of all for defeating and extirpating heresy was brought to maturity in Spain. But as it sometimes happens to private persons that the physician is able to cure a disease, but that when the disease is thoroughly conquered the patient dies, so it happened in Spain, that no sooner was heresy extirpated than the state declined and perished. In fact the Spanish Inquisition, by making every exertion of the mind dangerous, all theological learning penal, and all social intercourse beset with unseen pitfalls, extinguished the mind of the nation, destroyed liberty in its parliament, valour in its armies, wisdom in its statesmen, and made one of the proudest and bravest nations in the world a bye-word for imbecility, ignorance, and apathy.[1] But let us mark the chief events in this story. Till near the end of the fifteenth century heresy was encountered in Spain by argument, by learned writings, by friendly discussion. But about the year 1480 Queen Isabella conceived the hope of obtaining from

[1] See Macaulay's account of Charles II. of Spain in the fifth volume of his history.

the pope a bull for the establishment of the Inquisition in Castile. Queen Isabella had the same devotion to the Church of Rome, and the same belief that heresy led to the destruction of body and soul, which animated Mary Tudor of England. But the character which acquired for the English Queen the name of Bloody Mary, exalted the fame of Isabella, and she and her husband Ferdinand were celebrated as *Los Reyes Cattolicos.* Isabella, thus inspired, entreated the pope to give a permanent form to the Inquisition, and to make its judgments final without appeal to Rome. Hence the papal bull of August 1483, which gave to the Spanish Inquisition the form of a permanent tribunal, and named the orthodox Torquemada Inquisitor-General.

The fruits of this measure were not long in being gathered. Mariana, himself a Jesuit, affirms in his 'History' that in the first year of its existence the Inquisition of Seville burnt 2,000 persons. Andrea Berceldon computes that between 1482 and 1489, 700 persons perished by fire, and 5,000 underwent penitentiary punishments. A more public authority, namely, the Court of the Inquisition of Seville itself, placed in the front of its palace in the year 1524 an inscription, where it is recorded to the glory of the institution and the edification of the faithful, that 'from the time of the expulsion of the Jews and Moors up to that date, more than 20,000 heretics had abjured their criminal errors, and that more than a thousand persons, obstinate in their heresy, had been delivered to the flames.'

It is added, 'after being condemned in conformity to the laws.' The writ de hæretico comburendo was in Spain no idle formality.

It is possible that the former of these numbers may have been magnified, and the latter reduced in order to display at once the efficacy and the mercy of the tribunal. In the inscription the favour and approbation of popes Innocent VIII., Alexander VI., Pius III., Julius II., Leo X., Adrian VI., and Clement VII. are recorded to sanctify and hallow this holy persecution.

Outside the walls of Seville there was assigned, and there remained in my own day, a square surrounded by a low wall, where heretics were burnt, and which, in conformity with its purpose, was called the *Quemadero*. At Valladolid, at Jaen, at Saragossa, and other chief towns of Spain, the cruel punishment of fire was inflicted upon many of the best Spaniards; the most learned authors, the men who dared to think and to enquire, the most virtuous fathers of families, the most unspotted from the world among the wives and daughters of Spain.

But dreadful as was the sacrifice of life offered up to the Moloch of superstition, still more injurious to the nation was the systematic injustice perpetrated by the Inquisition. For instance :—

1. Anonymous accusations were at all times received. Besides the danger of thus giving a sanction to malignant conspiracies hatched by hatred and revenge, the usual consequences of such a proceeding were awful. A witness was summoned, and in his terror and perplexity was asked whether he knew of

any persons whose language or habits of life, or whose daily worship, or omission to attend worship, made him suspect them of heresy. The witness in his alarm might mention persons other than those whose conduct had been denounced to the tribunal. Thence fresh accusations, new enquiries, unexpected condemnations. Then again, the court would interrogate new witnesses, and make a detailed enquiry into the daily life, the accustomed studies, the familiar conversation of persons who were quite ignorant that they had become objects of suspicion.

2. The members of the tribunal were often priests who had sought by becoming inquisitors to avoid the discipline of their bishops and lawful superiors, but who were themselves quite destitute of theological learning. Thence, the researches of pious men, who had gathered, from a study of the Fathers, doctrines often profound and not seldom orthodox, were denounced by malicious accusers and condemned by ignorant judges.

3. The inquisitors, besides being illiterate or imperfect scholars, were often men of sinful habits and licentious appetites. Thence the property of rich men, the homes of chaste women, the integrity of faithful domestics, were assailed by the passions and the lusts of those who were specially appointed to guard religion and morals.

4. If the enquiries made did not furnish the hunters after heresy with sufficient materials for a sentence of death or imprisonment, torture was applied to fill up the charges requisite for condemnation. It is well known

that torture of a witness proves not that the accused is guilty, but that the witness is human. Galileo, under torture, was willing to admit that the earth did not move; the most pious and virtuous men and women of Spain were burnt to death because the nerves of the persons called upon to convict them could not bear the pain of torture.

Yet let us not suppose that all these evils—the death of many thousand victims; the extinction of the moral and intellectual life of hundreds of thousands more; the decay of public virtue; the loss of military glory; the abasement of the intellect; the corruption of morals, were entirely without excuse on the part of those who were thus the authors of the decline and fall of the Spanish monarchy. It is stated that many, nay, most of the inquisitors, were men of conscientious convictions and of blameless lives.

No doubt these men had read the words of the creed of St. Athanasius, commonly so called: ' Whosoever will be saved, before all things it is necessary that he hold the Catholic faith, which faith except every one do keep whole and undefiled, without doubt he shall perish everlastingly.' Then after many subtle propositions of scholastic metaphysics it is proclaimed :—

' This is the Catholic faith : which except a man believe faithfully, he cannot be saved.'

If, therefore, this creed, which is accepted by the Church of Rome, was the sincere belief of the kings and queens, archbishops and bishops of Spain, can we wonder that they upheld the Inquisition and its works? For they may have argued, ' Is it better that a whole nation should be eternally saved, or that military glory, literary fame, worldly prosperity, should be bought at the expense of living and unborn millions of innocent souls? Is it not better to forego temporal advantages, proficiency in trade, science, letters,. and arts, than to allow our people to fall into damnable heresies, and permit a multitude of erring and diverging sects? But if it is better to preserve the purity of the faith, how can it be done except by a tribunal which can search out every error, detect every secret aberration, pursue with vigour every departure from sound doctrine, and punish with inflexible severity every obstinate persistency in errors, which lead those who hold them to perish everlastingly? '

I think we must conclude, that if in defiance of the teachings of Christ we believe the Athanasian Creed, we may in our weakness tolerate error ; but that in strict logic we must conclude that the course of the Spanish Inquisition and of the Spanish Monarchy was the most consistent and the best calculated to insure what the Church and State believed will be the eternal happiness of the Spanish people.

So thought the Spanish people themselves. I have heard a Spanish priest tell a number of peasants that without the Inquisition the faith could not be preserved ; the obedient spirit of his hearers testified to their concurrence in this intolerant judgment. But what was the source of this judgment? Let us never forget that this unity of faith, this inflexible loyalty to the Roman Church, was obtained by a fatal departure from the obedience due to the commandments of Christ

The ambition of Julius II., the incestuous passions of Rodrigo Borgia, the love of pleasure of Leo X., the flagrant sins of a hundred popes, might safely be indulged, provided only that the equality of God the Son to God the Father was firmly maintained ; the procession of God the Holy Ghost from the Father and the Son was asserted boldly ; and the conversion of bread and wine into the flesh and blood of Christ was accepted with unhesitating faith. So likewise the murder of Philip II., and the licentious adulteries of Louis XIV., were readily absolved by courtly confessors, provided heretics were burnt in Spain, and Huguenots cut to pieces in France. Such were the consequences of the transformation of the religion of the heart and mind taught by Christ into a scheme of scholastic logic.

While such was the fruit of the attempts to carry into effect the lessons taught by the schoolmen, and to establish unity of faith, instead of unity of Spirit, all over Europe, we must endeavour to mark the symptoms of revolt which appeared in Germany, in the Low Countries, in Holland, and in England. There is much to admire in the courage and determination with which Luther and Calvin, John Knox the leader of the Presbyterians of Scotland, and Zuinglius, the apostle of the Swiss, sought to revive obedience to the gospel, as the great rule of faith left by Christ to the world. But there is much to lament in the errors which they committed by the partial adoption of the lessons which ought to have been accepted in their integrity. Christ had promised to his disciples that the Holy Ghost would aid with his Spirit the pen of those who should record his sayings and report his doctrines. But it is one thing to have the letter of the sayings and doctrines of Christ, it is another thing to divide the letter which killeth from the Spirit which giveth life.

St. Augustine relates that this precept was the text continually referred to by St. Ambrose, and enforced with all the eloquence and power of that illustrious prelate. The question remained for the times of which we are now treating, whether Christ had left a living apostle who should bequeath to his successors for all time a power to declare his will without error and without diversity. The adherents of the Church of Rome declared, and endeavoured to carry into effect by force, the belief that such a power existed, and was to be worshipped and adored in the person of an infallible pope. The Reformers of the sixteenth century were equally confident in their assertion, that the interpretation of Christ's doctrines was left to the private judgment of instructed men, who, by continual study of the Holy Scriptures, would discover the path of salvation, and, by constant examination of their own lives, would be able to discover whether their conduct was in conformity with the rules which they professed to obey. It is this faith which was affirmed or denied by the blood of martyrs, and appealed to in fields of battle by the armies of Europe.

But much as modern times have softened the spirit of contending churches and varying sects, I cannot refrain from declaring over and over again that the spirit which induced men to punish by law what they deem heresy, and even the mental conviction which induced them to refrain from participation in holy rites, or social intercourse, with those they call heretics, be they Unitarians or Baptists, or those they call Atheists, be they Pantheists or Socinians, followers of Spinoza or declared unbelievers, is a spirit contrary to the lessons of Christ and the true spirit of the Christian religion.

The influence of the religious orders was felt in the fourteenth and fifteenth centuries most particularly, and was pointed out and confessed very openly in the sixteenth at the Council of Trent, both with regard to dogma and with regard to the practical government of the Church. Thus, when it was laid down that all mankind were involved in the original sin of Adam, and were only redeemed by the atoning sacrifice of Christ, the Franciscans would only agree to the propositions wherein this doctrine was contained, on condition that an exception was made in favour of the Virgin Mary, who, they contended, was born without sin. To which the Dominicans replied, that if an exception were made for the Virgin Mary, there must likewise be an exception for her parents, and for the whole race of David, and possibly for all the seed of Abraham. So that by force of exceptions the whole dogma would vanish into obscurity. An ambiguous phrase saved the dogma, and the difficulty was evaded.

Then again when the non-residence of the bishops and clergy was complained of as a great practical abuse, the Cardinal del Monte, comparing the Church to a ship and the bishops to the steersmen, said, that

if there was no one to hold the rudder how could the
ship pursue her course? This observation was at first
approved, but when Giacomo Cortesi, bishop of Veson,
spoke, he said he agreed in all that was said of the
evil of a want of guidance, but that the evil was not
in the non-residence of prelates, but in their want
of authority. In the first ages of the Church the
bishops guided all their clergy, but in later times the
regular orders had acquired so much authority that
they could preach any doctrines they pleased, and
the residence or absence of the bishops was a matter
of indifference. Thus the disorders of Germany had
arisen from the preaching of Brother John Tetzel and
Brother Martin Luther, and those of Lombardy from
the preaching of Brother Janson of Milan. This
remark, whether made by Cortesi or any other bishop,
struck the assembled fathers as founded on truth.

If now we proceed to distribute praise and blame,
gratitude and reproach, among the communities of
Christians, we may say, ' The Roman Church, venerable
from its antiquity, has been built up with stone
and stubble; is adorned with the most variegated
marbles, with precious stones, and with painted images
of wood, which are held more holy than the foundations laid by Christ and the commandments of God.
The Church of Rome has pretended to govern the
world, and has substituted foul tyranny for justice
and peace. She has sought to elevate herself above
Pagans and Protestants by laying down moral laws
of divine origin and pure doctrine, and has vitiated all
those laws by dispensations and absolutions in com-

pliance with the most atrocious crimes, and the most abandoned vices.

Yet with all her failings, and with all her forgeries, and all her impostures, the Roman Catholic Church has preserved the precept, 'Faith, Hope, Love, these three, but the best of these is Love.' There is among Roman Catholics in their relations to each other a pure essence of affection, which does not appear in the moral writings of Greece or of Rome; a kindness apart from the pride of the Stoics, or the effeminacy of Epicureans; apart from human self-sufficiency, and from the conceit of academical learning. The Roman Catholics who have never practised, or have relinquished the vices of an erring youth, are humble, loving, compassionate, abounding in good works, kind to all classes of their fellow-creatures, ever ready to say, 'Lord, be merciful to me a sinner;' ready to give of their substance to the needy; ready to forgive others their trespasses, and to kneel in humble devotion to their Maker.

On the other side, the Huguenots of France, the Reformers of Switzerland, the Lutherans of Germany, the Presbyterians of Scotland, while they assume no merit for their good works, are often distinguished by a stern and consistent morality. Intolerant to all who will not tread their narrow path, they follow a standard of purity, held aloft before them, which they keep steadily in sight. Like Regulus, their martyrs have gone to torture and death with the complacency with which they would return to their flocks and herds, to their peaceful cottage, or their undisturbed repose. Shaking

M

off a slavish obedience to pope and prelate, to king and dictator, they preserved for mankind the germ of free thought, and the right of maintaining liberty for their family, their village, their town, their nation.

Thus amid the dominant Churches, and the rebellious sectaries of modern times, there is, as in all human affairs, a web of the brightest virtues, twined with the most odious vices. The pure river and the turbid stream flow on together, and he who follows their course must meet much that provokes his disgust, with much that excites his admiration.

Happily the days of bloody persecution are past. Neither in Spain nor in Italy, neither in France nor in Germany, are men or women subjected to any penal infliction for holding opinions which are deemed heretical. In England the writ *de hæretico comburendo* has been long abolished. In fact, the zeal which impelled men to denounce heresy to a tribunal erected for the purpose of punishing erroneous opinions, and the ferocity of manners which led them to assist at the spectacle of burning the heretic, have both disappeared. It is no longer thought in Spain that all who hold opinions beyond the pale of the orthodox Church will be condemned to everlasting flames. Still less is it thought that it is the business of a temporal government to punish opinions on religious matters which, in the opinion of the Church, savour of heresy.

It would be well if we in England could settle our minds upon this subject. If a man steal to the value of forty shillings in a dwelling-house, it is cruel to condemn him to death; but there is no doubt he has committed an offence to which some punishment is rightly affixed. If, however, he has given an opinion with respect to one person of the Trinity, whom he refuses to acknowledge, or if he entertains views with regard to the substance of Christ different from those expressed in the Nicene Creed, if he entertains notions with regard to the origin of man, or the nature of life, which are not agreeable to the Church of England— these are matters of speculation which are not properly in the purview of the criminal law. Let Mr. Darwin and Professor Huxley explain their opinions as freely as the Archbishop of Canterbury or Mr. Spurgeon. We may feel sure the truth will ultimately be the gainer from freedom of discussion.

In this respect, and in many others, the age is improving; the promotion of one of the most en- lightened authors of the ' Essays and Reviews ' to the bishopric of Exeter, is a proof that we have got beyond the time when Lord Melbourne was afraid to recom- mend the preferment of Dr. Arnold to the Crown, lest he should incur the hostility of the clergy of the High Church. The present Lord Derby gave an excellent example to the nation when he declined to preside at the following anniversary of the British Associa- tion, and pointed out Professor Huxley as the more appropriate president for the year. Those who have read the admirable address delivered on that occa- sion, have derived the benefit of Lord Derby's dis- cernment and Professor Huxley's knowledge from this act. The State is not so far-sighted. I had hoped to pay a permanent homage to science by conferring on Sir John Herschel, with the sanction of the Crown, the office of the Master of the Mint, which had been held by Sir Isaac Newton. When the office was again vacant, Lord Palmerston followed my example by the appointment of an eminent chemist. But when that distinguished man died, the precedent of appointing a man of science was disregarded. The appointment of Professor Huxley or Dr. Lyon Playfair would probably have saved the lives of many children who have fallen victims to the small-pox. But it was argued on the part of the British Government that while an expenditure of seventy millions was a scandalous waste of public money, an expenditure of seventy millions minus two thousand pounds would constitute a wise and virtuous administration. So it has been decreed.

It has frequently been said and repeated that Christianity is the law of the land, and it is added that while works of calm reasoning may be freely permitted to circulate, the law must not allow the religion of the nation to be treated with ridicule or contempt. But I confess it appears to me that the writer who should treat the nation with scurrility or vulgar abuse would incur the sentence pronounced by Samuel Rogers, when Mr. Croker attempted to destroy the fame of Macaulay's ' History of England.' Mr. Rogers said, ' He meant to commit murder, but he has only committed suicide.' Let opinion decide ; opinion—queen of the world. ' L'Opinione, Regina del Mondo,' should be the ultimate court of appeal in these cases.

Opinion for a time may make an erroneous judgment, but in one way or other the judgment of sensible men has a magic influence over mankind, and, in time, rallies the majority, and enables them to reverse a foolish or prejudiced opinion. The remark of Dr. Temple, that a barbarous or ignorant opinion is corrected by advancing wisdom, is, to be sure, liable to exceptions. The coast of Africa bordering on the Mediterranean shows no improvement over the time when St. Augustine was an inhabitant of Carthage, or when he was Bishop of Hippo. But with regard to the civilised portions of the globe, to England under her constitutional monarchy, to France and Germany, to Portugal under Dom John of Braganza, to Sweden and Denmark, to India under the British Government, to the United States of America, it may be said, as Galileo said of the earth when his torture had been relaxed, ' Nevertheless it moves.'

ESSAY XI.

LEO X. ADRIAN VI. CLEMENT VII.

THE anarchy and violence which swayed everything in
the middle ages had, in the process of time, yielded to
the influence of letters ; the improvement of manners
had, in process of time, driven away these open and
abominable scandals.   Learned men had occupied the
seat of St. Peter; the commerce of the Italian cities ; the
order which distinguished Venice; the talents which,
in the persons of Dante, and Petrarch, had illustrated
Florence; the revival of letters, and finally, the invention of printing, had prepared the mind of Europe
for great changes.

It seemed impossible that the dark superstitions
which had gained strength and power during the middle ages, should not be visited, and in some degree dispersed by the coming light.   It was, therefore, of the
utmost importance that the see of Rome should be
occupied by a prelate who might be at once pious and
enlightened ; who might reform the notorious abuses
of the Roman Catholic Church, and reconcile the advancement of letters, the progress of society, and the
refinement of manners, with the pure spirit of that
religion over whose ministers it was his duty to preside ; and whose ceremonies and sacraments it was in

his power to elevate, and to direct to the worship of an Almighty God, and the practice of an unblemished morality.

Who was Leo X., thus called upon to perform a most difficult task at a momentous crisis?

The republic of Florence was one of the most powerful of those States which had brought to pass, by its wealth, its commerce, and its love of the fine arts, the civilisation of Italy, when the greater part of Europe was in the chains of the feudal system, divided by private wars, sunk in ignorance, and suffering from poverty and barbarism. Florence, with Venice, Genoa, Pisa, and some other cities, exhibited in those times the most costly articles of manufacture; and in its churches displayed works of sculpture and painting, giving assurance of difficulties overcome, and promise of those wonders of art which in the days of Michael Angelo and Raphael astonished and enchanted Europe.

The political constitution of Florence was far from perfection. It fluctuated, as Machiavel has observed, not between liberty and servitude, but between servitude and licence. Some of the richest merchants, placing themselves at the head of different political parties, gained by turns a supremacy which was not limited by law, or restrained by moderation.

Among these, Cosmo de' Medici, while he was conspicuous by his wealth and extensive connections in various parts of Europe, was also remarkable for his political sagacity. Observing that the nobility availed themselves of their power to exempt their property from a due share of the public burthens, he made him self very popular by proposing what was called the Catasto ; namely, a valuation of all landed property, and a tax of half per cent. on the capital which each landed estate was estimated to be worth. Supposing estates to have yielded 5 per cent., an income of 2,000 florins would have represented a capital of 40,000 florins, and would have paid 10 per cent. on the annual income. Supposing the capital to have returned only 2 per cent., 100,000 florins would have paid a tax of 500 florins, or 25 per cent. on the income.

The Medici after this rose to unequalled power in the republic. It was usual in the peaceful revolutions of Florence, effected by a public assembly called a *Balia*, to expel the chiefs of the defeated party, who were what was called *confinati*—that is to say, banished to a fixed place in a foreign State, which they were bound not to leave. The cell or small chamber in which Cosmo was detained previously to his banishment, on one of the occasions when his party were routed, is still shown in the Palazzo Vecchio of Florence.

Lorenzo succeeded quietly to the power of his father, and increased his power after the failure of the conspiracy of the Pazzi, for taking part in which the Archbishop Salviati was hanged out of the window.

The authority of Lorenzo was long undisturbed. He governed with the assistance and by the influence of three hundred citizens of his own party, who met from time to time to deliberate on public affairs. It was at this period a question with the most patriotic statesmen of Florence whether the temperate authority of Lorenzo was not preferable to the turbulent liberty which had before prevailed. The manifest defect was that the merit of Lorenzo's rule depended on his own personal moderation, his good sense, and his readiness to listen to the counsels of the best men of his party.

While Lorenzo lived he was the Pericles of the Tuscan Athens. Laurentius Valla, Pico Mirandola, and other men of letters surrounded him, and shared in the discussions which revived the philosophy of Plato, and emulated the lyrics of Bion and of Moschus. More than one Aspasia welcomed Lorenzo as a favoured lover ; and when he stood forth in the streets of Florence, reciting

> Ben venga Maggio
> È il Gonfalonier selvaggio,

the age of political and social happiness seemed to have arrived.

Nor was Lorenzo less careful of the peace of Italy, and its immunity from the invasion of foreigners.

I have said that, before the Reformation was attempted, the Rome of Christianity had become as foul with crime and depraved morals as the pagan Rome, which St. Paul has described in terms of eternal reprobation.

Thus, if Caligula and Nero had blasted the fame of the Roman empire by incest and murder, Alexander VI., and his son Cæsar Borgia, had given to sacerdotal Rome the same infamy of incest and murder.[1] It is said that of the Pope's offspring, two of whom he acknow-

---

[1] Guicciardini.

ledged as his sons, the elder, the Duke of Gandia, was thrown a corpse into the Tiber one night by order of his brother. But we may quit this disgusting history.

Before we arrive at the time of the Reformation, however, it is necessary to take some notice of Julius II. His mind was devoted to two objects—the one to drive the barbarians, as he called them, out of Italy; the other to make Rome a great metropolis of art, and the church of St. Peter a temple of unequalled magnificence. His military forces were quite unequal to the first of these objects; in respect to the second, he laid the foundation for debts which, instead of retarding, hastened the progress of the Reformation.

The son of Lorenzo, afterwards Cardinal de' Medici, and finally Leo X., was brought up with great care, and was well instructed in classical learning. Politian was charged with his education.

His father, when he was still young, wrote him a kind and paternal letter, full of good advice. But although he was destined for the Church, it is remarkable that there is not, in Lorenzo's letter to his son, any reference to the Christian religion.

He became a cardinal at the age of fourteen, and was thenceforth much employed in the political negotiations and intrigues in which the reign of Julius abounded. When he became Pope, in the year 1513, he presently showed his diplomatic skill and his conciliatory temper by making peace with France, and reconciling to the Holy See the cardinals who had been at open war with his predecessor. His favour to literature and the arts was splendid and discriminating; his feasts were magnificent, his liberality large and popular. He spent his time in hunting and hawking; in listening to the most exquisite music, and partaking of the most refined conversation. These occupations became him as a secular prince, but serious clergymen and abstemious monks complained that there was something wanting. Paolo Sarpi, after praising his learning and his munificence, adds with some humour: 'He would have been a perfect Pope, if with these gifts he had united some knowledge of the affairs of religion, and somewhat more of a pious disposition— in neither of which matters did he take much interest.' Probably he was better instructed in the dialogues of Plato than in the doctrines of Christ, and had more knowledge of Virgil and Ovid than of the gospel.

His conversation was literary; his Court composed of jovial and merry men of letters. One of them who was idle wrote this distich :—

> Qual che dica la gente, il mio gran diletto
> È di non far mai niente e stare a letto.   .

Otherwise
> Il mio gran diletto, qual che dica la gente,
> È di stare a letto, e non far mai niente.

One of his poetical guests, finding his wine and water too weak, wrote, and sent up to his host at table, these lines :

> In poculis nostris Nympha est conjuncta Lyæo,
> Sic Dea juncta Deo, sed Dea major eo.

This story was related to me by Mezzofanti, the great linguist, afterwards cardinal.

It was a pity, however, that as he was most liberal in spending money, he should have looked at his pon tifical power only as a means of acquiring it. Being much in need of supplying his treasury, in order to continue his profuse hospitality, he looked to Lorenzo Pucci, Cardinal of Santiquattro, to furnish him with th means. His predecessor, Urban II., had, in the yea 1100 and following years, granted plenary indulgenc and a remission of all sins to those who went to th Holy Land for the purpose of delivering the sepulchr of Christ from the infidels. Afterwards the same in dulgence and remission were granted to those who con tributed sums of money sufficient to maintain a soldie in the Holy Land. Subsequent popes extended and abused the power of granting forgiveness of sins; the convenience of this mode of raising money was highly prized, and the purposes for which the money had bee destined were forgotten. The popes made a crusad against the Turks or the King of France, or the need of a large sum to build a church, the pretence fo granting the remission of sins to those who were willing to pay for their exemption from the pains of purgatory and their admission within the gates of Paradise. Bu it seems never to have occurred to Leo X. or Lorenzo Pucci that times were changed; that a spirit of enquiry was abroad; that the ignorance of the dark ages wa giving way before the approaching light; that learne men might examine the pretences for the new indul gences, and that even humble but pious men migh search in the gospels for the warrant by which th infallible pope might seek to cover his cupidity.

reserve for another Essay the resistance made by
I her to the open sale of indulgences, and an account
o the support he found in Germany; I propose to
st e in this place the various modes by which the
R nan Court endeavoured to abate the Northern heresy.

,eo was disposed at first, as his manner was, to be
c eless and indifferent; to let the Augustinian and
I ninican monks fight among themselves, and to be
s(citous only as to the amount of money he should
c ect from this branch of the papal revenue. But
w en he was told that great scandal was raised by the
o n sale of the forgiveness of God for ducats, and that
tl authority of the Holy See might be rudely shaken
b popular indignation, he began to view the matter
n re seriously, and took counsel with the most prudent
o is advisers. Finding after a time that Luther was
n to be persuaded or intimidated, and that he had
a wered Cardinal Gaetano, the Pope's legate, with
q ttations from Scripture—Leo determined to put
d vn the rising heresy with the infallible decree of
tl Holy Roman Church. He therefore issued a bull
o November 9, 1518, in which he affirmed that, as
tl successor of St. Peter, and the Vicar of Christ, he
li l the power to forgive the sins both of the living
a l the dead.

It so happened that Cibo, a gentleman of Milan, had
s nt large sums to obtain a cardinal's hat for Leo,
v en he was a boy of fourteen years old, and that the
s(ie Cibo had married the Pope's sister, Maddalena;
s' that Leo thought to recompense Cibo for his outlay
b granting to his sister the revenue to be derived from

Saxony by the sale of indulgences. But as these indulgences were sold by the subordinate agents of the Dominican friars in public-houses, and given in payment for the hire of horses, and in other discreditable ways, this gift to his sister only injured more deeply the Pope's reputation, and increased the scandal of selling for money Christ's forgiveness of sins.

Leo, however, having entered on the path of putting down opposition by the authority of the Holy See, did not feel inclined to stop or falter in his path. But all who observed his conduct blamed him in this crisis of the Church for giving up his time to hunting and hawking, to musical concerts and luxurious feasts, unbecoming the sanctity of his high office, and apparently to the neglect of those serious duties which it became the Holy Pontiff to fulfil, with a solemn regard to his position as the Vicar of Christ upon earth.[1] Leo, indeed, made it part of his duty to fast on Wednesdays and Fridays, and to show much outward devotion. But he evidently seemed to look rather to the pomps and pleasures of the popedom than to its responsibilities, and the critical position in which it was then placed.

Leo at this time thought the contumacy of Luther a matter of little importance. Martin Luther on his side went with a safe-conduct to the Diet of Augsburg, where he stoutly maintained his doctrine, supporting it by quotations from the Holy Scripture. But the scholastic theologians being little versed in Scripture, Cardinal Gaetano had recourse to violent and abusive

[1] Guicciardini; Paolo Sarpi.

language—upon which Luther, recollecting what had happened to Huss at Constance, retired from Augsburg and returned to Wittenberg.

Leo at this time, and in the same spirit, sent a bull of indulgences to Switzerland, where he was to encounter the opposition of Zuinglius, one of the wisest and ablest of the Reformers.

The next step was to issue a condemnation of the doctrines, the person, and the works of Luther. For this purpose a numerous conference was summoned of the theologians and canonists, or, in other words, the priests and lawyers of Rome. The canonists agreed to censure the unsound doctrines of Luther, but they argued that his person and his works ought not be condemned without a hearing. They quoted in support of their argument the act of God Himself, who, when Adam had sinned, came down to the garden of Paradise and called out, ' Adam, where art thou ? ' in order to hear his defence.[1] In the same way the Almighty, after the murder of Abel, called to Cain, ' Cain, Cain, where is thy brother ? ' But the arguments founded on justice and supported by the book of Genesis, had little weight with a pope who did not chose to be diverted from his hunting parties and his musical entertainments for the mere purpose of doing what was right, and preventing or delaying a rupture in the Church. But this summary proceeding in a matter of so much importance, not founded on the decision of any council, and without the promise of any reform of abuses, shocked all the more moderate adherents of the

[1] Paolo Sarpi.

Church, who greatly blamed the precipitation of the Supreme Pontiff.

On June 15, 1520, was issued the bull which condemned the errors of Luther. This bull was in its style very obscure, condemning forty-two errors, but not specifying whether all these errors were equally fatal. The penalty, however, was very clear. Luther and his adherents were to recant their errors within a certain time, and if they failed to do so were condemned to be burnt.

After this papal condemnation, which was much criticised by men of sense and judgment, the most remarkable event was the meeting of the Diet of Germany at Worms. Luther was summoned to this Diet, was heard, and was permitted to depart to his own house. On May 8, 1521, an edict was issued relating that, as it was the duty of the emperor and the princes of Germany to protect religion and to extinguish heresy, they had considered the bull which had been communicated to them by the Pope's legate, condemning Luther and his writings. The Diet, after reading the bull and hearing Luther, concurred in the justice of this condemnation, and declared that he had incurred the penalties to which, by the laws, heretics are subject.

At the end of the year Leo died. On January 9, 1522, Adrian was elected pope. Adrian was born in Holland, in the same country as Erasmus ; but though not far from adopting the moderate opinions, he was very far indeed from following the unambitious example of Erasmus. The antecedents of Adrian as the preceptor of Charles V. and as a cardinal attached to the court of the emperor were embarrassing and critical.

Isabella had succeeded to the crown of Castile, not without some doubts as to her title, and had strengthened herself by her marriage with Ferdinand, King of Aragon, one of the most politic and perfidious of princes. Upon the death of Isabella the crown of Castile reverted by right to Juana, her second daughter, whose brother and elder sister had both died. But this princess had married Philip, the eldest son of Maximilian of Austria ; and unfortunately for her welfare and happiness, her father and her husband conspired to deprive her of her rights, and to condemn her to imprisonment for life. With this view Ferdinand, from jealousy of his daughter, had spread a report in Flanders that she was mad. Her husband, Philip, at first indignantly denied the truth of this rumour, and set out for Spain with his wife, in order to claim for her the crown of Castile. But he had been a careless and cruel husband, spending her income upon boon companions and paramours. Ferdinand reckoned surely enough that such a man would not be very scrupulous, if, by sacrificing his wife, he could obtain a prospect of power for himself. Accordingly he sought an interview with Philip in a church in the village of Villafafila, and by a solemn treaty, which he swore upon the Gospel to observe, bound himself to give up to Philip the government of Castile. An hour after this he made a declaration, equally solemn, though secret, that he had been compelled by force to sign the treaty with Philip. For this allegation of force there seems to have been no foundation.

The protest against the treaty not being known to

N

the public, great surprise was caused by the news that Ferdinand, who was known to be able and ambitious, should have given up the government of Castile, which he had declared he would keep during his life, to his son-in-law. But the mystery was soon cleared up. An Aragonese attendant on the king was sent to Philip. Ferdinand himself proceeded to embark for Naples, but before he reached the Neapolitan Court Philip was no more. He had died of an illness which lasted from Sunday to Friday.

In the treaty with Ferdinand it had been affirmed that Juana refused under any circumstances to assume the government, but, if she should do so, it would lead to the ruin of the country, 'on account of her infirmities and passions which decency will not allow us to describe.'[1] This allegation was contained in the treaty signed by Philip, who had affirmed in the Low Countries that the allegation of Juana's mental infirmity was false, and who had come to Spain for the purpose, as he professed, of asserting her title to the crown, and her right to exercise the government of Castile.

With respect to the real state of mind of Queen Juana, it is almost impossible to ascertain the truth. It appears pretty clear, however, that she was not mad. The women who had been put about her, and those who saw most of her during her long and troubled life, all refused to say that she was mad. Mosen Luis Ferrer, to whose guard she was confided by her

---

[1] 'Segun las enfermedades y pasiones, que aquí no se espresan por la honestidad.'—*Memorial of Bergenroth*, p. 228.

father, administered to her a torture called *la cuerda*. This torture consisted in hanging the body in the air by ropes, while heavy weights were attached to the feet. The question naturally arises, on what pretext was this torture applied ?

The answer to this question reveals a curious and painful history. Juana, the wife of Philip the Arch-luke, when living in Flanders, showed an inclination to abandon the Church of Rome. Her mother Isabella, who was in the habit of burning her subjects for their want of Catholic faith, was uneasy at the reports she heard, and sent a confidential friar to Flanders to report on her daughter's state. He reported that the Archduchess was well, and handsomer than ever ; that she appeared at mass, but refused to go to confession. When she went to Spain she appeared to be still of the same mind, but her scruples had become stronger; and she declined to attend mass. It was for this malady that Mosen Ferrer prescribed torture.

Ferdinand died in January, 1516, having kept his laughter in prison nearly ten years, and permitted horrible cruelties to be perpetrated against her. Her son Charles succeeded to the crown, and Cardinal Cisneros (Ximenez) was entrusted with the regency during the absence of Charles in Flanders. Mosen Ferrer was deprived of his post of gaoler, ' because he was suspected of endangering the health and life of her highness.'

Cardinal Adrian, born at Utrecht in 1449, of poor parents, had been named, on account of his learning and acquirements, tutor to Charles, and upon his

N 2

reports the young king, then under seventeen years old, was sure to frame his opinion, and settle his plan of behaviour to his mother.

Adrian at first seemed disposed to ascertain the truth, and inform his master of the result. But some years elapsed before he was in a position to do so. At first Charles rejected with some haughtiness the interference of Cardinal Cisneros and the Bishop of Majorca. Afterwards, when in Spain, he appointed the Marquis of Denia and his Marchioness to superintend his mother's household. They seem to have executed their charge in no kindly spirit. The house at Tordesillas in which Juana was confined, had in it a large room looking over the Duero, and having a distant view of vineyards and cornfields. But Juana was not allowed by the Marchioness of Denia and her daughters to go into this room, and, except when on a visit to her daughter Catalina, was kept in her own dark apartment, where she could not communicate with any persons without the house. The Marquis was instructed by Charles to write him double reports: one to be shown to the Privy Council, and known to the world ; the other private, for the eyes of Charles alone.

The insurrection of the commons in Castile made a break in these arrangements. Padilla entered Tordesillas with his army. The women, twelve in number, who had been attendants or watchers upon Queen Juana, were examined as to her state of mind. The report containing these examinations has been unfortunately lost. The result was that the crown was offered to her by the commons, but she was too scrupulous or too much frightened to enter into opposition to her son.

When the royal army and the Marquis of Denia returned to Tordesillas the imprisonment of Juana was made more severe than before. Cardinal Adrian was desired to report faithfully to Charles the state of his mother. He sent the examinations of the women in attendance, saying that among them was a gossiping husband of one of the women, a licentiate at Madrid. They all agreed that Juana was not and never had been insane. The outer world agreed in this opinion. But Adrian, being quite as prudent as he was truthful, asked Charles whether he would like to wait for the death of his mother before he was permitted to govern Spain. Of course the question itself negatived the supposition of Juana's insanity. Adrian, having ascertained that Charles was by no means disposed to give up his position and his power to his mother, never again expressed a belief in Queen Juana's sanity. He never saw her, and contented himself with echoing the reports of her madness made by the Marquis Denia. The poor captive's imprisonment became more rigorous ; a secret letter of her daughter Catalina to Charles, complaining of her mother's sufferings, was left unnoticed, and during the thirty-five years of her second imprisonment, she was ill-used, and deprived of all society. At length her reason gave way ; sometimes she refused to eat or to leave her bed. The Marquis Denia for four years made a secret of her father's death, in order, as he alleged, to use his name to procure her compliance with his wishes.

At length this poor princess died, a victim to the injustice, the perfidy, and the cruelty of her father, her husband, and her son.

Returning now to the history of the Reformation, it is to be recorded that in 1520 Cardinal Adrian was elected pope. His arrival in a Court where his person was unknown created much curiosity and not a little consternation. But it soon appeared that Adrian, though he perceived and approved of what was right, was always willing to follow what was wrong. As a learned and discreet theologian this pope had arrived at the conclusion that the indulgences granted by the Church would only remit the punishment of sin so far as the sinner should comply with the terms of the indulgence and perform some good work prescribed by the act of forgiveness. So that a man might be relieved, by a partial performance of the conditions imposed, from the punishment due to some of his sins, and still be subject to the penalty due to others for which he had not atoned.

This was a very subtle distinction, and Frate Tommaso di Gaeta, cardinal of San Sisto, a consummate theologian, dissuaded Adrian from his project of making it public. He said the doctrine was plausible, but doubtful, and had not yet been fully adopted by the Church. Even if adopted, he thought it ought to be kept secret; that its publication would tend to diminish the value of indulgences granted by the Church, and thus lower the authority of the Holy See. The cardinal added, that having reflected much on this matter, and having discussed it at Augsburg when he was the Pope's legate there, with Luther, he had arrived at the opinion that the only way to remedy the existing difficulties and disorders, was to restore the ancient discipline of the Church. According to the old canons, certain penances—the recital of so many prayers, the giving of sums of money in alms, the abstinence from such or such favourite sins—were enjoined as the terms of forgiveness imposed by the Church. If this ancient discipline were restored, morals would be reformed, Holy Church respected, and the heresies favoured by Luther would be restrained by the authority of a purified and venerated universal Church.

The Pope was well pleased with this advice, and consulted many of his cardinals as to the mode by which the ancient discipline could be restored. The cardinals were much embarrassed in the endeavour to find a mode of restoring the ancient discipline of the Church. But while they were pondering over their difficulties, Lorenzo Pucci, the cardinal of Santiquattro, who had been much trusted by Leo X., interposed.

In speaking of Pope Leo, Thuanus (De Thou) says, ' While he was inclined of his own will to every species of licence, he was impelled by Lorenzo Pucci, a cardinal, a man of turbulent nature, to whom he listened too much, to require immense sums of money from every quarter of the Christian world, by means of decrees promising at a fixed price the pardon of every kind of crime, and as the price of eternal happiness.' It was not likely that the inventor of the scheme for selling a general forgiveness of sins and eternal happiness

at a fixed money price would shrink from his work.
He was encouraged by the general assent of the cardinals, and urged upon the Pope his opinion that the
plan proposed would never succeed. He said that the
ancient canon laws had gone out of use; for as the fervour and sincerity of the ancient times were wanting,
so the effects were wanting; and in order to have the
same effects it would be necessary to restore the ancient
zeal and charity. 'Methinks,' he said, 'I hear one saying, as St. Peter said, "Now, therefore, why tempt ye
God to put a yoke upon the neck of the disciples
which neither our fathers nor we were able to bear?"'[1]
After thus misapplying the words used by St. Paul in
reference to the ceremonial law of the Jews, and per-
verting them to the whole doctrine of penitence for
sin, Pucci went on to argue that so far from discourag-
ing the Lutherans by such concessions, it was the very
mode of giving them fresh strength and energy. The
mass of the people, who always argue from the event,
when they should see the Pope giving way to Luther
in some points, would say that, as Luther had proved
to be right in some articles, he might be right in
greater points also. The princes of Germany who
favoured Luther would likewise take fresh heart, and
acquire new importance from the concessions made to
their favourite. In fine, the only way to extinguish
heresy was by crusades, and by urging sovereign
princes to extirpate it. In this way Innocent III. had
suppressed the heresy of the Albigenses; in this way
the Waldenses, and the followers of Arnold of Brescia,

---

[1] Acts, chap. xv. 10.

the Piccardi, and Paduasi, and other heretics, had been punished, and their heresies extinguished.

The Pope, speaking to his most intimate friends, William Eckenwort and Theodore Her, bewailed his condition, and lamented that, with every desire to reform abuses, he could not do it. He directed the agents of indulgences to distribute them sparingly. But this was a vain precaution. Luther was informed in confession by those who had bought the plenary indulgence, that they had not only obtained pardon for their past sins, but that those who had committed adultery were permitted to live on in the habit of adultery; and those who practised embezzlement had obtained a licence to continue to embezzle the property of others.

This licence for future sins was not only a violation of Christian precepts, but was a flagrant contradiction of the rules of the Roman Church itself. In fact, it resembled rather the act of Judas, who sold Christ for thirty pieces of silver, than the conduct of a true Vicar of Christ.

The arguments of Lorenzo Pucci, which had so much weight with the Court of Rome, are nothing but the staple of the enemies of reform at all times, and on all subjects. There is no doubt that concession gives rise to demands for fresh concession, and it is right that it should be so. The true limit is, that all that it is just to concede should be conceded; all that it is true to affirm should be affirmed; but that which is unjust should be rejected, and that which is false should be denied.

Adrian, thus yielding to counsels which he did not approve, sent Francesco Chieriento, bishop of Teramo, in the Abruzzi, to the Diet of Nuremberg. This delegate was furnished with a letter, in which the Pope pointed out all the mischief which had been done by Luther, a small friar, and exhorted the Diet to imitate what had been done to John Huss and Jerome of Prague, and cut off the peccant member. The leaders of the Church party in those days thought little of the objection that Huss had been burnt in violation of a safe-conduct which had been granted him; on the contrary, they always held up the breach of faith as an example to be followed, and to be applied especially to Luther.

Adrian was, however, far from being a willing follower of these violent counsels. On the contrary, he instructed his legate to admit that, while Luther had committed a mortal sin in publishing errors in matters of faith, the origin of the confusion in the Church arose from the sins of men, and especially of prelates and of priests, who had admitted many abuses in spiritual things, and were guilty of many excesses in morals, and finally everything had been turning to evil.

This ingenuous confession pleased no one. The Catholic party blamed the imprudence, and disputed the truth of the blame imputed. The Protestants gave little credit to admissions of wrong which were not followed by active remedies and substantial reforms.

The Diet of Nuremberg answered the nuncio in no conciliatory tone. They noted that annates had been collected for hundreds of years under the pretence of

making war on the infidels, but had never been
applied to that purpose. After recounting many of
the grievances of Germany, they concluded by requesting the Pope to summon a council 'pious, free, and
liberal.'

Pope Adrian had scarcely received this answer of
his legate when his life came to an end. He died on
September 18, 1523.

His intimate friend and confidant, Cardinal Eckenwort, wrote his epitaph, which thus commences :—' Hic
situs est Adrianus VI., qui nihil sibi infelicius in vitâ
duxit quam quod imperaret.' [1]

The pope elected in the place of Adrian was a
nephew of Lorenzo de' Medici, and a cousin of Leo X.,
who took the title of Clement VII.

It happened, fortunately for the Reformation, although
it says little for the credit of the spiritual and temporal
princes who professed so great a regard for the unity
of the Apostolic Roman Church, that the attention of
the popes, emperors, and kings of this period was very
much engrossed by their separate and selfish objects.
Clement VII. was the son of Julian, the brother of
Lorenzo, who had been murdered in the conspiracy of
the Pazzi. It was much doubted whether Julian had
ever been married to the mother of Clement, and the
Pope was afraid that if a General Council should meet,
he might be told that, as a natural son, he was not
admissible to the priesthood, and therefore disqualified
to be pope.

For this reason, as it was said, he constantly, so long as

[1] *Paolo Sarpi*, Florence, 1558, p. 61, note 1.

he ruled, postponed the meeting of the Council. Besides
this personal interest, he was, for family reasons, as much
concerned for the establishment of the Medici at Florence as for the good of the Church. His successor,
Paul III., was a Farnese, and was much bent on the
acquisition of the Duchy of Milan for his family. This
desire gave rise to many political intrigues, and the
marriage of his son, a boy of fourteen, to the Princess
Margaret, a natural daughter of Charles V., produced
much scandal, violent quarrels, and fresh political
designs.[1]

Charles V., on his side, designed the union of the
tiara with his imperial crown, and was ceaselessly
employed in negotiations with Italian princes or in war
against the Holy Father. His general, the Constable of
Bourbon, took Rome by assault and made the Pope a
prisoner. Charles wished to exhibit his Holiness at
Madrid, where the King of France had been seen as a
captive; but the pious feelings of the Spanish people
would have been shocked by the exhibition of the
Pontiff as a prisoner, and the project was prudently
renounced. A short time afterwards he was again an
ally of the emperor, and obtained large concessions in
payment for his assistance in the war against France.

The King of France was bent on defeating the ambitious designs of universal empire attributed to Charles,
and even allied himself with the Turks for that purpose.

Henry, King of England, was, above all things, bent
on his divorce from Catherine of Aragon, and his marriage with Anne Boleyn. As he proceeded in this

[1] See Bergenroth.

affair somewhat hastily, and even concluded it without
clerical sanction, he was by Pope Clement excommu-
nicated, and formally deprived of his title to the crown.
But the separation of England from all subjection to
the see of Rome, and the independence of that kingdom,
proved a new source of strength to the Reformation,
and a bulwark for the Protestants of Europe, which
neither the Guises nor Philip II., neither the murders
of Henry III. and Henry IV. of France, nor the expedition of the Grand Armada from the coast of Spain,
were able to overthrow.

But it is not our present business to enter into that
stirring and eventful narrative. I shall only say, therefore, that Clement VII. died without extirpating heresy,
and that Paul III., after many years of hesitation, of
negotiation, and reluctance, summoned a Council to
meet at Trent on March 15, 1544. He was impelled
to this decision by Charles, who had made peace with
France, fearing that his rule over Germany would pass
away from him unless he was secure on his French
frontier. Charles was also impelled to this course by
the Protestant princes and party, who called loudly for
a Council, and by his own danger from reforms of the
Church, which, if not made with his consent, might be
made without him. Henry VIII. of England, and the
Protestant princes of Germany, had repeatedly demanded that laymen, as well as bishops and clergy,
might be summoned to the Council. But against such
a demand the Pope, in a letter to the Emperor, had
solemnly protested, and in this respect his wishes had
been gratified. I do not propose in this place to give

any history of the Council of Trent. I will content myself with the judgment of Fra Paolo Sarpi, the ablest historian of that Council, who says, that whereas it was asked for with a view to put an end to the schisms which had sprung up, and to give greater liberty and power to the bishops, it terminated by confirming all the schisms which it found struggling for existence, and by placing the bishops in a state of complete subserviency to the pope. The further remark of Sarpi, that the Church was left by the Council more stained and corrupted by abuses than ever, is matter of more controversy; the truth, perhaps is, that while some abuses utterly indefensible and irreconcilable with the decrees of the Church were reformed, the great vices of the Church of Rome—which gave rise to the separation of Luther and Calvin ; of a great party in France ; of the whole of England, Sweden, and Denmark ; of Prussia, and many German princes ; which armed Gustavus Adolphus, and which struck deep the roots of religious liberty in Europe—remained unacknowledged, unreformed, as vigorous, as powerful, and as poisonous as ever.

ESSAY XII.

THE REFORMATION. LUTHER. CALVIN. ZUINGLIUS.

THE cardinal doctrines of Christianity—the existence
and the unity of God, the Trinity, the Divinity of Christ,
the Atonement, the promise of Immortality—had never
been denied by those who professed and called themselves Christians.

But when scholastic theologians, defining the relations of Christ to God the Father, and of the Holy
Ghost to God the Father and God the Son, declaring
that the substance of the Spirit of Christ was the same
as the substance of the Spirit of God the Father ; that
the Holy Ghost proceeded not only from the Father,
but from the Father and the Son ; that the Atonement
of Christ was accepted as a satisfaction, like the ancient
sacrifices of the heathen, for the sins of man ; that the
promise of immortality was only held out to those who
professed certain abstruse and metaphysical articles of
belief, which, by a perversion of the language used by
Christ, were called Faith—then divisions in abundance
sprang up.

One of the first divisions among Christians related
to the choice of a bishop. Although this dissension
caused violent contests, yet, arising from a personal
cause, it could not be lasting.

The difference between Athanasius and Arius arose from a deeper cause, and was attended with more serious and more permanent effects.

Jesus Christ, while He laid down rules the most comprehensive respecting the conduct of men to each other, revealed with great reserve, and very partially, the nature of God. Like Moses, He taught there was only one God, who had commanded his chosen people, ' I am the Lord thy God ; thou shalt have no other gods but me.' The Jewish people, in obedience to their interpretation of the second commandment, had refrained from making, as the Greeks and Romans had done, any image of the Lord and Father. This departure from the usage of other nations was begun in the time of Pompey. Tacitus relates, ' Romanorum primus Cn. Pompeius Judæos domuit: templumque jure victoriæ ingressus est. Inde vulgatum, nullâ intus deûm effigie vacuam sedem, et inania arcana.' [1]

In the last days He said to his disciples, ' I go to my Father and to your Father.' So likewise He said, ' If ye loved me, ye would rejoice because I said, I go unto the Father, for the Father is greater than I.' [2]

But theologians ambitious of fame were not content with these indications. They did not think of God as one of our great poets thought—

> Thy throne is darkness in th' abyss of light,
> A blaze of glory which forbids the sight.

They were determined to penetrate into this darkness ; to ascertain the inscrutable nature of the Supreme

---

[1] Tacitus, *History*, lib. v. 9.   [2] St. John, chap. xiv. 28.

Being, and to prescribe a form of belief to which all Christians should be bound to adhere under pain of eternal damnation.

When Christ was upon the earth, He said to his disciples, 'Then if any man shall say unto you, Lo, here is Christ, or there; believe it not. For there shall arise false Christs and false prophets, and shall show great signs and wonders; insomuch that, if it were possible, they shall deceive the very elect. . . . Wherefore, if they shall say unto you, behold, he is in the desert; go not forth: behold, he is in the secret chambers, believe it not.' [1]

From these various causes we have seen that there arose a complete change in the aspect of Christianity. Christ had left to his disciples—1. A simple theology founded on the Unity and Supremacy of God. 2. A pure morality. 3. A law of love and charity, by which all men were to be bound. In place of these the Church had introduced—1. A complex and unintelligible theology, combined with the ancient Polytheism of Greece and Rome. 2. A corrupt morality, giving an exemption from the penalties of sin for money. 3. Persecution of all who did not obey the Church.

With the revival of letters and the progress of civilisation, men began to read the Gospel and to ask for reform of abuses. Three men led the way to the Reformation—Erasmus, Luther, and Calvin. The Reformation in Switzerland and in England followed the traces of these three men.

Some account of each of these Reformers, and the

[1] St. Matthew, chap. xxiv.

O

work they did, and the work they left undone, may be
here given.

Luther was a great man—one of the reformers of
European religion and morals. It was not his opposition to Leo X.'s bull of indulgences which made him
great—though his opposition to that bull has been very
unjustly attributed to the jealousy entertained of the
Dominican by the Augustine order of friars. It was
highly to the credit of his judgment and his courage,
that he perceived at once that the bull of Leo was
inconsistent with Christianity, and that he appeared at
Augsburg to maintain his opinion. He knew well that
the burning of John Huss at the Council of Constance
had been approved by the strongest party at Rome,
and he had no reason to trust that Charles, if he saw
his interest in the burning of Luther, would have hesitated to commit an offence so light in his eyes as a
breach of faith. Luther, however, with the innocence
of the dove had some of the wisdom of the serpent.
In an age which was opening its eyes to enquiry,
and when the midnight of the dark ages was gradually
yielding to light, Luther, by his incessant activity, by
his preaching and his writing, by collecting disciples
among the hearers of his lectures, and by his earnest
exhortations to some of the most spirited and enlightened princes of Germany, was securing to himself
friends, and many who did not venture openly to
adopt his opinions gave him secret assurances that he
would not be abandoned.

The inestimable service, however, which Luther
rendered to the religion and morals of Europe and

the world, was by opening the Bible. Paolo Sarpi says
that when in his discourses and arguments Luther
appealed to the Scriptures the Cardinal Legate declined
to argue with him, as the canonists and theologians had
not been accustomed to search the Scriptures as the
authority for their religion.[1] In fact, theological
opinions and decrees were not founded on the Scriptures. A Scotch bishop said he had never read the
Bible, and did not see the use of it. Luther himself
perhaps did not at first perceive that when once the
reading of the Bible and the invention of printing
furnished the minds of Germany and of Europe with
ample stores of religious instruction, no partial reform
of abuses would suffice.

Yet Luther before long threw off his subjection to
the Pope, and entered into open rebellion against the
Church of Rome.

The fault of Luther was, that in the very beginning
of this mighty contest, he attempted to erect a new
Church, to cover it with something like infallibility,
and to defend it by persecution.

It was a necessary part of priestcraft that, after miracles
had ceased, the visible Church on earth should invent
a theory by which they should say, Lo, Christ is here;
Lo, Christ is there; and assume to themselves the

---

[1] 'Martino, con salvocondotto di Massimiliano, andò a trovar il
legato in Augusta, dove, dopo una conveniente conferenze, sopra la
materia controversa, scoprendo il Cardinale che con termini di teologia
scolastica, nella professione della quale era eccellentissimo, non poteva
esser convinto Martino, che si valeva sempre della Scrittura divina,
la quale da' scolastici è pochissimo adoperata, si dichiarò di non
voler disputar con lui,' &c.—*Paolo Sarpi*, lib. i. p. 21, edit. 1858.

power and even the very presence of Christ. The
last words of Christ, as recorded by St. Matthew, were,
'All power is given to me in heaven and in earth.
Go ye therefore and teach all nations, baptising them
in the name of the Father, and of the Son, and of the
Holy Ghost; teaching them to observe all things whatsoever I have commanded you : and lo, I am with you
alway, even unto the end of the world.   Amen.'

A few days before, at the Last Supper, when Jesus
was giving them to eat and to drink, ' Jesus took bread,
and blessed it, and brake it, and gave it to the disciples,
and said, Take, eat; this is my body.   And he took the
cup, and gave thanks, and gave to them, saying, Drink
ye all of it ; this is my blood of the new testament,
which is shed for many for the remission of sins.   But
I say unto you, I will not drink henceforth of the fruit
of the vine, until that day when I drink it new with
you in my Father's kingdom.' [1]

In the same manner it is recorded by St. Mark that
He said to his disciples, ' Verily, I will drink no more
of the fruit of the vine, until that day I drink it new
in the kingdom of God.' [2]

In nearly the same words St. Luke relates that
Jesus said, 'for I say unto you, I will not drink of
the fruit of the vine, until the kingdom of God shall
come.' [3]

Although Christ had in these sublime yet simple
lessons told his disciples to teach all nations whatsoever He had commanded unto them, and has pointedly

---

[1] St. Matt., chap. xxvi.   [2] St. Mark, chap. xiv.
[3] St. Luke, chap. xxii.

called the wine he drank the fruit of the vine, the
Church which assumed his name, and said, ' Lo, Christ
is here,' founded upon those two sayings their pretensions to miraculous powers.

Although Christ had told them to teach all nations
whatsoever he commanded, they taught that, by the
rite of baptism, they could communicate to children
of a day old, who were incapable of understanding a
word of his commandments, a right to inherit the
kingdom of heaven, and if these infants had not
received this miraculous gift, they, innocent and un-
intelligent as they were, would be condemned to everlasting and eternal punishment.

In the same spirit, although Christ had expressly
called the wine he drank the fruit of the vine, the
priesthood pretended that the bread which Christ distributed to his disciples was, at the moment He sat
before them, changed into his body, and that the
wine he drank was changed then and there into his
blood.

Moreover, the Church pretended that, for all time to
come, they, the priesthood duly ordained, had the
power of changing the bread and wine, prepared by
their hands, into the body and blood of Christ, and to
obtain the Real Presence of the Saviour in the celebration of the Sacrament.

There was thus a sacrifice made, not once by Christ
of his life upon the Cross, but a sacrifice daily and
hourly made by the priest for the redemption of mankind. Had the Christians of early times been sufficiently instructed in the Scriptures they would have

easily understood both the rite of baptism and the celebration of the Lord's Supper.

They would have easily concluded that when a whole household were baptized it might be convenient to admit the infants of a family into the Church of Christ by baptism, but that no miracle attended that ceremony, and that it was not till the infants reached fourteen or fifteen years of age that they could properly comprehend the story of Christ's life, the gratitude due for his sufferings, and the duty of obeying his commandments.

In the same way they would gladly have partaken of the bread and wine, in commemoration of his Last Supper, and would no more have concluded that Christ was in the bread and wine than that He was a vine, or that He was present in the body when a cup of water was given to a child.

But these simple interpretations did not answer the purpose of the priesthood. Luther was a monk; Calvin a student of theology, and the broken links of their chains hung about them while they were striving to set themselves free.

> Luctata canis nodum arripit, attamen illi
> Dum fugit a collo trahitur pars longa catenæ.

ESSAY XIII.

ERASMUS.

TOWARDS the close of the fifteenth century everything was preparing for one of those changes in the state of the world which are destined to influence for a long period subsequent generations. The great authors of Greece and Rome, whose works had been neglected or buried for centuries, were discovered anew, and revealed to the eyes of admiring nations. A passion for learning seized the minds, not only of studious men, but of the daughters of the aristocracy of Europe; there being few authors of the age or of the day whose style was polished and whose matter was interesting. The works of Homer and of Plato, of Virgil and of Cicero, attracted the attention and occupied the time of Lady Jane Grey, of Victoria Colonna, of the Princess Elizabeth of England, and of many noble ladies in different countries of Europe; but if these studies were the occupation or the recreation of illustrious ladies, were they not sure to absorb the vigilant studies of scholars, of professors, and of poets? But further, if profane authors of past times were the objects of enquiry and curiosity, was it not certain that the sacred books, which contained the miraculous flight of Moses from Egypt, and the records of the first beginnings of

Christianity, would excite the vigilant attention of scholars, and be deeply studied by the pastors of the community and the monks of the cloister? The new art of printing gave fresh food to the appetite of scholars, and fresh information to a curious and ardent world.

It seemed for some time doubtful what would be the result of these new steps in civilisation. The great citizen of Florence, who had raised himself to a position of supreme power, and governed the State over which he presided with so firm, yet so tranquil a mastery, found time for philosophy as well as for government, for poetry as well as for learning. The celebrated historian Guicciardini has left a dialogue, after the manner of Cicero, in which an interlocutor praises the condition of Florence as one of happy enjoyment and peaceful security, as one not so much of despotic rule as of a willing concert of the best men of Florence to govern without destruction of property or of oppression to person. But it was doubtful whether Lorenzo and his friends wished to inculcate a real belief in Christianity, or whether they were not more disposed to adopt the Deism of Plato, leaving the ceremonies of the Church and the sermons of the priests rather as a matter of reverence to the educated classes of society than as the actual faith and religious creed of earnest men. It is certain that Lorenzo, in his letter of advice to his son, who was destined to the ecclesiastical profession, and who rose to be bishop, cardinal, and pope, does not lay a stress upon the Christian religion as a matter of serious import. We

lave seen, on the authority of the best historians, how
his son, when he became pope, gave up his time to
'easts and music, to hunting and light literature, to the
great scandal of those who thought that at so critical
a period the head of Christianity ought to devote his
ife to religious studies, and to examine with the
greatest care the line of policy which it was his duty to
adopt. It is said, indeed, that Leo scrupulously observed
he fasts of the Church. But this may have been from
notives of health, or intended to gain outward respect,
and make up for more serious deficiencies.

While the son of Lorenzo was undergoing his edu-
·ation in Italy, there was born in the city of Rotterdam,
n Holland, a boy who was destined to be a great
cholar, and to prepare the road to the Reformation
by his studies, no less than Leo by his negligence.
Jerard, the father of Erasmus, was one of ten sons,
born of decent but not opulent parents at Gouda
Tergau), in Holland. Gerard formed a passionate at-
achment to the daughter of a physician; this daughter,
Marguerita, finding their marriage prevented by the
opposition of the parents of her lover, fled to the city
of Rotterdam, where, on October 28, 1467, she gave
birth to a son, born to immortal fame. Gerard was
ome weeks after this time alarmed by a rumour that
he object of his love, and his hoped-for bride, was dead.
In a fit of despair he severed himself from the world,
and took the irrevocable vows of a priest. On his
·eturn to Gouda he found his destined wife in perfect
health; he was faithful to his love; and Marguerita,
on her side, preserved from thenceforth an unsullied

fame. At nine years old her son was sent to school at
Deventer, accompanied by his mother, who obtained
for him lessons in design and drawing.

It has been said that the mother of Erasmus had
previously borne a child to Gerard, who became a
stupid and profligate monk ; he died early, and may
be forgotten. The son of Gerard, whose name was
Latinized into Desiderius, and Desiderius again repeated
in the Greek Erasmus, made good progress at Deventer,
and gave early promise of future eminence. Sinheim,
the sub-rector, was the first to understand this promise,
and on one occasion said to him, ' Go on as thou hast
begun, and before long rise to the highest pinnacle of
letters.' Rudolph Agricola, the first who brought
Italian learning across the Alps, and was an eminent
Greek scholar, having, on a visit to Deventer, put a few
questions to Erasmus, and having looked at his eyes
and the shape of his head, · dismissed him with the
words, ' You will be a great man.' Erasmus himself
has recorded that at Deventer he went through the
whole course of scholastic training—logic, physics,
metaphysics, and morals ; and that he had also learned
Horace and Terence by heart. Every art was used
to induce him to join the institution permanently
and become a monk, but in vain. The boy was
obliged to leave Deventer by the death of both his
parents. He was cast upon the world an orphan, with
faithless guardians, who robbed him of his small inheritance. There remained, however, certain bonds or
securities, which furnished a temptation to the brotherhood of Bois le Duc to endeavour to drive him into

ıe cloister. They endeavoured to frighten him by
ıccssant tales of wild beasts, goblins, and devils; to
ear him out by the infliction of corporal punishment,
ıd to attract him by an advantageous opening in the
ıonastery of Sion, near Defta. But Erasmus replied
ıat he was still young, he knew not himself, nor the
loister, nor the world; he wished to pursue his studies;
ı riper years he might determine on conviction and
xperience on his course of life. A false friend achieved
ıat which had been attempted in vain by threats and
ıverity. Verden was a youth a few years older than
imself, astute and selfish, but high-spirited and am-
itious : he had gone to Italy, and, on his return, had
ntered into the monastery of Stein, which he described
ɔ his friend as a paradise for a man of letters. Thus
ersuaded he entered the cloister. But very soon his
yes were opened; the quiet, the indulgence, the un-
ıroken leisure were gone. Yet, although he was in the
ıidst of coarse and profligate men, he gave much of
ıis time to study. Among modern authors his admi-
ation was excited by Laurentius Valla. Laurentius
Valla was one of the scholars of Florence who, in his
ıanly and arrogant style, and by the boldness and
ıriginality of his thoughts, had most thoroughly ex-
ɔosed the fiction of the fabulous gift of Constantine to
he good pope Sylvester. In this place Erasmus passed
ive years; the brotherhood looked on him with
ealousy, and he regarded them with aversion. Both
ɔarties were willing to escape from their contract, and
when the Bishop of Cambrai meditated a journey to
Rome in hopes of obtaining a cardinal's hat, and, in

want of a secretary skilful in writing the Latin language, offered the post to Erasmus, it was eagerly
accepted.   His friend Herman alone lamented the
solitude in which he should be left :

> Me sine solus abis, tu Rheni frigora et Alpes,
> Me sine solus adis,
> Italiam, Italiam lætus penetrabis amœnam.

Erasmus was at length induced to enter into holy
orders.   He continued his studies, and as a scholar
made some valuable friendships.   At length, after five
years not wasted—but still to him not profitable years—
he hoped to obtain the one grand object of his ambition
—residence and instruction at one of the great universities of Europe.   Paris, the famous seat of theological
learning, seemed to open her gates to him.   The bishop
not only gave permission, but promise of support.   The
eager student obtained what may be called a pensionate
or bursary in the Montagu College.   But new trials
and difficulties awaited him.   The bishop was too poor,
too prodigal, or too parsimonious to keep his word.   His
allowance to Erasmus was reluctantly and irregularly
paid, if paid at all.   The poor scholar had not where-
withal to pay fees for lectures, or for the purchase of
books ; but he had lodging, and such lodging !—food,
but how much, and of what quality !   Hear his college
reminiscences :—

'Thirty years since I lived in a college at Paris,
named from vinegar (Montaceto).   " I do not wonder,"
says the interlocutor, " that it was so sour, with so
much theological disputation in it ; the very walls, they
say, reek with theology."   Erasmus : " You say true ; I

ideed brought nothing away from it but a constitution all of unhealthy humours, and plenty of vermin." Over hat college presided one John Standin, a man not of a bad disposition, but utterly without judgment. If, having himself passed his youth in extreme poverty, he had shown some regard for the poor, it had been well. f he had so far supplied the wants of the youths as to nable them to pursue their studies in credit, without pampering them with indulgence, it had been praiseworthy; but what with hard beds, scanty food, rigid vigils and labours, in the first year of my experience, I saw many youths of great gifts, of the highest hopes and promise, of whom, some actually died, some were loomed for life to blindness, to madness, to leprosy. Of these I was acquainted with some, and no one was exempt from the danger. Was not that the extreme of cruelty? . . . Nor was this the discipline only of the poorer scholars; he received not a few sons of opulent parents, whose generous spirit he broke down. To restrain wanton youth by reason and by moderation, is the office of a father; but in the depth of a hard winter to give hungry youths a bit of dry bread, to send them to the well for water, and that foetid and unwholesome or frost-bound! I have myself known many who thus contracted maladies which they did not shake off as long as they lived. The sleeping-rooms were on the ground-floor, with mouldy plaster walls, and close to filthy and pestilential latrinæ.'

In Paris, the name of Erasmus as a distinguished scholar soon became famous. He took private pupils, and many of the wealthiest youths of England profited by his tuition. Lord Mountjoy added friendship to the relations of a pupil; he removed Erasmus from the unhealthy precincts of the college to purer air, and some time after settled on his master a pension, which he held for life. In an excursion from Paris, he became acquainted with the Marchioness of Vere, whose son he instructed, and from whom also he received a pension. From time to time he visited his native Holland, which he called in contempt, 'Beer and butter land.' He despised the banquets of epicurean plenty on the one hand, and the mean jealousy of learning on the other. In 1498 he paid his visit to England, on the invitation of Mountjoy; his accounts of this country, both as regards the climate and the state of learning, were singularly favourable. 'You ask,' he writes to Piscator, an Englishman at Rome, 'how I am pleased with England. If you will believe me, my dear Robert, nothing ever delighted me so much. I have found the climate most agreeable and most healthful, and so much civility (*humanitas*, a far wider term), so much learning—and that not trite and trivial, but profound and accurate—so much familiarity with the ancient writers, Latin and Greek, that, except for the sake of seeing it, I hardly care to visit Italy. When I hear Colet, I seem to hear Plato. Who would not admire Grocyn's vast range of knowledge? What can be more subtle, more deep, more fine, than the judgment of Linacre? Did Nature ever frame a disposition more gentle, more sweet, more happy, than that of Thomas More?' On his host, Mountjoy, Erasmus is gratefully loquent : ' Whither would I not follow a youth so courteous, so gentle, so amiable—I say not to England, would follow him to the infernal regions ! '

We have arrived now at the great question, what vas the conduct of Erasmus in regard to the Reformaion? There can be no doubt that while Erasmus was n enemy of the scholastic system, and that while he lamed not only with a free spirit but with the most iting wit, and general popularity, the abuses of the Jhurch, he was utterly averse to any revolution by orce, and was content to leave the work of the Reormation to people formed by reason, by the progress if knowledge, and by the general humanity which night be expected to follow the revival of letters. The great poet Goethe, the eminent historian Macaulay, and some other men of note, have wished that Erasmus had been successful; that the German eruption of Luther and the French triumph of Calvin had not disturbed the peaceful progress of reform, and that the sixteenth century had come to its close amid the undisputed predominance of the Church of Rome. Yet it seems to me that these complacent authors have rather consulted their own preferences as men of letters, to their sagacity as interpreters of past events. The Church of Rome had, up to the appearance of Luther and his bold defiance in Germany, been as intolerant and as sanguinary as ever. John Huss had visited Constance in possession of an inviolate safe-conduct ; Jerome of Prague relied upon the faith of princes who guaranteed his safety—both were burnt. Leo X. and his successor Adrian had consulted the

most trustworthy of their cardinals on the policy to be
pursued towards Luther; examples were quoted to
them in abundance of the extinction of heresy by fire
and sword. The disappearance of Arianism ; the defeat
of the Albigenses ; the very punishments of Huss and
Jerome of Prague, the forerunners of the restoration
and triumph of the Church in Bohemia, were pointed
out as models of the true policy to follow, and the sure
proofs that the heresies of Germany, of England, of
Spain, and of Italy, would be happily extinguished,
if the popes would but follow the happy lessons
of persecution which had been derived from their
predecessors.

I therefore arrive at the conclusion, that if Luther
and Calvin, Zuinglius and Knox, had quietly submitted
to the paternal admonitions of their spiritual chiefs,
they would have been consigned to the flames with the
numerous victims of the Spanish Inquisition—with
Cranmer, Hooper, Latimer, and Ridley—to the great
joy of Philip of Spain, of Mary Queen of Scots, of the
Duke of Guise, and the Roman Catholic Church in
Europe. But we must do no injustice to Erasmus. I
will extract from the works of Milman, late Dean of St.
Paul's, and of Mr. Froude, a living writer, a summary
of the great works performed, and the great lessons
taught by Erasmus. He was truly the precursor of the
Reformation, and held aloft the light which caused the
obscene birds of prey to fly back to the dark recesses
in which their ignorance and sloth had hitherto lain
buried. To begin with Dr. Milman :—

' Erasmus was no less the declared opponent, and

took great part in the discomfiture, of scholasticism, and of the superstitions of the middle ages.

> At length Erasmus, that great injured name,
> (The glory of the priesthood and the shame,)
> Stemmed the wild torrent of a barbarous age,
> And drove those holy Vandals off the stage.'

Pope's 'wild torrent' is not a very happy illustration of the scholasticism which had so long oppressed the teaching of Europe; 'a stagnant morass' or an 'impenetrable jungle' had been a more apt similitude. Few, however, did more to emancipate the human mind from the Thomism and the Scotism, the pseudo-Aristotleism, which ruled and wrangled in all the schools of Europe. Erasmus fell in, in this respect, with the impatience and the ardent aspirations of all who yearned for better days. In Italy the yoke was already broken : the monks, especially on this side of the Apennines, fought hard in their schools and in the universities, in which they had still the supremacy. But the new universities, the schools founded especially in England out of the monasteries suppressed by Wolsey, or out of ecclesiastical wealth, as by Bishop Fox, or by Colet, who hated scholasticism as bitterly as Erasmus, were open to the full light of the new teaching. Erasmus served the good cause in two ways : by exposing barrenness and uselessness, in his serious as well as in his satirical writings; and by supplying the want of more simple, intelligible, and profitable manuals of education. Against the superstitions of the age, the earlier writings of Erasmus are a constant grave or comic protest,

P

though he was not himself always superior to such
weaknesses. In his younger days he had attributed
his recovery from a dangerous illness to the intercession of St. Genoveva, to whom he addressed an
ode. The saint, it is true, was aided by William
Cope, the most skilful physician in Paris. When at
Cambridge he made a pilgrimage—it may have been
from curiosity rather than faith—to our Lady at
Walsingham. But his later and more mature opinions
he either cared not, or was unable, to disguise. The
monks, the authors and supporters of these frauds, are
not the objects of his wit alone, but of his solemn,
deliberate invective. Severe argument, however, and
bitter, serious satire had been heard before, and fallen
on comparatively unheeding ears ; it was the lighter
and more playful wit of Erasmus which threw even
the most jealous off their guard, and enabled him to
say things with impunity which in graver form had
awakened fierce indignation. Even the sternest bigots,
if they scented the danger, did not venture to pro-
scribe the works which all Christendom, as yet un-
frightened, received with unchecked and unsuspecting
mirth. Let the solemn protest as they will, there are
truths of which ridicule is the Lydian stone. The
laughter of fools may be folly, but the laughter of
wise men is often the highest wisdom. Perhaps no satire was ever received with more universal applause, in
its day, than the 'Praise of Folly.' Let us remember that
it was finished in the house of More, and dedicated to
one who was hereafter to lay down his life for the
Roman faith. To us, habituated to rich English

humour and fine French wit, it may be difficult to
do justice to the ' Moriæ Encomium ; ' but we must
bear in mind that much of the classical allusion, which
to us is trite and pedantic, was then fresh and original.
The inartificialness and, indeed, the inconsistency of
the structure of the satire might almost pass for consummate art. Folly, who at first seems indulging in
playful and inoffensive pleasantry, while she attributes
to her followers all the enjoyments of life unknown
to the moroser wise, might even, without exciting
suspicion, laugh at the more excessive and manifest
superstitions — the worship of St. Christopher and
St. George, St. Erasmus and St. Hippolytus ; at indulgences; at those who calculated nicely the number
of years, months, hours of purgatory; those who would
wipe off a whole life of sin by a small coin, or who
attributed magic powers to the recitation of a few
verses of the Psalms. But that which so far is light,
if somewhat biting wit, becomes on a sudden a fierce
and bitter irony, sometimes anticipating the savage
misanthropy of Swift, but reserving its most merciless and incisive lashes for kings, for the clergy, for
the cardinals and the popes. Folly, from a pleasant,
comic merry-andrew, raising a laugh at the absurdities
of the age, is become a serious, solemn, Juvenalian
satirist, lashing its vices with the thrice-knotted
scourge, drawing blood at every stroke, and, as it
were, mocking his prostrate victims. Of this work
twenty-seven editions were published during the life-
time of the author, and it was translated into many
of the languages of Europe. The ' Colloquies ' were

P 2

neither less bold nor less popular ; they were in every
library, almost in every school. We have accounts of
an edition of above 20,000 copies said to have been
struck off by one .adventurous printer ; and yet in
these 'Colloquies' there was scarcely a superstition
which was not mocked at—we say not with covert, but
with open scorn ; and this with a freedom which in
more serious men, men of lower position in the world
of letters, would have raised an instant alarm of deadly
heresy, and might have led the hapless author to the stake.
In the 'Shipwreck,' while most of the passengers are
raising wild cries, some to one saint, some to another,
there is a single calm person, evidently shown as the
one true Christian, who addresses his prayers to God
Himself, as the only deliverer. In the 'Ichthyophagia,'
the eating of fish, there is a scrupulous penitent, whom
nothing, not even the advice of his physician, will
induce to break his vow, and eat meat or eggs, but
who has not the least difficulty in staving off the payment of a debt by perjury. In the 'Inquisition concerning Faith' there is a distinct assertion, that belief
in the Apostles' Creed (which *many at Rome do not
believe*) is all-sufficient; that against such a man even
the Papal anathema is an idle thunder, even should
he eat more than fish on a Friday. 'The Funeral'
contrasts the deathbed and the obsequies of two men.
One is a soldier, who has acquired great wealth by
lawless means. He summons all the five orders of
mendicants, as well as the parish priest, to his dying
bed. There is a regular battle for him : the parish
priest retires with a small share of the spoil, as also do

three of the mendicant order. Two remain behind. The man dies, and is magnificently buried in the Church in the cowl of a Franciscan; having forced his wife and children to take religious vows, and bequeathing the whole of his vast wealth to the order. The other man dies simply, calmly, in humble reliance on his Redeemer: makes liberal gifts to the poor, but bequeaths them nothing; leaves not a farthing to any one of the orders; receives extreme unction and the Eucharist without confession, having nothing on his conscience, and is buried without the least ostentation. Which model Erasmus would hold up as that of the true Christian, cannot be doubted. In 'The Pilgrimage,' not only is pilgrimage itself held up to ridicule, but even the worship of the Virgin. In the letter which, by a fiction not without frequent precedent, he ascribes to the blessed ' Deipara,' there is a sentence, in which the opinion of Luther, denying all worship of the saints, is slily approved of, as relieving her from a great many importunities and troublesome supplications. The 'Franciscan Obsequies,' perhaps the finest and most subtle in its satire, while it openly dwells only on those who, to be sure of Paradise, dying, put on the weeds of a Franciscan, and think to pass disguised, was in its covert sarcasm an exposure of the whole history of the order, and, with somewhat contemptuous homage for the holy founder, scoffs even at the Stigmata, and lashes the avarice and wealth of this most beggarly of the begging fraternities. He thus galled to the quick this powerful brotherhood, who had provoked

214 HISTORY OF THE CHRISTIAN RELIGION.

him by their obstinate ignorance, and became still
more and more his inveterate and implacable foes.
A scholar could fill pages from his various writings
with denunciations against these enemies of sound
learning and true religion.

Erasmus was the parent of biblical criticism. His
edition of the New Testament first opened to the West
the Gospels and the Epistles of St. Paul in the original
Greek. Preparation had been made for the famous
Complutensian edition, but it had not yet appeared to
the world. For its age, in critical sagacity, in accuracy,
in fidelity, in the labour of comparing scattered and yet
unexplored manuscripts, the New Testament of Erasmus was a wonderful work. The best and latest of our
biblical scholars—Tischendorf, Lachmann, Tregelles—
do justice to the bold and industrious pioneer, who
first opened the invaluable mines of biblical wealth.
It was no common courage or honesty which would
presume to call in question the immaculate integrity,
the infallible authority, of the Vulgate, which had
ruled with uncontested sway the Western mind for
centuries; to appeal to a more ancient and more
venerable, as well as more trustworthy canon of the
faith. To dare in those days to throw doubt on the
authenticity of such a text as that of the 'Three
Heavenly Witnesses,' implied fearless candour, as rare
as admirable. Such a publication was looked upon, of
course, with awe, suspicion, jealousy. Some with
learning, some, like Lee, with pretensions to learning,
fell upon it with rabid violence; but Erasmus had
been so wise, or so fortunate, as to be able to place

the name of the Pope, and that Pope Leo X., on the front of his work ; he under that protecting ægis fought manfully, and with no want of controversial bitterness against his bigoted antagonists. The names of these adversaries have sunk into obscurity, though Lee became Archbishop of York, and was, according to his epitaph—we fear his sole testimony—a good and generous man.[1] But to the latest times theological learning acknowledges the inestimable debt of gratitude which it owes to Erasmus. But it was not only as editor, it was as interpreter also, of the New Testament, that Erasmus was a benefactor to the world.

In his notes, and in his invaluable paraphrases, he opened the sense, as well as the letter, of the long-secluded—if not long-sealed—volume of the New Testament. He was the parent also of the sound, and simple, and historical exposition of the sacred writings. He struck boldly down through the layers of mystic, allegoric, scholastic, traditional lore, which had been accumulating for ages over the holy volume, and laid open the vein of pure gold—the plain, obvious, literal meaning of the apostolic writings.

Suffice it for us to say, that Erasmus is, in a certain

[1] Compare More's letters to Lee on his attack on Erasmus. More had known Lee's family, and Lee himself in his youth; but he scrupled not to castigate the presumption of Lee in measuring himself against the great scholar. In his last letter, after alluding to Pope Leo's approbation of the New Testament, he adds, ' quod ex arce religionis summus ille Christiani orbis princeps suo testimonio cohonestat, id tu monachulus et indoctus et obscurus ex antro cellulæ tuæ pestilentâ linguâ conspurcas.'—Jortin, *Life of Erasmus*, *App. II.*

sense, or rather was in his day, to the Church of England, the recognised and authenticated expositor of the New Testament. The translation of the paraphrases, it is well known, was ordered to be placed in all our churches with the vernacular Scriptures. Nor was there anything of the jealousy or exclusiveness of the proud scholar in Erasmus. His biblical studies and labours were directed to the diffusion and to the universal acceptation of the Scriptures as the rule of faith. Neither Luther, nor the English Reformers, expressed themselves more strongly or emphatically on this subject than Erasmus : ' The sun itself should not be more common than Christ's doctrine.'

'I altogether and utterly dissent from those who are unwilling that the Holy Scriptures, translated into the vulgar tongue, should be read by private persons (*idiotis*), as though the teaching of Christ were so abstruse as to be intelligible only to a few theologians; or as though the safety of the Scriptures rests on man's ignorance of it. It may be well to conceal the mysteries of kings; but Christ willed that His mysteries should be published as widely as possible. I wish that simple women (*mulierculæ*) should read the Gospel, should read the epistles of St. Paul. Would that the Scripture were translated into all languages, that it might be read and known, not only by Scots and Irishmen, but even by Turks and Saracens ('*Paraclesis in Nov. Testamentum I*')[1]

Erasmus was justly averse to the logical refinements and subtle definitions introduced by the schoolmen of

[1] Milman's *Life of Erasmus*, p. 122.

a past age. To one of his correspondents, an archbishop, he writes :—' Let us have done with theological refinements. There is an excuse for the Fathers,
because the heretics forced them to define particular
points ; but every definition is a misfortune, and for us
to persevere in the same way is sheer folly. Is no
man to be admitted to grace who does not know how
the Father differs from the Son, and both from the
Spirit? or how the nativity of the Son differs from
the procession of the Spirit? Unless I forgive my
brother his sins against me, God will not forgive me
my sins. Unless I have a pure heart—unless I put
away envy, hate, pride, avarice, lust, I shall not see
God. But a man is not damned because he cannot
tell whether the Spirit has one principle or two. Has
he the fruits of the Spirit? That is the question. Is
he patient, kind, good, gentle, modest, temperate,
chaste? Enquire if you will, but do not define. True
religion is peace, and we cannot have peace unless we
leave the conscience unshackled on obscure points on
which certainty is impossible. We hear now of questions being referred to the next Œcumenical Council—
better a great deal refer them to Doomsday. Time
was, when a man's faith was looked for in his life—not
in the articles he professed. Necessity first brought
articles upon us, and ever since we have refined
and refined till Christianity has become a thing of
words and creeds. Articles increase—sincerity va-
nishes — contention grows hot, and charity grows
cold. Then comes in the civil power, with stake and
gallows, and men are forced to profess what they do

not believe—to pretend to love what, in fact, they hate ; and to say that they understand what, in fact, has no meaning for them.'

Again, to the Archbishop of Mayence, Erasmus writes—' Reduce the dogmas necessary to be believed to the smallest possible number ; you can do it without danger to the realities of Christianity. On other points, either discourage enquiry, or leave everyone free to believe what he pleases—then we shall have no more quarrels, and religion will again take hold of life. When you have done this, you can correct the abuses of which the world, with good reason, complains. The unjust judge heard the widow's prayer. You should not shut your ears to the cries of those for whom Christ died. He did not die for the great only, but for the poor and for the lowly. There need be no tumult. Do you only set human affections aside, and let kings and princes lend themselves heartily to the public good. But observe that to the monks and friars be allowed no voice; with these gentlemen the world has borne too long. They care only for their own vanity, their own stomachs, their own power ; and they believe that if the people are enlightened their kingdom cannot stand.'

Once more, Erasmus writes to the Pope himself : ' Let each man amend first his own wicked life. When he has done that, and will amend his neighbour, let him put on Christian charity, which is severe enough when severity is needed. If your Holiness gives power to men who neither believe in Christ nor care for you, but think only of their own appetites, I fear there will be danger. We can trust your Holiness, but there are bad men who will use your virtue as a cloak for their own malice.'

'The stupid monks,' he writes, 'say mass as a cobbler makes a shoe; they come to the altars reeking from their filthy pleasures. Confession with the monks is a cloak to steal the people's money, to rob girls of their virtue, and commit other crimes too horrible to name! Yet these people are the tyrants of Europe. The Pope himself is afraid of them.'

Erasmus was delighted with the manners of English women, which at that time, though free from immorality, had a warmth of welcome which in later days was thought inconsistent with propriety and dignity of behaviour.

'English ladies,' he says, 'are divinely pretty, and too good-natured. They have an excellent custom among them, that, wherever you go, the girls kiss you. They kiss you when you come, they kiss you when you go, they kiss you at intervening opportunities; and their lips are soft, warm, and delicious.'[1]

But Erasmus, who liked so much the excellent custom of the young ladies, to kiss him when he came, to kiss him when he went, and to kiss him at intervening times, was not fated to pass his days in such pleasant pastimes. The time arrived when he was

---

[1] Dean Milman's *Life of Erasmus*, p. 94. Dean Milman says simply, 'It seems that in the days of Henry VII. our great-great-great-grandmothers, at meeting and at parting, indulged their friends, and even strangers, with an innocent salute. On this usage Erasmus enlarges to his poetic friend, in very pretty Latin,' &c. &c.

called upon to assert the opinions he had through life
professed. Let it be remembered that he had signified
his wish to have in the Church no other creed than the
short declaration called the Apostles' Creed ; that he
had ridiculed with biting wit the superstitious worship
of saints, and the gifts to propitiate senseless images ;
that he had refuted and exposed the logical refinements of the schoolmen, and had endeavoured to sim-
plify the faith of the Church.

Besides all this, he had openly expressed an opinion
that simple women, and even Saracens and Turks,
should be encouraged to read the Bible. He had himself translated the Scriptures from Greek into German.

Possibly his jests were still more offensive to priests
and monks than his arguments for reform. When the
image of a saint was insulted and burnt, Erasmus, with
a quiet sneer, said, ' It is a marvel there was no
miracle. The saint worked so many in the good old
times.'[1] So when he was told by the adherents of
Rome that from the marriage of Luther with a nun
Antichrist must be born ; ' Nay,' said Erasmus, ' if
monk and nun produce Antichrist, there must have
been legions of Antichrists these many years.'[1]

But although these gibes deeply offended the Church
militant, they did not satisfy Luther. The time was
come when a man must either declare for the Reformation or withhold his aid. The question was not
whether particular articles of faith should be embraced,
whether free will or predestination should be accepted,
whether faith alone was sufficient for salvation, whether

---

[1] *Short Studies on Great Subjects*, Erasmus, Luther.

public worship should be connected with the images
of saints or freed from unmeaning and superstitious
ceremonies. No. The question was wider and more
absolute. The freedom to read the Scriptures, the
rejection of Transubstantiation, the worship of Christ
or of the Pope as His image on earth—such were the
questions which divided those who protested at Augsburg from those who adored at Rome.

Luther felt the importance of obtaining the suffrage
of Erasmus on this question. He wrote in the most
conciliatory terms to Erasmus, but he wrote as a man
confident and resolute in his purpose, and he wrote as
a brave man to a timid man.

When such great issues were pending, it is melancholy to find that the man who ploughed the field was
about to separate from the man who was sowing the
seed, and might hope to reap the harvest. The correspondence which preceded the rupture between
Luther and Erasmus is read by the friends of religious
liberty with the same pain which is felt by the friends
of political freedom when they peruse the debate which
heralded the separation of Burke and Fox ; and while
men attached to political freedom feel compelled to
adhere to Fox, so men attached to religious liberty
must find themselves bound to give their verdict in
favour of Luther.

The letter of Luther, making allowance for his fiery
nature, and extreme confidence in his own judgment,
was calm and conciliatory. He acknowledges gratefully
the services which Erasmus had rendered to the reform
of religion, and limits his demands upon the older and

more experienced advocate of truth to such require-
ments as may, he thinks, be complied with without a
sacrifice of personal consistency.

Thus he says, and says truly : 'The whole world
cannot deny the magnificent and noble gifts of God
in you; for which we should all give thanks that
through you letters flourish and reign, and we are
enabled to read the Holy Scriptures in their purity. I
never wished that, neglecting or forsaking your own
measure of grace, you should enter into our camp.
You might have aided us much by your wit, and by
your eloquence; but since you have not the disposition
or the courage for this, we would have you serve God
in your own way. Only we feared lest our adversaries
should entice you to write against us, and that necessity should compel us to oppose you to the face. We
have held back some among us who were disposed and
prepared to attack you,' &c. . . .

'Our friends, yourself being judge, do not easily
bear your biting words, because human infirmity thinks
of and dreads the authority and reputation of Erasmus;
and it is a very different thing to be attacked by Erasmus, and by all the papists in the world.'

The letter ends almost affectionately—'Pardon my
childishness, and farewell in the Lord.'[1]

The question was fairly put to Erasmus, and Erasmus had time to consider his reply. Had the question
referred to freedom of the will, or to the doctrine that
salvation was to be obtained by faith alone, without
love or good works, the friends of liberty might hesi-

---

[1] Milman's *Life of Erasmus*, pp. 138, 139 ; Jortin's *Erasmus*.

tate, or even lean to the side of Erasmus, with his learning, and deep knowledge of theology. But the question really was, 'Are the Scriptures to be read, and
the abuses of the Roman Church to be warred against?
or is the Pope to continue the sale of indulgences, the
open venality of bishoprics, the worship of images, the
idolatry of bread and wine in the Sacrament?' The
voice of truth must, without a doubt, be in favour of
Luther.

Erasmus lived several years after his declaration of
war against Luther, and his reconciliation with the
papal system. He survived the execution of More
about a year.

Erasmus died at Basle, July 12, 1536.

ESSAY XIV.

LUTHER. COUNCIL OF TRENT.

WE have now arrived at the name of one of the great champions of the Reformation. Martin Luther was born in 1483. His father and mother belonged to a family of miners. They had lived in the village of Mora, near the forest of Thuringia; they had gone from there to Eisleben in Saxony, where they gained their bread as miners. Luther has himself mentioned that he was born and baptized at Eisleben; he was not six months old when his parents left Eisleben to establish themselves at Mansfeld. The mines of Mansfeld were at that time much celebrated; his mother often carried wood upon her back in order to obtain the moderate wages of the family. Luther complains that he was brought up with severity; and it appears that his mother was obliged to interfere to temper the harshness of his father, who had taken too literally the maxim of the wise Solomon, that he who loves the child will not spare the rod. At school, Martin was treated with frequent punishments; but having a bold and resolute spirit, the fire of genius was not quenched by this harsh discipline. As he grew near the age of manhood, he displayed much ability. At the age of seventeen, after he had already distinguished himself by his

learning, his enthusiastic nature and religious zeal led
him to form a determination, unknown to his father,
that, in order to accomplish his salvation, he must embrace the profession of a monk. He accordingly rose
in the middle of the night, and obtained admission into
a monastery of the order of St. Augustine. Intent
upon conquering the passions of youth and the weakness of the flesh, he subjected himself to the most cruel
privations, and hoped by self-inflicted punishments to
overcome the world, the flesh, and the devil. But it
was all in vain. Yet Luther continued to study, and
was much struck with a work of St. Augustine, entitled ' Of the Letter and of the Spirit.' He knew almost
by heart the works of Pierre d'Ailly, and was very
much impressed with the remark of that writer, ' that,
if the Church had not decided to the contrary, it would
be far better to admit that in the Holy Supper bread
and wine were received, and not mere accidents.'
About the year 1502, the Elector Frederic of Saxony
founded, in Wittenberg, a new university. Luther
had been three years in his cell at Erfurt, when he was
named professor at the University of Wittenberg. It
was then that he was obliged to devote himself to
the study of the scholastic philosophy of Aristotle.
These studies, though disliked by Luther, were afterwards of great use in furnishing him with arms to
combat the errors of the schoolmen. In 1510 or 1511
he was despatched by the order to which he belonged
to Rome, and instructed to arrange a dispute which
had arisen between the Vicar-General and seven monasteries of the order. When he arrived at the rich con-

Q

vent of Benedictines, situated on the Po, he was surprised, not only with the beauty of the architecture,
but with the abundance of meat which covered the
tables on a Friday—a fast-day of the Church. He
spoke out, but with mildness. 'The Church and the
Pope,' he said, 'forbid these things;' but the porter of
the convent warned him that he exposed himself to
danger by his remonstrance. He escaped to Bologna,
where he fell dangerously ill. After recovering from
this illness, he proceeded to Rome; but there he was
destined to be still more shocked by the riotous manners and open mockery of their religion, which were
characteristic of the prelates and priests of Rome. One
day in particular, having been invited with several
bishops to a dinner of ecclesiastics, they told him, without disguise, that when they were before the altar saying mass, instead of the sacramental form they used
these words of derision: '*Panis es, et panis manebis;
vinum es, et vinum manebis*'—(Thou art bread, and
thou wilt remain bread; thou art wine, and thou wilt
remain wine).[1] The disregard of the Church's injunc-
tion to fast shown in the Benedictine monastery of
Lombardy, and the open ridicule of the sacrament of
the Lord's Supper at Rome, must have given Luther
strange notions of the insincerity practised by the
clergy, both secular and regular, of the Church presided over by the Pope. The progress of the great
reformer made him at length declare that by faith
alone can the salvation of man be assured. This
declaration makes it necessary to pause, and consider
whether Luther had rightly understood the whole

[1] *Hist. de la Réformation*, vol. i. p. 187.

of the teaching and commandments delivered by Christ in the name of God, when at the end of his mission he declared to his disciples, ' I go to my Father and to your Father.'

The religion taught by Christ Himself to man, and repeated by His apostles in various shapes, comprehended three great lessons. The first was, to love God with all the heart and soul; the second, to love his neighbour as himself; the third—and not the least important—that if, from the strength of human passion or the weakness of human powers of resistance, he should fall into sin, his position might be recovered by sincere repentance, and a real determination to sin no more, and to lead for the rest of the period of his dwelling on earth a pure and virtuous life.

It will be observed by anyone who attentively reads the New Testament, that these lessons are scarcely ever allowed for a day to drop out of sight. In the prayer to ' Our Father which art in Heaven,' we are commanded to pray that ' our trespasses ' may be forgiven, ' as we forgive those who have trespassed against us.' There are few instances of severity recorded in the parables of our Saviour; one of the most striking is the instance of the servant who, having been forgiven by his lord a debt of ten thousand talents, refuses to forgive his fellow-servant a debt of three hundred pence. Such severity, whether in parable or in reality, is almost unexampled on the part of our Saviour. The woman guilty of adultery is told, ' Neither do I condemn thee; go, and sin no more.' The father of the prodigal son exclaims with

joy, upon his repentance, 'My son was dead, and is
alive again.' The acts which were singled out by our
Saviour, when He says that in all future time He shall
be in the midst of the doers of good works, are all acts
of kindness, of charity, and of love. St. Paul, when he
says that 'Love worketh no ill to his neighbour,' takes
care to enumerate acts of wrong which are inconsistent
with love. St. Paul, in his epistle to the Corinthians,
writes, according to the translation of Stanley, Dean of
Westminster, and the translation of Alford, Dean of
Canterbury, 'And now abideth faith, hope, love, these
three; but the greatest of these is love.' In the lexicon
of Liddell and Scott the word is translated, 'brotherly
love;' but whether we take the single word, or the
two words, brotherly love, it is impossible to think
that St. Paul considered faith as the greatest quality of
a Christian, when, after enumerating faith, he says so
expressively that love, or brotherly love, is the greatest
of the three.

Indeed it is impossible to think that Christ and His
apostles could have laid so much stress upon acts of
love and forgiveness, as works in conformity with the
commandments of God, and yet have left it as a matter
of indifference, when the great sacrifice of Christ had
been completed, whether those acts of love and repentance should or should not be performed.

I conclude, therefore, that Luther, in exalting faith,
to the exclusion of love and repentance, has divided
religion, which he ought to have kept entire; and has
omitted, in order to give undue prominence to faith,
many of the most impressive lessons which Christ, in

His sermon on the Mount, in His various parables, in His lessons to His disciples, and in His last words delivered to the most faithful among those who had attended Him in life and were ready to imitate Him in death, had delivered as the commandments of God. The abuses of the Roman Church, the untrue doctrine of Transubstantiation, and the adoration of a living man—often an ambitious and profligate priest—as a being to be approached with worship and deemed infallible as a God, have worked deep and extensive mischiefs in the various countries of Europe which have submitted to the spiritual and temporal government of the Pope. But the errors of Luther and of Calvin, however rebuked by other enquirers, have done much to alienate Christians from the great doctrine of love. It is to be hoped that, casting aside passion and prejudice, men will arrive at a period when the whole of the Bible will be searched for the doctrines by which they can be guided in this life, and upon which they can base their hopes for the future.

Having made these remarks upon the general course of Luther, to which I shall afterwards recur, I now follow the narrative of the great work of the Reformation.

In the year 1517, John Deizel or Tezel, the son of a goldsmith of Leipsic, who had studied in his native town, and had in 1489 entered the order of St. Dominic, invaded Germany, armed with 'Indulgences,' and assumed the character of an inquisitor of heretical pravity. He had been appointed by Pope Leo X. specially to collect money by the sale of indulgences, in order to

supply the expenses of the Pope, the costs of his
sumptuous feasts, his harmonious concerts, his hunting
parties, his patronage of letters, and all the excesses of
a luxurious Court.   Leo X., as we have already said,
was an accomplished scholar, a hospitable landlord, and,
with the exception of the Bible and the Christian religion, a Pope well versed in every kind of learning.
Tezel took care, while he supplied the daily wants of a
pompous and profuse Court, to obtain sufficient money
for his own expenses and those of his retinue.   He
himself bore a red cross, and in a loud voice proclaimed the benefits of the indulgences he was authorised to distribute.   He declared that he had saved
more souls than the apostle St. Peter by his lessons.
He proclaimed that, in the place of confession and absolution, and a penance of seven years to be endured,
those who came to him would have to pay only a small
piece of money, and would be relieved from the burdens
of the greatest sins—from the guilt of adultery and
murder, of rape and parricide.   Nay, they would be
relieved from all punishment in the next world on
account of crimes which they had not yet committed,
but which they intended hereafter to commit.   In the
same manner, the vicious would obtain the power of
continuing a life of fraud, or of persevering in habits
of adultery, and the indulgence of vices of all kinds.
Tezel then passed on to another subject.   The indulgences, he said, freed not only the living but the dead.
' Priest, noble, tradesman, wife, young girls, young men,
your relations cry to you from the pains of purgatory,
A small sum of money would save us from a dreadful

martyrdom, and you refuse to give it!' Numbers attended this auction of eternal happiness in the place of purgatory and hell. The greediness of the multitude, and the eagerness to be deceived, drove whole flocks of people into the hands of the impostor, and induced them to pay their money for this imaginary benefit. Some, however, were not so easily deceived. A Saxon gentleman asked Tezel whether he could be sure of granting him pardon for an act of revenge which he proposed to perpetrate against one who had injured him. Tezel assured him that his absolution was infallible, and received the money for his pardon; but going with his servants into a wood, the Saxon gentleman waiting for the passing of Tezel, when he came up, beat him soundly, and robbed him of the treasure he had collected. This was not a solitary example of incredulity and the infliction of punishment for the frauds, swindling, and cheating of which Tezel was the chief promoter. But the retaliation of the benighted and plundered world did not stop here. Luther knew very well that absolution for sins which had not yet been committed, and the substitution of impunity for future crimes in place of deep and sincere repentance, to atone for the weakness of the flesh in past days, was as contrary to all the precepts of the Church of Rome as to the religion of Christ. The Pope had indulged his pomps and vanities somewhat too long; while the Church of Rome had advanced in the confidence that the burning of John Huss and Jerome of Prague could be repeated without stint, and that the whole earth might be bathed in blood to maintain the pride of a Julius, or the feasts of a Leo. A spirit had awakened in Germany, in England, and in Switzerland, which was destined to set at defiance the stake in Bohemia, the fagots in Smithfield, and to arm the Elector of Saxony in Germany, Latimer in England, and Calvin in France, with the means of overthrowing the most powerful instruments of papal tyranny.

Luther himself was at this time full of respect for the Church and the Pope. He says, ' I was at this time a monk, one of the most stupid of papists; so much intoxicated with the doctrines of Rome that I would willingly have assisted, if I had been able, to punish anyone who had had the audacity to refuse the least in the world obedience to the Pope.'¹ But this blind obedience was soon to be corrected. Luther was one day seated in the confessional at Wittenberg: the penitents confessed themselves guilty of every kind of sin; some of adultery, others of dissolution of morals, unjust possession of property, and other crimes. When Luther told them they must repent and forsake the sins which it had been their habit to practise, to his astonishment they told him they had obtained an indulgence to persist in them. Luther said that in that case he could give them no absolution. These persons returned to Tezel, and told him that the monk Luther had refused them absolution. Tezel preached against him with great violence, had a great fire lit in the market-place, and declared that those who would not conform to his teaching should be burnt as heretics in that fire. The words of Luther produced little effect.

¹ *Hist. de la Réformation.*

Luther believing that the indulgence proclaimed by Tezel would not be sanctioned by the Pope, on the eve of the Feast of All Saints posted on the door of the principal church ninety-five propositions. The gist of these propositions was that the Pope cannot remit the condemnation of any sin, but can only declare and confirm the remission that God Himself has made, except in certain special cases reserved to the Pope; if the Pope does otherwise, the condemnation is not altered. In these and other propositions the Pope is treated with the utmost respect.

The Pope himself regarded these propositions lightly, and seemed inclined to take the part of Luther against the Dominicans; but throughout Germany, and, a fortnight later, in Italy, this open declaration of opposition excited the greatest ferment. Erasmus highly approved the conduct of Luther, and the princes of the House of Saxony applauded and protected the bold monk. Wise men felt that a revolution in the religious opinions of Europe was impending.

In fact, the preparations now about to be made were the beginning of a contest which was to separate Europe into two great camps—those who were ready to support the Church of Rome with all its existing abuses, and those who were ready to protest against such abuses, and to place themselves under different leaders. It was obvious that this separation could not take place without a long contest, without revolutions in various States, without conflicts of argument, to be followed by conflicts of the sword, and cruel punishments, inflicted by bigotry on the one side and suf-

fered by conscientious faith on the other. In the year
1516 this strife was about to begin; in 1619, more
than a century afterwards, began that great contest of
the different States of Europe, led by Gustavus Adolphus on behalf of the Protestants ; by the Emperor of
Austria, by Wallenstein, and other great warriors, on
behalf of the Roman Church.   This war, properly
called the 'Thirty Years' War,' was terminated by the
Peace of Westphalia in 1649, but its spirit lasted in
various shapes for a century longer. The expulsion of
James II. from the throne of England was a part of
the dispute in favour of the universal Roman Church
on the one hand, and of liberty of conscience and
the free exercise of private judgment on the other.
This separate contest was decided by the battle of
Culloden in 1746, and the general though silent acknowledgment of the right of George III. to the throne
of England in 1760.

Such were the mighty issues which, unknown to the
principal parties to be engaged in the struggle, were at
this time depending.   Yet it cannot be said that the
preparations were inadequate or unfit for so vast an en-
terprise.   The Pope, on his side, summoned Luther to
attend him in Italy, but these preliminary proceedings
were complicated by various political interests which
animated the contending parties, and the Emperor
Maximilian was intent, above all things, on the ag-
grandisement of his family and the elevation of his
grandson, already King of Spain and Naples, to the
imperial throne. With this object in view he feared
to alienate the Elector of Saxony, who was a known

ipporter of Luther. The Pope, for a similar reason,
shing to stop the advancement of so powerful a
ince as the King of Spain, already master of the
etherlands, to the imperial throne, was willing to
ine to some compromise with the German heretic, in
der to preserve the independence of Germany. But
ents were too quick for the procrastinations of
erman formalities and Italian artifice. Authority,
vour, confidence, reputation, fame threw themselves
1 the side of Luther, whose firmness and courage
eatly increased the number of his supporters. Leo
., fearing that if allowed further indulgence his victim
ould escape him, instituted at Rome an ecclesiasti-
il court, charged with the trial of Luther, at which
uther was summoned to appear before his greatest
nemy, who was at once the accuser and the judge.
n August 7, Luther received his summons at Wit-
enberg. The commotion it excited, not only at
Vittenberg, but in all the neighbouring States of
iermany, was ardent and sympathetic. 'Shall he
vho has told the truth,' it was said, 'go without any
ecurity for his life to this-great city, already drunk
vith the blood of the saints and of the martyrs of
Jesus Christ?' On August 8, Luther wrote to Spa-
atin requesting him to solicit the Elector of Saxony
o employ his influence to have the cause tried
n Germany and not in Italy. What had passed at
he Council of Constance was known to all Germany,
and it appeared certain that if Luther went to Italy
he would very speedily be condemned and burnt, in
order that the Pope might obtain means to defray

the expenses of his feasts and his concerts, his hun
ing parties in the morning and his literary court i
the afternoon.

Fortunately for Luther, he was not without assist
ance; the University of Wittenberg wrote to th
Pope himself, alleging in excuse for Luther his weak
ness of body, and his health impaired by study. Th
Elector of Saxony sympathised with his people, an
was unwilling to allow the light of learning in Ger
many to be extinguished to promote the maintenanc
of Italian diversions. Happily, time brought to th
aid of Luther a young man, whose ardour for stud
made him equal to any encounter of argument ii
Greek or Latin, and whose natural prudence and dis
cretion fitted him admirably to temper the excitabilit
of Luther, and the undoubted pugnacity of his disposi
tion. George Schwarzerd was a skilful armourer o
Bretten, a small town of the Palatinate; his wife wa
the daughter of a worthy magistrate named John
Reuter. On February 14, 1497, this couple had a
son born to them, who was christened by the nam
of Philip. The father of the wife, the magistrate
Reuter, brought up Philip and his brother George
with his own son, and gave them for a tutor John
Hungarus, who was not only an excellent scholar, but
a man devoted to the study of the Holy Scriptures.
The name of Schwarzerd was changed into that of
Melanchthon, the harmonious Greek translation of his
German name. Brought up in Bretten, the young
man distinguished himself by his rapid acquisition of
the Greek and Latin languages, to the admiration of

e travellers who passed that way and examined him to his progress. Suspicion was excited when he went Tubingen, by observing that between the services ' the Church he read a volume, which was supposed , be the work of some profane author. But on ex- nination, the book was found to be a copy of the oly Scriptures, lately printed at Bâle, by John Fro- enius. Knowledge and learning were accumulated 1 all sides. Erasmus wrote, ' I have the most distin- uished opinion and magnificent hopes of Melanchthon. et Christ allow that this young man may survive us a ong time ; he will entirely eclipse Erasmus.' In 1514 e was made a Doctor of Philosophy, and by the grace f his language and the charms of his conversation ontributed greatly to the increase of learning. When e was twenty-one, Frederic, Elector of Saxony, con- ceived the idea of appointing a professor of ancient inguages at his favourite university of Wittenberg. Ie addressed himself to the famous Reuchlin, who amed Melanchthon as best fitted for this task. The Elector, delighted to promote his favourite institution by adding to it a popular name, at once appointed Melanchthon to be professor. From this time Me- anchthon became the bosom friend and counsellor of Luther, who, in the rude battle he was about to sustain, required not only his own ardour, but the best advice that prudence could afford ; that every determination should be weighed, and every step be the result of the most enlightened judgment. The Pope had now agreed, with a view to his own influence in Germany, and especially in hopes to influence the election of an emperor, that the legate should be sent to Augsburg provided with a pardon for Luther, but only on condition that his submission was entire and complete. The person sent to Augsburg was called Thomas de Vio, surnamed Cajetan, of the town of Gaeta. He was an able and a learned man, but he relied entirely on the doctrines of Thomas Aquinas. Luther, on the other hand, based his faith on the express words of the Holy Scriptures. Hence the certain failure of this attempt at a compromise. Thus when Luther obtained an audience, the legate relied altogether on a constitution of Pope Clement in favour of indulgences. Luther, upon hearing this constitution quoted as a supreme authority, said, ' I cannot receive such constitutions as proofs of such great things, for they twist the Holy Scripture, and never quote it properly.'

De Vio. 'The Pope has authority and power over everything.'

Luther. 'Except the Scriptures.'

De Vio. 'Except the Scriptures! The Pope, do you not know it, is above councils. He has recently condemned and punished the Council of Bâle.'

Luther, holding firmly to the ground he had taken, said, soon afterwards,

' As to indulgences, if it can be proved to me that I am mistaken, I am ready to be instructed ; but as to the article of faith, if I were to yield anything it would be to deny Jesus Christ. I therefore cannot yield on this point, and with the grace of God, I will never yield.'

The next day there was a further conference, but Luther held firm to his declaration, and quoted Panor-

ıitanus,[1] who maintains that in what regards the
[oly Faith, not only a General Council, but every
ıember of the Church is above the Pope, if he can
ıote better authorities and urge better reasons than
he Pope.[2] Luther held this doctrine. Luther gave in
declaration in writing, and the legate on the other
and said to him, ' Retract, retract; if you do not,
send you to Rome before judges who are empowered
ɔ hear and decide on your cause.'

When this conference was over, Luther, seeing that
ıothing could be effected, determined to fly. He got
ıpon a borrowed hackney before day, without a bridle
ɔ his horse, without boots, without spurs, without
rms. His horse was led by a servant of the chief
ıagistrate of Augsburg. They rode through the
ark by a small door in the walls. He pressed his
ıorse into a gallop, and arrived on October 26 at
ɟraefenthal, where he received the hospitality of
ᴧlbert de Mansfeld.

I do not propose to follow the history of the
ᴧeformation; I therefore pass at once to the great
ıpoch of the Confession of Augsburg in the year
.530. There was a great assembly at Augsburg
ıı that year, and the Confession of Faith prepared by
ᴧelanchthon was read to a numerous assembly in the
ıresence of the Emperor of Germany.

Bruck and Bayer appeared before this assembly, the
ıne with a copy in Latin, and the other with a copy in

---

[1] 'Panormitanus' (Luther désignait par ce nom Ives, auteur
ᴧu fameux recueil de droit ecclésiastique intitulé *Panormia*, et
vêque de Chartres à la fin du onzième siècle).

[2] *Hist. de la Réformation.*

German of the Confession of Faith. The Emperor
asked that they should read the Confession in Latin.
The Elector of Saxony rose and said, ' We are Germans, and upon German territory ; I hope, therefore,
your Majesty will allow us to speak German.' Bayer,
one of the secretaries, then began to read the Confession, slowly, gravely, distinctly, in a sonorous
voice, and in a manner to make a great impression
on his auditory. In the prologue he said that those
who had signed the Confession wished to establish
one sole true faith ; but in case religious dissen-
sions could not be terminated amicably, he offered
to his Majesty to explain their cause in the presence of
one universal, free, and Christian council. After giving
in their adhesion to the doctrines of the Holy Trinity,
and the incarnation of the Son, true Man and true
God, he proceeded : ' We teach, moreover, that we
cannot be justified before God by our own strength,
our merits, and our works, but that we are so justified
on account of Christ, by grace, by means of faith,
when we believe that our sins are remitted by virtue of
Christ, who by His death has rendered satisfaction for
our faults. This faith is the justice that God imputes
to the sinner. We teach at the same time that this
faith ought to produce all the good works which God
has commanded us to do, for the love of God, and not
in order to obtain by them the grace of God.'

Such was the celebrated Confession of Augsburg.
It may be as well, before we go further, in examining
and giving an opinion upon that important document,
that we should contrast the declaration made at Augsburg on the question of salvation by faith and not by

works, to record the decision of the Council of Trent upon the same subject. In 1546, that is to say, sixteen years after the Confession of Augsburg, the Roman Catholic bishops and theologians assembled at Trent, took into consideration what they called the propositions of the Lutheran doctrine, in order to censure and condemn those which they considered it necessary and decent to condemn. These propositions, according to one historian, Fra Paolo Sarpi, were twenty-three, and according to another historian, Cardinal Pallavicini, were twenty-five. But these propositions, whatever their number, were not taken literally from the Confession of Augsburg, nor from any authentic declarations of Luther. They were founded, as it was supposed, partly on the writings of Luther, and partly on those of Zuinglius, the Swiss Reformer. The two first propositions thus stated are :

I. Faith alone, excluding all other works, suffices for salvation, and alone justifies.

II. The faith which justifies is the confidence with which it is believed that sins are remitted by Christ, and the justified are bound to believe with certainty that their sins are remitted.

When these propositions were submitted to debate by forty bishops and forty-five theologians, it appeared that there were several able men who would not concur in the condemnation until the reasons on both sides had been fully weighed. Among these were Fra Ambrosio Catarino, Andrea de Vega, Antonio Marinari. Some time was spent in enumerating the various kinds of faith, of which one of the fathers reckoned nine, and

R

another as many as fifteen. Fra Domenico Soto, opposing
the others, said there were but two significations of
faith, the one meaning the truth and sincerity of him
who asserts and promises, the other the assent of the
person who hears : that the first belonged to God, and
the second to man. That the mere confidence of him
who believes is an abuse of the word faith, and differs
little from hope ; but it was an undoubted heresy of
Luther to employ justifying faith to mean nothing
more than a certainty in the mind of the Christian that
his sins were remitted by Christ. He added, and was
followed by the majority, that such a confidence could
not justify, that it was nothing more than a temerity
and a sin ; for man could not, without presumption,
hold it as certain that he possessed the grace of God,
that being a point upon which he must always be in
doubt. Catarino, on the other hand, maintained with a
considerable following, that although confidence could
not justify, yet that the just man might and ought to.
believe that he lived in the grace of God. A third
opinion was put forth by Andrea Vega. He held that
such an opinion was not temerity, and still less certain
faith, but that a conjectural persuasion might be entertained without sin. Thereupon arose a long and warm
dispute with regard to the second article. The opinion
was general among the fathers that there were two
kinds of faith, the one being a dead faith that might
be held by sinners, and signified mere assent; the
other which was accompanied by charity or love, and
which formed an efficient and lively faith. When this
faith was spoken of, Marinari said that he could not

ıpprove the term, faith informed by charity, as that erm was not used by St. Paul ; the only proper term vas, faith operates by charity.

If we look to the result of these discussions it is clear hat the difference between the two sets of theologians,)etween Melanchthon and Marinari, and their respective ollowers, depended rather on the want of charity existng on both sides than on any real theological distinctions. The Protestants of Augsburg had fully admitted hat there might be a faith held by bad men, and even)y devils, which amounted to a mere assent to propoitions which they could not refute. On the other ıand, the Protestants of Augsburg maintained that, hough faith alone were sufficient for salvation, good vorks were absolutely necessary to form the character ıf a just man.

The error of Luther was thus rather that of admiting terms which might be perverted to unsound and angerous conclusions, than of laying down doctrines bsolutely false.

In order to look a little more closely, as well as ırgely, into this question, we must return to the eneral sense of the other propositions maintained by hé Protestants of Augsburg.

When Bayer had terminated the summary of the loctrine professed in the Protestant churches, and vhen he had declared that this doctrine was in no way)pposed to the scriptures, to the universal Church, nor ven to the Roman Church, such as it was known rom their writers, he concluded, that to reject the

B 2

Protestants as heretics is to offend against unity and charity.

He then went on to the part of the confession destined to denounce and to expose the errors and the abuses which had arisen; he denounced the division into two kinds in the sacrament of the Holy Communion; he attacked the compulsory celibacy of the priests; he declared that in the Evangelical Churches the Holy Supper was only given to those who had first confessed their sins. He denounced the celebration of certain feasts, the fixing certain days of fasts, and the number of orders and ceremonies which assumed the name of a spiritual and Christian life, as so many abuses.

The greatest profession of which Bayer was the organ, was the distinction that he drew between the jurisdiction of bishops and that of temporal princes. He declared that the office of bishops was to preach the scriptures, to pardon sins, to exclude from the Christian Church all who rebelled against the law; but the only weapons he was to employ were preaching and teaching by words, without any employment of human power. It was the office of kings and princes, on the other hand, to govern their states and to punish those who violated the laws. It has been understood in later times, that the Protestant princes renounced all power to punish spiritual offences, or in any way to permit persecution. But the doctrine of toleration, if then proclaimed, seems to have been lost in the wars, discord, and confusions which followed the period of which we are treating. The confession ended by a declaration, that the bishops were not to be obeyed if they taught

,nything contrary to the canonical scriptures inspired
)y God Himself.

The confession of Augsburg was a great and me-
norable act. Schiller, the historian of the ' Thirty
(ears' War,' has said, with great appearance of reason,
hat it was too early to lay down the regular articles of
ı new creed, or to found a new Church. He adds
hat twenty-six years afterwards, in 1556, the doctrines
)f Zuinglius and Calvin had very much altered the
)revailing articles of belief, and that Protestants were
u the dilemma, either of adhering to a hard and fast
article which had already ceased to influence their
ninds or to be condemned as the adherents of a vari-
ıble and fluctuating religion. But, in fact, the Pro-
estants of that day had hardly a choice, for the Pope
vas prepared to condemn them as heretics, and the
Emperor Charles V. to punish them as rebels ; they
vere, therefore, forced to stand on their defence and
ıppear in arms to vindicate their rights of judgment.
.t would indeed have been better, had they contented
hemselves with denouncing the errors and abuses of
.he Church of Rome, and reserved for more mature
leliberation the specific confession of their own faith.

The remaining events relating to the Diet at Augs-
ɔurg and the Council of Trent, belong rather to political
than to ecclesiastical history. The Pope was intent
upon employing the army of the empire to extirpate all
diversities of faith. The Emperor was still more determined not to employ his army for any such purpose.
He therefore denounced the Protestant princes as rebels,
and assured them that if they would obey their legiti-

mate emperor, he would not inquire too strictly into
their religious scruples.   Unluckily for the Pope,
Charles V. was the more crafty statesman of the two.
He had, by force and fraud together, destroyed the
liberties of Spain, which were growing up under the
forms of a popular representation ; he had extinguished
all liberty in the republican constitution of Florence ;
he had so craftily promoted despotic power in Austria
and in Brandenburg as to leave scarcely any vestiges
of political freedom in Germany.   By means of the able
generals who commanded his forces, he had done much
for despotism in the Low Countries ; and, when the
Prince of Parma captured Antwerp, scarcely a vestige
of liberty was left in Flanders.   Holland survived, and
by means of the House of Orange asserted the independence of a free republic.   But, generally, we may
affirm that Charles V. established despotism in by far
the greater part of Europe from the end of the sixteenth
to the end of the eighteenth century, when the eruption
of the French Revolution scattered flames and ashes on
every side.

Yet, even Charles V. was obliged to own a master in
duplicity and treachery.   Maurice of Saxony, pretending
to be the devoted servant of the emperor, undermined
his power ; and, at the peace of Passau, obtained for the
Protestant princes of Germany freedom of conscience,
which was confirmed nearly a century afterwards by
the Treaty of Westphalia.

Another effect of the manœuvres of Maurice, was the
breaking up of the Council of Trent.   No sooner was
it known at Trent that Maurice had taken up arms,

nan a general consternation seized the Fathers of the
'ouncil. The German prelates were anxious to be at
ome, each to defend his own immediate interests
gainst his new enemy, and the legate of the Pope
ladly seized hold of the opportunity to postpone a
.earing of the Protestant divines, who, in their appli-
ations for an audience, were supported by the imperial
mbassadors. On April 28, 1552, the Council was pro-
ogued for two years, and, in fact, the prorogation lasted
or ten years. The attempt to reconcile the Protes-
ant Reformers to the Roman Church had entirely
ailed. The King of England and the Parliament of
}cotland, the Protestant Princes of Prussia, and the
_eaders of the Republic of Holland, were finally
:stranged from the Roman Church. Had Louis XIV.
ind James II. succeeded in planting the Roman Catholic
:aith in England; had the Prince of Orange failed in
nis expedition at Torbay; or had the Duke of Marl-
oorough lost the battle of Blenheim; the Protestant
Church of England would have been destroyed, and such
men as Baxter and Calamy and Bunyan would have been
crushed by imprisonment or still more severe penalties. New victims, who might have attempted to follow
the example of Hampden, Pym, and Sidney, would
have perished on the scaffold, and the cause of civil
and religious liberty, instead of being fixed on an enduring basis, would probably have yielded to a second
Cromwell, or would have been the prey of a continental
Napoleon.

ESSAY XV.

CALVIN.

JOHN CAUVIN or Chauvin, who is generally known by the Latinised name of Calvin, was born at Noyon, in Picardy on July 10, 1509. His father, Gerard, was a notary in the ecclesiastical court and secretary to the bishop. John was one of three brothers, Charles, John, and Anthony. He received the first rudiments of instruction in his native town; and at the age of fourteen went to Paris, where he became a pupil of the celebrated Corderius.

John was intended, like his brothers, for the Church, and at the age of twenty had already received the tonsure, and the cure of Pont l'Evêque, where he had sometimes preached. But his father, whether alarmed at the disturbed state of the Church, or apprehending some want of caution from the fiery nature of his son, at this time turned his studies to the law, which he studied at Orleans and Bourges.

It has been conjectured rather than proved that at this time he wished to reform, and not to destroy, the Church. But his nature was not to be controlled by the mere change of his profession. In 1532, when he was twenty-three years of age, he composed for his friend, Nicholas Cop, recently chosen Rector of the

Jniversity of Paris, an oration in which he defended
he doctrines of the German Reformers. When this
ration was publicly read, a great tumult arose ; Calvin
ras forced to escape by a window, and to leave Paris.
t is related that as he was flying away, he met a
lerical friend, who advised him to return and submit.
It is too late,' said Calvin, and, shaking his friend's
iand, pursued his journey..

After many wanderings Calvin found himself at
3asle, where Erasmus, the light of the age, and the
precursor of the Reformation, exercised a great sway
over the men of letters of that place of refuge. Here,
n 1536, appeared the ' Institutio Religionis Christianæ,'
the great work in which Calvin sought to build up the
Reformed Church where Luther had left little more
than ruins. Unfortunately, as I consider the matter,
he passed in the same year through Geneva, where
Farel, an ardent Reformer, but distasteful to Erasmus
from his fanatical violence, found him. Farel urged
him to stay and join in the work he was doing, and
when Calvin declined to leave his learned retirement,
and enter upon the heat of controversy, Farel exclaimed, ' May God curse your life, and your learned
leisure, if you do not now come to His help in this
necessity.' Calvin consented.

At first the rule of Calvin was light and not un-
reasonable. He drew up a Confession of Faith, in
twenty-one articles, the chief purpose of which was
to define and justify the separation of the Reformed
Church of Geneva from the Papal Church of Rome.

But having been banished in 1538, he retired to

Frankfort, where he lived for some years. In May, 1541, he was recalled by a decree, and in September of that year he made a triumphal entry into Geneva. His absolute power was from this time exercised in the name of a theocratic republic, joining the spiritual tyranny of Torquenada to the political despotism of Philip II. In one character or the other he bent to his will the religious observances, the dress, the mode of arranging the hair, the number of dishes at feasts, the regulations for weddings, the jests and idle talk, the belief and the behaviour of all the citizens of Geneva. The wife of the captain of the town, who was found guilty of dancing at a wedding, was sent to the common prison with prostitutes and thieves. The gaols were occupied to such an extent that in March, 1545, the gaoler reported that the prisons were full, and could hold no more. In the four years from 1542 to 1546, fifty-eight persons in that small community were sentenced to death, and seventy-six to exile. The imaginary offence of witchcraft was subject to capital punishment, and in three months thirty-four miserable beings were executed for that unreal crime. Calvin's health was bad, his temper was irritable; he punished heterodoxy, he punished irreligion, he punished adultery with death, and dancing with imprisonment.

But of all his acts of cruelty the execution of Servetus was the most inhuman. Servetus was a Spaniard, born in the same year as Calvin. He studied medicine, and is said to have anticipated in some degree the discovery of Harvey. He began early to doubt the infallibility of the Roman Church, and entered into a confidential correspondence with Calvin on many points of theology. In answer to his doubts, Calvin referred him to an oracle which could not err, his own work on the 'Institutes of the Christian Religion.' Servetus sent to Calvin his copy of the work, with many notes written in the margin. Calvin renounced all correspondence with one whose opinions differed so widely from his own. On the same day, referring to a visit which Servetus had proposed to make to him, he wrote to his friend Farel, 'If he comes I shall never permit him to depart alive, provided my authority be of any avail.' At this time Calvin's power at Geneva was absolute and supreme. Nor did he ever forget his threat.

His vengeance was long delayed, but at length his gratification was complete. In 1553 Servetus published anonymously a book called ' Restitutio Christianismi,' a work very heterodox. He had written many private notes to Calvin, as he himself said, for information and 'brotherly correction.' These notes Calvin gave up to the Papal Inquisition, and hounded on the persecution of Servetus, then living under the name of Villeneuve, at Vienne, near Lyons. Forced to fly, he alighted, on July 19, 1553, at a little inn on the banks of the Lake of Geneva. He meant to go away the next day, but stayed imprudently three weeks. Calvin had in his own hands the temporal as well as the spiritual government of Geneva ; he set a syndic on the track of Servetus, had him arrested, and, in order to deprive him of all chance of escape,' conducted himself a prosecution for heresy. Servetus was condemned to be burnt at the stake. On the morning of the execution Calvin visited Servetus, but the heretic would not recant his errors and was burnt the same day on a green eminence behind the town of Geneva, called Choupel.

The triumph of Calvin was complete. He had denounced his opponent to the Inquisition, he had given up confidential papers, he had prosecuted the heretic to conviction, he had burnt him! The Papal Inquisition could have done no more. Nothing seemed to be wanting. Yet though Bullinger, Peter Martyr, and Melanchthon justified the deed, Calvin felt that some over-scrupulous persons might censure this act of rigour. He therefore wrote and published his 'Fidelis Expositio Errorum M. Serveti et brevis earumdem Refutatio; ubi docetur jure gladii cremandos esse hære-ticos.' So signally did the Reformers, as well as the Roman Catholics, abjure the doctrine of religious liberty.

If a Spaniard renounced the errors of the Church of Rome he was burnt at Seville, or at Valladolid. If a friar refused to acknowledge the spiritual supremacy of Henry VIII., he was burnt in England. If a learned Italian doubted the temporal supremacy of the Pope, he was burnt at Rome. Such was the unhappy condition of Europe. In 1545, at the very time when Calvin was preaching persecutions of Roman Catholics at Geneva, some unhappy villages in Provence and Languedoc had instituted from the old worship of the Waldenses and the new doctrines of Zuinglius some rude imitations of Protestant worship. A French letachment of troops, aided by Papal guards from Avignon, and instructed by the king's advocate-general of Provence, advanced upon those villages, ravished the women, and put to death the old people and the infants. In Cabriera in the Venaissin, and Merindol in Provence, more than 4,000 persons were put to death. Francis I. on his death-bed repented of this barbarity; the advocate-general was condemned and put to death for his participation in persecution.

The spirit of persecution which Calvin, beyond all other of the leading reformers, taught in Geneva, was taught likewise in Scotland and in Holland, and penetrated deeply among the Huguenots of France. Henry IV., though he became a Catholic, was imbued with one of the best elements of the Reformation—that which affirmed the right of every man to govern his relations to God by the dictates of his own conscience, and the wrong of every government which endeavours to disturb that right. Hence the tolerant spirit of the edict of Nantes. Richelieu, himself a bishop, and afterwards a cardinal, acted in the same spirit. He promoted the Protestants of station and ability to high offices in the army and in the State ; he banished and deprived of their sees those Catholic bishops who were the turbulent agitators for persecution. But the priestly persecuting spirit which was curbed and discountenanced by the secular rulers of France, took refuge in the clerical leaders of the Reformation. No longer moderated by the lay chiefs, whom they denounced as deserters and unfaithful shepherds, they forbade the attendance of their flocks at any Catholic marriages or Catholic

burials; they would not allow of marriages between
Catholics and Protestants; they suppressed, as far as
their power extended, Catholic places of worship; they
prohibited theatres, and dances, and regulated the dress
of their flocks, according to the most approved Calvinistic standard. One of their community, who doubted
the infallibility of their synods, was ejected and given
over to Satan. To hate their brethren appeared to
them the true version of the commandment of Christ.

It has pleased the Almighty Maker of heaven and
earth to place man upon a planet, fruitful of all that is
necessary for his sustenance, and to give him faculties
for obtaining the means of nutrition and of enjoyment.
Thus, with a due exercise of his bodily strength and
mental powers, he can procure corn and flour for his daily
bread; he can nourish himself with vegetables which
are at once wholesome and succulent; he can pluck
the most delicious fruits from creeping vegetables, from
bushes laden with delicious berries, from trees whose
produce can be improved by judicious cultivation. He
can convert the wild grass into fertile pasture, where
cattle and sheep can be fattened by his care, and afford
him strengthening and palatable food. Some animals,
such as the horse and the dog, the camel and the ass,
seem specially intended for his use—to carry his person
or his baggage, to assist him in subduing wild animals,
to help him in his pursuits, and to obey his commands.

Thus, placed on a globe destined for his benefit,
man naturally desires prolongation of his existence.
'Health and long life!' says the Irish peasant; 'May
you live a thousand years!' is the exclamation of the

Spaniard who wishes well to his fellow-creature. It is ascribed as the merit of Solomon, that he did not ask for long life, as that would have been a petition too obviously selfish. Men who have gone through a career too prosperous or too unhappy ; women, who have lost the sun and solace of their lives ; have wished for death as a relief to their sorrows, or as an end to painful disease. But for the great mass, it is otherwise.

> For who, to dumb forgetfulness a prey,
> This pleasing anxious being e'er resign'd,
> Left the warm precincts of the cheerful day,
> Nor cast one longing, lingering look behind ?

For, besides the ordinary enjoyment of life, God has given to man the capacity to derive from his senses, from sight, from hearing, from smell, from taste, from touch, the most delightful emotions—the view of the sublime mountain and the vast ocean ; the rapture inspired by music ; the scent of a thousand flowers, which ' Nature boon '

> Pour'd forth profuse on hill, and dale, and plain.[1]

So also on the vine-covered hills, and gay regions of France ; in the sierras of Spain, in Persian groves, in the valleys of Italy, the violin, the guitar, and the lute inspire the national dance, and diffuse the gaiety of the village.

When Christ appeared upon earth, while He taught man with divine wisdom to check his passions, to be constant to the partner of his bosom, and to restrain his animal appetites, He gave his sanction to innocent amusement, made ceremonial subject to human happiness, and human observance subordinate to the great

[1] Milton's *Paradise Lost*, Book iv.

ends of human society. He taught that the sabbath was made for man, and not man for the sabbath ; that it is not the kind of food which goeth into the mouth, but the kind of language which cometh out of the mouth that defileth a man. His first miracle was performed at a wedding feast ; and when, in the parable, the father of the prodigal received his lost son, the fatted calf was killed, and when the elder son returned towards his home, he heard the sound of music and dancing, and was told by his father, ' It was meet that we should make merry and be glad, for this thy brother was dead and is alive again, and was lost and is found.' It was in a world thus made for innocence and enjoyment, repentance and forgiveness, for glee and for concord, that the pretended followers of Christ introduced the contrivance of an elaborate creed, and declared,not that those who led a wicked life and did not repent ; not those who being forgiven by their Lord, refused to forgive their fellow-servant ; not those who refused a cup of water to the thirsty, and a crust of bread to the hungry ; but those who did not embrace all the articles and particles of their unintelligible creed : those who did not allow infallibility to Pope and Council, or to Luther, or to Calvin, should perish everlastingly.

It cannot be too often repeated that there is no foundation in truth or scripture for this monstrous perversion. Origen, one of the most able of the fathers, maintained that pagans might be saved. Baxter, one of the best among the learned Christians of modern times, when he accepted the greater part of the Thirty-nine

Articles of the Church of England, declared that he would not assent to the damnatory parts of the Athanasian Creed, and that he would not take upon him to affirm that good and pious heathens, who had never accepted the teaching of Christ, might not be eternally saved. Samuel Clarke, one of the most enlightened members of the Church of England, affirmed that Socrates, Plato, and Aristotle, might all be saved by the mercy of God. It is easy to fix the charge of heresy on these men, but the real heresy was on the part of those who made dogmas of their own invention the test of Christianity. This pernicious theory once accepted, it was obvious to say that it was an act of mercy to a nation to enforce unity of faith; for the punishment by fire of a few obstinate unbelievers might ensure the eternal salvation of millions upon millions of unborn generations.

The only way, therefore, to get rid of persecution is to destroy its root. There may be good foundation for the doctrine that those who are not forgiving, who are not merciful, who hate their brethren, and blaspheme their Maker, will be punished in a future life. There is no foundation for the doctrine that any form of belief is required to obtain eternal salvation, or to avoid the penalties of eternal perdition.

The first error of Calvin was the prohibition of the enjoyments and innocent pleasures which Providence has bestowed upon mankind. With this gloomy doctrine was connected an austere and mournful celebration of the Lord's Day, on which Christ rose from the dead. I remember in the year 1811 or 1812, being

at Kinneil with Dugald Stewart, that kind and benevolent philosopher told me that the parish contained
a number of men, who having been buried in the
coal mines all the week, used to walk on the Sunday
with their wives and children along the banks of the
Firth of Forth. But the Calvinist minister of the
Kirk, shocked at this indulgence, preached against
a practice which was at once in accordance with family
affection and with enjoyment of the natural beauties
granted by the Almighty to that fair land. Thus the
spirit of man mars the works of his Creator.

The next great error of Calvin was the doctrine of
Predestination. His creed on this subject is well expressed by Dr. Chalmers, speaking of 'the world of mind.'
'If this class of events,' he says, 'if the movements of
intelligent and animated nature, can be referred to no
moving forces directed by and dependent upon Him, of
whom we have been taught to believe, that He hath
ordained the mechanism of the world, and presides
over all the evolutions of it—if amid the diversity
of the operations by which we are surrounded, those
of the will and of the mind form an exception to the
doctrine that it is God who worketh all in all—then
by far the most dignified and interesting of all his
creations is wrested from the dominion of Him who
gave it birth—and in the most emphatic sense of the
term might it be said that there is a universe without
a Lord—an empire without an imperial sovereign to
overrule its destinies.' [1]

Dr. Chalmers adds very justly that both the power

---

[1] Chalmers, *Institutes of Theology*, vol. ii. pp. 351, 355.

and the prescience of God are involved in this question.

But M. Guizot most truly observes, ' God, they say, is an absolute monarch, and in no part of his realm, from no one of his subjects, will he allow of any intervention, any action, or any will opposed to his own law, and because of this inexorable and universal law they deny the free will of man. Strange denial! which has been condemned beforehand by God himself! God is infinitely more powerful and more incomprehensible than Calvin and Chalmers have imagined him to be. Among the infinitude of his creatures there is one being whom he has created and placed high above all others on this earth, and whom he has distinguished by his own mark placed upon him. God has thought fit to create man, and to make him *in his own image*, that is to say, a free being, capable of deliberate acts of intelligence and will.' [1]

It appears to me, I confess, as it does to Guizot, that the theory of Calvin, far from exalting the Deity, tends to degrade Him. It seems to me a lower exertion of power to make a locomotive engine fit to travel along a railway than to create an eagle able to soar to the clouds, and view with undazzled eyes the sun's effulgence; less a proof of supreme intelligence to make an automaton capable of playing at chess than to create a man qualified to choose between good and evil, and only directed in the magnificent liberty of his will by the visible and all-pervading laws of a gracious and benevolent God.

[1] Guizot, *St. Louis and Calvin*, p. 199.

Another error of Calvin, shared with many learned men, was the assertion of the plenary inspiration of the Holy Scriptures; the doctrine that not only the thoughts, but the words in which they are clothed are divinely inspired, every word on every subject, the language as well as the doctrine.

Upon this subject Guizot remarks, ' This assertion seems to me to indicate a deplorable confusion, giving rise to profound misconceptions as to the meaning and aim of the sacred volume, and causing its authority to be very seriously compromised. God never intended to teach men grammar by a supernatural process, and he no more intended to teach them geology, astronomy, geography, and chronology than grammar. Not on these do the rays of divine light fall, but on the relation of man to his Creator, and on the laws of his faith and life. God dictated to Moses the laws which regulate the duties of man towards God, and towards his fellow man; He left it to Newton to discover the laws which govern the universe. The inspiration of the sacred volume relates not only to religion and morality, but to religion and morality alone, and apart from any mere human science.' [1]

The doctrine of Election as explained by Calvin, or in other words, ' Calvin's theory of Free-will and Pre-destination,' appears to me founded on a most deplorable error. We recognise the freedom of the will at the very moment of its exercise. We have the same knowledge of our freedom as of our existence. We feel and know that we are free. To suppose, as Dr.

[1] *St. Louis and Calvin*, p. 183.

Chalmers has done, 'that all must be determinate, and all, both in the mental and material world, be under the absolute control of Him who made all, and who upholds all,' is to suppose that God has created a vast number of beings, some of whom are selected for eternal happiness and some for eternal condemnation; but to imagine that God has created a number of beings who are to be condemned for the sin of one, who existed four thousand years before, without the possibility of escape, either by a righteous life or by repentance, however heartfelt and sincere, is to suppose a God neither just nor merciful. It is to suppose a God totally different from the Being described by Christ, when He said to the scribe, that if he loved God with all his heart and soul and his neighbour as himself, this do and thou shalt live.' There is an entry in Wesley's journal, in 1767, where he asks, 'if it is not high time to return to the plain word—"He that feareth God and worketh righteousness is accepted with him."' In fact, the kind and benevolent heart of Wesley gave its vital worth to his character, his love of his neighbour and of mankind made him revolt from those hard and harsh doctrines, which have been accepted, apparently at least, by the Calvinists of the Church of Scotland, and by the Calvinists of England and the other countries of Europe. Mr. Froude relates in his ' Short Studies on Great Subjects,' that going into a place of worship in the west of England, he found a body of persons collected, who were persuaded that the Christian religion imposed upon them no duties, and asked from them no sacrifices; they were persuaded that Christ had done everything for them, that his sacrifice of Himself had appeased the wrathful God whom they worshipped, and that they had no more to do than to enjoy the benefit of his atonement. This seems to be a notion borrowed rather from the religion of Pagans, and the practice of offering hecatombs of oxen and of sheep, than from the religion of St. Peter and St. Paul. Yet, as Mr. Froude truly says, the Sunday once passed, the men and women whom he saw assembled would, during the remainder of the week, perform the usual duties of Christians, be grateful for benefits, punctual in returning money that they had borrowed, faithful in fulfilling the promises that they had made, so that a religion, which only influences one day out of seven, can hardly be said to be a practical religion.

Indeed, the doctrine of Calvin, which enabled him to put to death Servetus and all who offended against his intolerant laws, has not come down in its spirit to the present generation. Dr. Chalmers, if he had had the power of Calvin at Edinburgh, would have been shocked to use it as Calvin used his power at Geneva. The Calvinists of Scotland and the Puritans of England employed their influence in the seventeenth century rather for the purpose of resisting tyranny than for that of enforcing persecution.

We cannot conclude this account of the principal leaders of the Reformation without taking some notice of Zuinglius, who was the leader of the Reformers of Switzerland. In the mountainous district called Unterwald, there was, at the end of the fifteenth century, living in a district called Wildhaus, the ammann, or governor, or president of the community, called Zuinglius. His wife had already given him two sons, when, on the first day of the year 1484, seven weeks after the birth of Luther, a third son was born, who was called Ulric. Five other sons and a daughter completed this Alpine family.

Ulric, who is known to us by the name of Zuinglius, displayed from his early youth the greatest aptitude for learning, and an intense zeal for the study of the Holy Scriptures. He himself dated the commencement of the Reformation in Switzerland from the year 1516. At this time Zuinglius was thirty-two years old; he led, with a most intrepid courage, not only his flock at Zurich, but the armed troops of the Reformers. He was killed at the battle of Cappel in 1530; with his last words he confessed his faith in Christ.

There are only two points in the career of Zuinglius to which I desire to draw attention. The celebrated historian Merle D'Aubigné blames him for having fought with carnal weapons, and contrasts his career with that of Luther, appearing to think that the Swiss Reformers, by fighting in arms, lost the approbation of God, and that their defeat in battle showed clearly that it was by persuasion only that the Almighty had decreed that the cause of the Reformation should be triumphant.

Yet this assertion must appear not warranted by history. The Reformers of the Church of Luther never hesitated, being thoroughly in earnest, from maintaining the cause of right and justice, as well in the field of battle as in the field of controversy. The Lutherans, who made their confession at Augsburg, assembled not long afterwards an army of seventy thousand infantry and fifteen thousand cavalry to maintain their right of reading and interpreting the Bible against the organised forces of the Emperor Charles V. Maurice of Saxony, who obtained for the Reformers the privileges they had long sought, was an accomplished soldier, and died in battle. In the succeeding century, Gustavus Adolphus did not disdain the use of the arm of flesh, and by his great and immortal victories gave to Germany a fresh title as the great source and the main strength of the Reformation.

The failure of Zuinglius, therefore, in his courageous attempt to maintain at Zurich the banner of the Reformation, was no proof of the displeasure of God against the assertion, by force, of Protestant freedom ; but was owing entirely to the inferiority of his forces as compared with those of the legions on the side of the Pope. The mountain cantons refused to abandon their old faith ; Berne declined to join him ; the house of Austria sent fresh troops to overcome and to suppress the Protestant insurgents. But in Switzerland, as in other countries, it has proved true that—

> Freedom's battle once begun,
> Bequeathed from bleeding sire to son,
> Though baffled oft, is always won.

Not that Switzerland or Germany counts among its inhabitants none but champions of the Reformation but if we compare the armies assembled to maintain

the Protestant States of Europe in 1872, with the hosts
which overcame and put to death Zuinglius in 1530,
we shall entertain strong hopes that freedom of
enquiry, right of private judgment, the diffusion of the
Scriptures over the world, and the variations of Protestant sects against which Bossuet employed so much
eloquence and so much knowledge, are destined to
triumph, with the approbation and favour of God, over
all their enemies, and give to the cause of truth a final
and enduring victory.

Another question of great import to the human race
is connected with the name of Zuinglius.

The doctrine that Pythagoras and Plato might be
saved, might be admitted to eternal bliss, had been
put forward in early Christian times by Origen, and
after much bitter controversy, has been condemned
by the legislator Justinian.[1] At the time of the
Reformation, the doctrine that salvation was only to
be hoped for in the Church, was held by the Reformed Churches, by the Lutherans and the Calvinists,
as by the Roman Church. Calvin says, ' Beyond the
bosom of the Church no remission of sins is to be
hoped for, nor any salvation.' The Saxon Confession, presented to the Synod of Trent A.D. 1551,
the Helvetic Confession, the Belgic, the Scottish—all
avow that salvation is only to be had in the Church.
The Presbyterian divines, assembled at Westminster
A.D. 1647, in their ' Humble Advice concerning a Confession of Faith ' (c. 25), declare that ' the visible

[1] See article, ' Origen,' in Bayle's *Dictionary*; Gibbon's *Decline
and Fall*, &c.

Church, which is also Catholique and Universal under
the Gospel (not confined to one nation, as before under
the law), consists of all those throughout the world that
profess the true religion . . . out of which there is no
ordinary possibility of salvation.' The Independents
admitted the same. Nor was the position of the An-
glican Church at all different. The Athanasian Creed
was given an honoured place among the formularies,
and the doctrine which that creed distinctly asserts
was implied in several of the services of the Church,
and was strongly maintained by a long succession of
her divines.' [1]

Against this doctrine, which condemns the most
virtuous of the Greeks and Romans to eternal punishment, which declares that even in a Christian country,
infants who have not received the rite of baptism will
be found ' crawling along the pavement of hell ; ' and
that boys and girls of fourteen years old, whose Baptist
parents had delayed the period of their baptism, are
hardly entitled to Christian burial—against this doctrine, so revolting to the untutored reason, so horrible
to the loving heart, Zuinglius rose, and with intrepid
spirit taught a better, a more charitable, a more
Christian belief. In a ' Confession of Faith,' which
he wrote just before his death, he described with his
mind's eye, that ' assembly of all the saintly, the
heroic, the faithful, and the virtuous,' when Abel and
Enoch, Noah and Abraham, Isaac and Jacob, will
mingle with Socrates, Aristides, and Antigonus, with

[1] *History of the Rise and Influence of the Spirit of Rationalism
in Europe.* By Lecky. Vol. i. p. 419.

Numa and Camillus, Hercules and Theseus, the Scipios and the Catos; and when every upright and holy man who has ever lived will be present with his God.[1]

We know the comment of Roman Catholic Bishops and Protestant Reformers on this magnificent passage ; Bossuet quotes it, as if language so repugnant to faith and morals were sufficient to obtain from a jury of all mankind the condemnation of Zuinglius ; Luther on reading it, said he despaired of the salvation ·of Zuinglius.

A great ancient historian, commemorating the life and death of a virtuous man, thus indulges the hope that a future life may be reserved for the souls of the good. I give this passage in its entirety, without copying the paraphrase of Byron, or the expression of similar sentiments by the best men of our own English Church.

After describing the grief of the widow and the daughter of Agricola, Tacitus adds :—

'Si quis piorum manibus locus, si, ut sapientibus placet, non cum corpore exstinguuntur magnæ animæ ; placidè quiescas, nosque domum tuam, ab infirmo desiderio et mulieribus lamentis ad contemplationem virtutum tuarum voces, quas neque lugeri neque plangi fas est : admiratione te potius et immortalibus laudibus, et si natura suppeditet, æmulatu decoremus. Is verus honos, ea conjunctissimi cujusque pietas. Id filiæ quoque uxorique præceperim, sic patris, sic mariti memoriam venerari, ut omnia facta dictaque ejus secum re-

[1] Lecky, vol. i. p.. 420.

volvant, formamque ac figuram animi magis quam cor-
poris complectantur : non quia intercedendum putem
maginibus, quæ marmore, aut ære finguntur : sed ut
vultus hominum, ita simulacra vultûs imbecilla ac mor-
talia sunt ; forma mentis æterna, quam tenere et ex-
primere non per alienam materiam et artem, sed tuis
ipse moribus possis.   Quidquid ex Agricola amavimus,
quidquid mirati sumus, manet, mansurumque est in
animis hominum, in æternitate temporum, famâ rerum.
Nam multos veterum, velut inglorios et ignobiles ob-
livio obruet : Agricola, posteritati narratus et tradi-
tus, superstes erit.' [1]

[1] Tacit. *Agric* xlvi. Ed. Haase.

ESSAY XVI.

THE CHURCH OF SCOTLAND.

Queen Elizabeth died at her palace at Richmond, in Surrey, in the month of March, 1603.

While adverting to the character of James the Sixth of Scotland and the First of England, it may be well to describe the state of the kingdom over which he had for many years reigned, and where he had exercised a weak and precarious authority.

James the Fifth, his grandfather, having been thwarted by his nobles in a great plan for the invasion of England, and seen his influence daily vanish, broken by disappointments, fell into a slow fever, which put an end to his life in December 1542. He left his crown to Mary, his daughter just born, and the regency to Mary of Guise, his widow.

The power of governing Scotland did not, however, belong to the crown. It was divided between the great nobles, whose possessions were large, and whose followers were true and devoted, and the Roman Catholic clergy, whose riches were great, and whose influence was likewise considerable.

A new element, therefore, was introduced into the contest, which in no very long time prevailed over both the nobility and the existing clergy. Lord Maxwell, who had influence with the Earl of Arran—the most powerful

of the nobles—persuaded him to permit the translation of the Bible into Scotch or English. This great
innovation was sanctioned by the Scottish Parliament
in 1545.

About the same time occurred another event, not
strange to the barbarism of the times, and likewise connected with the reformation of religion. Cardinal
Beatoun, the most powerful and the most able of the
Scotch priesthood, was murdered by a party of nobles
in his own house at St. Andrew's. John Knox, a
young man at that time, took the part of the murderers,
was taken with them, and sent to work as a convict.
On his release, he was absent from Scotland for nearly
two years. On his return he found the Protestant Reformation in full triumph; yet he again left Scotland.
In 1559 he returned, and on the 11th of May he
preached at Perth. This sermon was followed up by
the destruction of the monasteries, and the total overthrow of the Established Church.

In 1560 the Parliament passed a law, making it penal
to say Mass, and another, repealing all the laws relating
to religion and the clergy. Thus rapid was the progress
of the Reformation in Scotland. The reformation of religion, however, was not the only work which was effected
by the new clergy. Men who had never been ordained
were placed in the pulpit, and preached democracy in
the State as well as in the Church. One minister compared kings to devils, and another declared that the
king was Satan himself. A third advised the people to
abolish kings altogether. When these ministers were
brought before the courts of justice they said that their

authority was spiritual, and they were not subject to any temporal jurisdiction !

Never had the Pope so openly trodden upon all thrones, and degraded secular monarchs, as these Calvinistic preachers.

A curious scene occurred when James, alarmed by the rumour that his mother would be put to death by Elizabeth, commanded the clergy to pray for her. The Archbishop of St. Andrew's being ordered to officiate before the king, James was much surprised on entering the church to see a certain Mr. John Cooper in the pulpit. Nevertheless he called out, ' Mr. John, that place is destined for another; yet since you are there, if you will obey the charge that is given, and remember my mother in your prayers, you shall go on.' He replied that he would do as the Spirit of God should direct him. But he obeyed the Captain of the Guard, who told him he should be pulled out.

Bishops were utterly abolished. In the First Book of Discipline superintendents were invested with a certain authority, but in the Second Book of Discipline entire equality was enacted, and every minister was made subject only to the Presbytery, and ultimately to the General Assembly.

The revenues of the Church fell chiefly to the nobles. They possessed themselves of the cathedrals, the churches, and the lands, and retained their hold. By Act of Parliament one-third of the Church revenues was divided between the State and the Church; out of the sixth thus assigned to the Church were to be provided the stipends of the ministers, their houses or

dwellings, and the teachers and schools for the poor—
for there was no subject on which Knox was more intent
than education.

The rest of the property of the wealthy Roman
Church fell to the nobles, not indeed without many
and strong protests from the ministers of the Calvinistic Church, but without any effectual opposition to the
new distribution.

While, however, the new Church failed in obtaining
the succession to the property, the cathedrals, the
abbeys, the lands, and the tithes of the Roman Church,
they did not become reconciled to the poverty to which
they were subjected ; but as they grew more and more
dependent on the popular will, they became more and
more democratic in their political opinions, more and
more stiffened in their spiritual pride, more and more
averse to the yoke of king and nobles, more and more
intolerant of any opposition to their narrow and
gloomy theology.

While such was the Church which James left behind
him in crossing the frontier of Scotland, he found a
Church totally different in its origin, far more richly
endowed with revenues, far more subservient to the
authority of the crown, in taking possession of the throne
of England.

The Reformation of the Church of England had from
the first been prompted and guided by the Crown.
Henry the Eighth, bent upon a divorce from Catherine of
Arragon, was not willing to waste his youth in prosecuting a slow suit in the legal labyrinths of Rome, and was
determined to make Ann Boleyn not his mistress, but

his wife. He found, with the aid of Cranmer, means of effecting his divorce without the sanction of Rome, and instantly married the object of his love. The Pope, angry at the denial of his supreme authority, and too much animated by resentment to hearken to prudence, at once broke with Henry, and formally deposed him: A quarrel with the King of England in these times was no light matter ; and instead of seeing the King kiss his toe and hold his stirrup when he mounted his horse, the Pope had to meet an open rebellion, and the defection from his Church of one of the principal States of Europe.

Henry was arbitrary and cruel. He made his kingdom independent ; he made himself the head of the Church in the place of the Pope.

The virtuous Sir Thomas More was beheaded ; a poor friar, who could not understand how a temporal sovereign could be his spiritual head, was burnt, to make him the better comprehend the nature of the Reformation.

Still, while Henry threw off the Pope's authority, he did not change the dominant religion. The law of the Six Articles, which he established by an Act of his subservient Parliament, established all the main articles of the faith of the Church of Rome.

In the reign of Edward VI., by the same royal authority the Reformation of the Church was introduced. But again, by virtue of the power of the Crown, Mary restored the Pope's supremacy in spiritual matters. Still she did not attempt to repeal the old laws, by which, before the accession of Henry VIII., the inde-

T

pendence of the Crown of England was affirmed ; Cecil, Bedford, and other reformers went to mass.

With Elizabeth came a new change. The spirit of the Reformation was not so deeply implanted in the minds of the people as it was in Scotland. But the clergy and the nation were, generally speaking, ready to adopt the new doctrines at the command of their sovereign.

Thus free, Elizabeth neither overthrew everything, like John Knox, nor restored everything, like her sister Mary.

Elizabeth herself loved the grandeur of Westminster Abbey and York Minster, and the Cathedrals of Canterbury and Lincoln. The pomp of the old worship was not distasteful to her ; she therefore preserved, as far as in her lay, the old buildings, and reserved a fund for their repair. At the same time she perceived the wisdom of the advice of Cecil to stand by the Reformation, as the seal of the validity of her mother's marriage and her only title to the crown.

There had arisen, however, during the reign of her sister two parties, which equally called for the reformation of the Church, but with far different objects. These parties had disputed at Frankfort during the prevalence of Queen Mary and the Roman Church ; they came to contend for mastery in England when a Protestant Queen had ascended the throne. One of these parties was for moderate and inevitable changes ; the other consisted of the followers of Calvin at Geneva, and of John Knox in Scotland.

The latter of these two parties came to be called by

THE CHURCH OF ENGLAND.   275

the name of Puritans ; Miles Coverdale was their leader, and is represented by Jack in Swift's 'Tale of the Tub.' A number of political patriots belonged to this party.

It could not long be doubtful to which of these two parties Elizabeth would give the preference. Unfortunately she gave that preference too absolutely, and excluded too openly the influence of the Puritanical party.

In the year 1562, the Articles of Religion, approved by the Queen, were ' deliberately read and confirmed again by the subscription of the hands of the Archbishops and Bishops of the Upper House, and by the subscription of the whole clergy of the Nether House in their convocation.'

The first five articles of the Church of England treat of the Trinity ; of God, of Christ, and the Holy Ghost, according to the doctrines of the Council of Nice.

The sixth article rejects tradition as a ground of faith in these words—' Holy Scripture containeth all things necessary to salvation ; so that whatsoever is not read therein, nor may be proved thereby, is not to be required of any man that it should be believed as an article of the Faith, or be thought requisite or necessary to salvation.'

The Article proceeds to name the Canonical Books of the Old Testament.   All the books of the New Testament are received.

The Articles proceed to state how far the commands of the Old Testament are binding on Christians (Art. vii.), and declare that the three creeds, the Nicene, that of Athanasius, and that which is commonly called

T 2

the Apostles Creed, may be proved by most certain
warrants of Holy Scripture (Art. viii.).

In the sixteenth article it is pronounced that sins
committed after baptism may be forgiven upon repentance and amendment.

In the seventeenth article Predestination is accepted
as a true doctrine. But it is at the same time declared
that ' for curious and carnal persons, lacking the Spirit
of Christ, to have continually before their eyes the
sentence of God's predestination, is a most dangerous
downfall, whereby the devil doth thrust them either
into desperation, or into wretchlessness of most unclean
living, no less perilous than desperation.'

Of the Church it is said, Arts. 19 and 20—'As the
Church of Jerusalem, Alexandria, and Antioch have
erred ; so also the Church of Rome hath erred not only
in their living and manner of ceremonies, but also in
matters of faith.' Again, ' Wherefore, although the
Church be a witness and a keeper of holy writ, yet as
it ought not to decree anything against the same, so
besides the same ought it not to enforce anything to be
believed for necessity of salvation.'

The 'errors of the Church of Rome are protested
against, not only in the general terms already quoted,
but in particular doctrines referred to. Thus in the
twenty-second article—' The Romish doctrine concerning purgatory, pardons, worshipping, and adoration, as well of images as of reliques, and also invocation
of saints, is a fond thing vainly invented, and grounded
upon no warranty of Scripture, but rather repugnant
to the Word of God.'

So likewise in the twenty-fourth article: ' It is a thing plainly repugnant to the Word of God, and the custom of the Primitive Church, to have public prayer in the Church, or to minister the sacraments, in a tongue not understanded of the people.'

The question of Transubstantiation is treated very positively in the twenty-eighth article—' Transubstantiation (or the change of the substance of bread and wine) in the Supper of the Lord cannot be proved by holy writ ; but is repugnant to the plain words of Scripture, overthroweth the nature of a sacrament, and hath given occasion to many superstitions.'

Queen Elizabeth took care not to assume any priestly office, or to prescribe anything beyond that which had been already read and confirmed again by the bishops and clergy of the Church of England. It is, therefore, plainly declared in the thirty-seventh article how far her authority extends, and what are the offices to which she does not pretend :—

' The Queen's Majesty hath the chief power in this realm of England, and other her dominions, unto whom the chief government of all estates of this realm, whether they be ecclesiastical or civil, in all causes doth appertain, and is not, nor ought to be, subject to any foreign jurisdiction.

' Where we attribute to the Queen's Majesty the chief government, by which titles we understand the minds of some slanderous folks to be offended, we give not to our princes the ministering either of God's Word or of the sacraments, the which thing the injunctions also lately set forth by Elizabeth our Queen do most plainly testify ; but that only prerogative which we see to have been given always to all godly princes in Holy Scriptures by God himself ; that is, that they should rule all estates and degrees committed to their charge by God, whether they be ecclesiastical or temporal, and restrain with the civil sword the stubborn and evil doers.'

' The Bishop of Rome hath no jurisdiction in this realm of England.' [1]

Such were the Articles of Religion, adopted by the bishops and clergy, sanctioned by the Queen.

Elizabeth took care not to alter those provisions of Acts of Parliament made in the time of her father, by which the State reserved to itself the independent power of explaining, limiting, and defining the meaning of the Articles of Religion. Secular judges were joined with spiritual prelates in the interpretation of the national standards ; the authority to admit within the portals of the Church the different schools of Calvinists and Arminians ; the power to arrest the tide of persecution by which all churchmen seem to be carried away. This most useful prerogative was retained by Elizabeth ; the imperfect tribunals constituted by Henry VIII. and his daughter have in our time been remodelled and reformed by the genius of Brougham. The Judicial Committee of the Privy Council is the only security we have that the spirit of Laud or the spirit of John Knox shall not indulge itself in prohibitions and exclusions, banishing from the Church such men as Clarke, Middleton, and Hampden, and narrowing within the strict limits of an uncharitable orthodoxy the large

[1] Art. 37.

and comprehensive Church which is rightly denominated the Church of England.

In looking at the Articles of Religion as a whole, we may see to lament several things contained in them.

We must regret that, instead of adopting the words of Christ, the Church of England sanctioned the metaphysical creeds of the Council of Nice, and the creed called of St. Athanasius, which if they may be proved by 'sure warrant of Scripture,' were most certainly never used by Christ, or by St. John, his beloved disciple, nor by St. Paul, to whom the Holy Spirit gave utterance.

Neither the Roman centurion, nor the Jewish scribe, whose words were blessed with the sanction of Jesus Christ, ever professed their faith in the language used by the Nicene Council or by the writer of the creed called the Athanasian.

It was, therefore, a mistake of the bishops and clergy of England to embrace so warmly and unconditionally those human inventions. But considering the opinions entertained in that age not only by the Church of Rome but by Luther and Calvin, and the great body of the German and Swiss Reformers, we cannot be surprised at the language adopted by the Church of England.

On the great questions upon which the Pope and the Reformers were divided, it must, I think, be admitted that the founders of the Reformed Church of England took a temperate and considerate line. They condemned what all Protestants considered as the obvious errors and glaring abuses of the Church of Rome : transubstantiation, worship of saints, purgatory, celibacy of the clergy, teaching religion in a language unknown to the people; all indulgences and pardons for sin granted by priestly authority. On the other hand, they condemned, though not sufficiently, the extremes of the Calvinistic doctrines.

The Church of England always opposed the Puritans, and endeavoured to restrain their zeal on behalf of the doctrines which belonged to Calvin rather than to any other chief. Lord Chatham said, with more wit than truth, that the Church of England consisted of a popish liturgy, Calvinistic articles, and an Arminian clergy. It may be said, with more justice, that of all the churches which may be called established, or which count among their adherents a great national community, the Church of England is that which follows with the most fidelity the spirit of the Gospel, and which combines in the general character of its members. It cannot be said that in the Articles of Religion the Church sanctions religious liberty. It is declared, that 'although the Church be a keeper and a witness of holy writ, yet as it ought not to decree anything against the same, so besides the same ought it not to enforce anything to be believed for necessity of salvation.' This declaration is ambiguous, for it is not clear whether although what is ' besides the same ' may not be enforced as necessary to salvation, it may or may not be preached by others without fear of temporal penalties. But in the Liturgy, in the prayer for all conditions of men, it is directed that 'more especially we pray for the good estate of the Catholic

Church, that it may be so guided and governed by Thy good Spirit, that all who profess and call themselves Christians may be led into the way of truth, and hold the faith in unity of spirit, in the bond of peace, and in righteousness of life.'[1]

Those who profess and call themselves Christians are Roman Catholics, Presbyterians, Lutherans, Calvinists, the Church of England, Baptists, Independents or Congregationalists, Quakers, Unitarians, and others. We are not directed to pray that they may hold the faith in unity of doctrine, but in unity of spirit, which may be the same in a Roman Catholic and a Unitarian, in a Fénélon and a Channing. Nor is anything declared to be necessary to salvation which is not contained in the Bible. The interpretation of the Holy Scripture is left to faith, guided by love and charity.

While the Articles and the Liturgy of the Church of England were becoming firmly established in the southern part of our island, James was carrying on a doubtful and difficult contest with the Presbyterian Church of Scotland. In 1592 Episcopacy was utterly abolished by the General Assembly of the Church. In 1596 James adopted a desperate expedient in defiance of his duty to his people, and of a nature to inflame to madness their resentment and disaffection. He turned into Edinburgh the most savage of the Highland clans, and supporting them with an armed force, gave them licence to plunder, to violate women, to slay men who should resist the destruction of his

[1] See the Book of Common Prayer; prayer when the Litany is not read.

own royal capital. For a time this violence succeeded, and the episcopal office was nominally recognised and restored.

But the determination, the perseverance, and the sagacity of the Scottish Lowlanders were not thus to be permanently subdued. Andrew Melville, a man of great talents and unflinching courage, took the place which the death of Knox had left vacant. For four years the contest was carried on, with great popular enthusiasm, against the office of bishop, a printed liturgy, and a distinction of ranks among the ministers of the Presbyterian Church. In 1600 James, finding himself overpowered by numbers as well as zeal, virtually surrendered, and allowed his enemies to govern Scotland against his own wishes. But in his succession to the Crown of England he perceived, as he thought, the means of gratifying his ambition, his ecclesiastical preferences, and his revenge.

Lord Dartmouth, in a note to 'Burnet's History of His Own Time,' says : 'The Earl of Seafield told me that King James frequently declared that he never looked upon himself to be more than King of Scotland in name till he came to be King of England, but now he said one kingdom would help him to govern the other, or he had studied kingcraft to very little purpose from his cradle to that time.' [1]

History tells us what that study of kingcraft produced.

It was a study, be it remarked, which was pursued by James I., his son Charles I., and his two grandsons, Charles II. and James II. The policy was varied in its

[1] Burnet, Oxford Ed. vol. i. p. 15.

path by the different tempers of these four kings, but it never varied in its ultimate object, to root out civil and religious liberty in Great Britain, and place in supreme authority the will of the House of Stuart.

Charles I. failed in his attempts to arrest the five members; had he succeeded and obtained, as he would have obtained, bad juries to condemn them, the five members would have had the fate which Russell and Sidney had to undergo. As it happened, the threat of Cromwell against Charles, 'I will cut off his head with the crown upon it,' was first fulfilled. But the execution of Charles I., by the pity it inspired, led to the Restoration; the Restoration gave scope to the tyranny and folly of James II., the tyranny and folly of James II. caused the Revolution. The Revolution speedily led the way to religious liberty.

It would not be ·just to leave unnoticed the re-proaches which have been cast upon a noble people by one[1] whose early death the world of thought must ever mourn, who has ventured to liken the bigotry of Scotland to the bigotry of Spain. The fact is that John Knox, who was one of the greatest men of his age, was engaged in leading the people of Scotland from a state of miserable religious and political servitude to a state of political independence, in which they could assert their freedom of worship and their political liberty against the perfidy and cruelty of the House of Stuart. In the course of this

[1] Mr. Buckle.

struggle, a religious creed was adopted which had no doubt much of the cruelty of Calvin and much of the bigotry of the age in which he lived. But when William III. had established in Scotland the Presbyterian worship, men arose, who, like Dr. Robertson, combined the most enlightened religious ˙toleration with the utmost freedom of discussion. Compare this with the slavery and darkness of Spain from 1600 to 1808.

The maintenance of the Inquisition in that country, less cruel than at its beginning, but not less pervading or less absolute, has been favoured by the Austrian kings of Spain and their successors of the House of Bourbon, down to the times of the Revolution which overthrew the throne of Isabella. Those who showed any inclination to become Protestants were imprisoned without mercy, and at Seville, even the English Protestants who resorted to the chapel in the Consul's house were not permitted to carry their Prayer-books openly through the streets. A Portuguese gentleman, with whom I was acquainted, told me, that having let fall some unguarded expressions at dinner, in the presence of his uncle, who was an Inquisitor, he was much alarmed the next morning at seeing some of the officers of that Holy Tribunal enter his bedroom. He was carried off to the prison of the Inquisition, but, being a relation of the judge, was let off with an admonition and a short confinement.

While such was the state of Spain and Portugal, let us ask what has been the domestic observance of religion in the families of Scotland. This is nowhere better described than in the poetry of Burns, who loved his country and knew its people. I cannot do better than extract some of his stanzas:—

> The cheerfu' supper done, wi' serious face,
>   They, round the ingle, form a circle wide;
> The sire turns o'er, wi' patriarchal grace,
>   The big ha'-Bible, ance his father's pride :
> His bonnet reverently is laid aside,
>   His lyart haffets wearing thin an' bare;
> Those strains that once did sweet in Zion glide,
>   He wales a portion with judicious care;
> And 'Let us worship God!' he says, with solemn air.

> They chant their artless notes in simple guise;
>   They tune their hearts, by far the noblest aim;
> Perhaps 'Dundee's' wild warbling measures rise,
>   Or plaintive 'Martyrs,' worthy of the name;
> Or noble 'Elgin' beets the heavenwards flame,
>   The sweetest far of Scotia's holy lays;
> Compared with these, Italian trills are tame;
>   The tickled ears no heartfelt raptures raise;
> Nae unison hae they with our Creator's praise.

> The priest-like father reads the sacred page—
>   How Abram was the friend of God on high;
> Or Moses bade eternal warfare wage
>   With Amalek's ungracious progeny;
> Or how the royal bard did groaning lie
>   Beneath the stroke of Heaven's avenging ire;
> Or Job's pathetic plaint, and wailing cry;
>   Or rapt Isaiah's wild, seraphic fire;
> Or other holy seers that tune the sacred lyre.

> Perhaps the Christian volume is the theme—
>   How guiltless blood for guilty man was shed;
> How He, who bore in Heaven the second name,
>   Had not on earth whereon to lay His head :
> How His first followers and servants sped;
>   The precepts sage they wrote to many a land :
> How he, who lone in Patmos banishèd,
>   Saw in the sun a mighty angel stand :
> And heard great Babylon's doom pronounced by Heaven's command.

Then kneeling down, to Heaven's Eternal King
  The saint, the father, and the husband prays:
Hope 'springs exulting on triumphant wing,'
  That thus they all shall meet in future days:
There ever bask in uncreated rays,
  No more to sigh, or shed the bitter tear,
Together hymning their Creator's praise,
  In such society, yet still more dear;
While circling time moves round in an eternal sphere.

Compared with this, how poor Religion's pride,
  In all the pomp of method, and of art,
When men display to congregations wide,
  Devotion's every grace, except the heart!
The power, incensed, the pageant will desert,
  The pompous strain, the sacerdotal stole;
But, haply, in some cottage far apart,
  May hear, well-pleased, the language of the soul:
And in His Book of Life the inmates poor enrol.[1]

[1] Burns' *Cottar's Saturday Night.*

ESSAY XVII.

GENERAL RESULT OF THE REFORMATION.

HAVING given a sketch of the sayings and acts of Luther, Zuinglius, and Calvin, we are enabled to take a view of the tendency and general result of the Reformation in the principal countries of Europe. Luther seems to have considered it as the great object of his mission on earth to open the Bible to all nations, and at the same time to declare the principal doctrines which the German Reformers deduced from the Holy Scriptures. This object was accomplished by the Confession of Augsburg. But there was a further object which was not attained by the Reformers in Germany, in France, in Sweden, in England, or in Scotland : this was the abstinence on the part of the clergy and the teachers of religion from any attempts to propagate their doctrines by violence or to imitate in any way the persecutions of the Roman Church. In the early ages of the propagation of the Christian religion, it was easy for the bishops to separate those whose faith was erroneous or whose conduct was immoral from the mass of the Christian community. Those who failed in their adherence to Christian doctrine or who disgraced themselves by their bad lives, fell into the general ranks of the Pagan community, and enjoyed the privileges of the other subjects of a pagan emperor. But when the emperor was himself a Christian, the spirit of persecution unfortunately arose, and the majority endeavoured, by fire and sword, to make the minority embrace what was considered the orthodox creed. Then arose the dogma, 'There is no salvation beyond the pale of the Church'—a maxim which was equally acceptable to popes desirous to propagate their faith, and to emperors and kings who wished to comprehend all their subjects under one uniform and despotic rule. Hence the bloody wars between the Athanasians and the Arians, which did not cease till the Arians were utterly subdued in the field of battle. Hence the persecutions of the Albigenses, and the cruel watch-word when a town was taken by assault by an orthodox army, 'Slay all—God will know his own.' Hence the massacres and executions which marked with blood various countries of Europe and led to the establishment of the Spanish Inquisition.

It was to be hoped that Protestants would, in conformity with their early declarations at Augsburg, endeavour to convert the followers of the Church of Rome by persuasion only. Above all, it was hoped by moderate men, that, resting their own right of protest on the privilege which every man inherits of guiding his conduct in matters of religion by the dictates of his own conscience, a Protestant ruler or Protestant assembly would grant the same liberty to those whose minds led them to differ upon articles of doctrine or upon ecclesiastical discipline and Church ceremonies.

Unhappily this has not been the case; the Reformation violated for centuries the sacred right of religious liberty. The reformers of England, under the guidance of Cranmer, persecuted those who would not submit to their tests of religion. A Protestant bishop commanded to be burnt, in his presence, a friar who refused to the king the title of 'Head of the Church.' In vain the poor friar protested that he could not understand how a temporal sovereign, himself a layman, could be the head of a spiritual community. Disdaining any answer to this reasonable doubt, the reforming bishop authorised the burning till the friar was consumed to ashes.

In Scotland, the spirit of the Calvinistic Church was not milder or more tolerant. Mr. Buckle has exposed, with a severity beyond measure, the narrow and in-tolerant spirit of the Presbyterian Church of Scotland. It is to be said, however, that in England and in Scotland the principles of the Reformation, in the course of time, overcame the passion of religious persecution. In England Elizabeth, being herself latitudinarian, refused to punish by death Roman Catholics who had not conspired to deprive her, by arms or by assassination, of her royal sceptre.

Oliver Cromwell, renouncing the lessons of the Presbyterians, and embracing the toleration taught by the Independents, refused to persecute, except on the ground of political hostility.

When William III. ascended the throne, his own favourite maxim that 'Conscience is God's province' induced him to favour religious liberty, both in England and Scotland. A bill introduced by Lord Nottingham,

U

which became law, gave the Protestant dissenters of England the right of worship, according to their own religious forms and doctrines, in chapels built by themselves. This Act, either with a view to conciliate the bigots, or to smooth the passions of the orthodox, was called the Toleration Act. But in fact it was an Act for the establishment of religious liberty. This is proved by Lord Mansfield's famous judgment, delivered in the House of Lords in 1768. In Scotland the Presbyterian Church was erected, and the English Liturgy banished from the State Church. But the English Church obtained for her sons the same liberty which the Presbyterians obtained in England after the accession of the House of Hanover: the Whig party Government, while it refused to Protestant dissenters political equality, gave them full liberty to worship God and educate their children according to their own opinions. This was a liberty which the Tory ministry of Queen Anne had denied to Nonconformists.

It would seem that from the beginning of the world it has been the ambition of men to learn the nature of the Supreme Being who created heaven and earth ; to penetrate into the secrets of Omnipotence, to climb the heights of heaven, and to sound with a plummet-line the depths of hell. Thus it is that Prometheus is represented as bound, and suffering perpetual agony, for stealing the celestial fire. Thus it is that the giants have been buried under Pelion and Ossa for their assault of Olympus. Thus it is that the ascent of Sisyphus is constantly baffled ; and in like manner the thirst of Tantalus is never assuaged. So likewise in

Holy Writ it is related in a passage, evidently allegorical, that the people said, ' Go to ; let us build a city and a tower, whose top may reach unto heaven ; and let us make us a name, lest we be scattered abroad on the face of the whole earth.'[1] A similar ambition animated the followers of the Church of Christ. He had never Himself said what was His essence or His substance ; the Council of Nice, eager to punish Arians, undertook to define. In like manner He had never said more of His relation as a Son to the Father, than that His Father was greater than He. The anonymous author of a third and anonymous creed was not satisfied with Christ's humility, and undertook to affirm that He was equal to the Father. With a similar ambition and equal presumption, Luther and Calvin undertook to point out the way to heaven, and throwing aside the words of Christ, and the teaching of St. John, St. James, and St. Paul, declared that by faith alone man could be saved. They disdained the words of Christ in reference to the Pagan centurion and the Jewish scribe ; they looked aside when they were reminded that God is Love ; they refused to accept the words of St. Paul, ' Faith, hope, and love, these three ; but the greatest of these is love.'

Happily there is a remedy. Talleyrand, when age and experience had taught him a prophetic strain, said in the Senate of France, ' There is somebody who has more cleverness than Voltaire, more cleverness than Bonaparte ; this somebody is everybody.'

[1] Genesis, c. xi. v. 4.

Now what does everybody say of the religion of Englishmen ? Let us consult a living writer, master of a powerful style, hostile to the Church of England, but candid in judging the English nation. ' Bible religion,' says Dr. Newman, ' is both the recognised title and the best description of English religion. It consists not in rites and creeds, but mainly in having the Bible read in church, in the family, and in private. Now I am far indeed from undervaluing that mere knowledge of Scripture which is imparted to the population thus promiscuously. At least in England it has to a certain point made up for grievous losses in its Christianity. The restoration again and again in fixed course in the public service of the words of inspired teachers, under both covenants, and that in grave, majestic English, has, in matter of fact, been to our people a vast benefit. It has attuned their minds to religious thoughts ; it has given them a high moral standard ; it has trained them in associating religion with compositions which, even humanly considered, are among the most sublime and beautiful ever written; especially it has impressed upon them the series of Divine providences in behalf of man, from his creation to his end ; and above all, the words, deeds, and sacred sufferings of Him in whom all the providences of God centre.'

Again, ' What Scripture especially illustrates, from its first page to its last, is God's providence ; and that is nearly the only doctrine held with a real assent by the mass of religious Englishmen. Hence the Bible is so great a solace and refuge to them in trouble. I repeat, I am not speaking of particular schools and parties in England, whether of the High Church or of the Low, but of the mass of piously-minded and well-living people in all ranks of the community.' [1]

I pass from Dr. Newman to Dr. Milman, the Protestant Dean of St. Paul's. Judging Latin and Teutonic Christianity in his balanced scales, he says :

' The subjective, more purely internal, less demonstrative character of Teutonic religion is equally impatient of the more distinct, and definite, and rigid objectiveness of Latin Christianity. That which seems to lead the Southern up to heaven, the regular, intermediate ascending host of saints, martyrs, apostles, the Virgin, to the contemplative Teuton obscures and intercepts his awful intuitive sense of the Godhead, unspiritualises his Deity, whom he can no longer worship as a pure Spirit. To him it is the very vagueness, vastness, incomprehensibility of his conception of the Godhead which proclaims its reality. If *here* God must be seen in the altar in a materialised form, at once visible and invisible ; if God must be working a perpetual miracle ; if the passive Spirit must await the descent of the Godhead in some sensible sign 'or symbol ; *there* on the other hand (especially as the laws of nature become better known and more familiar, and what of old seemed arbitrary variable agencies are become manifest laws) the Deity recedes, as it were, into unapproachable majesty.'

Again, ' As it is my own confident belief that the words of Christ, and His words alone (the primal inde-

<hr>

[1] Grammar of Assent, pp. 54, 55,

feasible truths of Christianity) shall not pass away, so I cannot presume to say that men may not attain to a clearer, and at the same time more full and comprehensive and balanced sense of these words than has yet been generally received in the Christian world.   As all else is transient and mutable, these only eternal and universal, assuredly whatever light may be thrown on the mental constitution of man, even in the constitution of nature, and the laws which govern the world, will be concentred so as to give a more penetrating vision of those undying truths.' [1]

In reflecting upon these words I cannot but perceive that the Latin Christian embraces his faith more with his heart than his understanding, and the Teuton more with his understanding than his heart.   Each has his strong foundation to rest upon.   The Latin or Roman Christian adores God with all his soul ; he bends with intense gratitude before the image of Christ, who gave His life to save mankind from the punishment of their sins, and he hastens to take in the stranger, to feed the hungry, to heal the sick as a proof of his acknowledgment of the propitiation offered for his sins, and as practical evidence that he loves his neighbour as himself.   The Teuton Christian learns from his Divine Master that God is a Spirit, and that it is his duty to worship Him in spirit and in truth. He searches the Scriptures to enlighten and fix his faith, and he acquires from his studies the conviction that if he hopes to be forgiven he must forgive.   He rejoices in his liberty, but he uses it only to perform

[1] Milman, *Lat. Christ.* vol. vi. pp. 631, 633.

with his whole mind and soul his duty to God and to his neighbour.

Among the Teutonic Christians must be reckoned the Lutherans of Germany, the Presbyterians of Switzerland and of Scotland, the Calvinists of France, the Congregationalists, the Baptists, and the Unitarians of England and of her colonies, and of the United States of America.

It is not probable that any one form of Christian doctrine, that any one Church, whether of Rome, of England, of Geneva, or of Scotland, will be embraced by the whole body of Christians.   It is not probable that the Roman Catholic population of Italy and Spain will join in the same worship or recite the same catechism as the Presbyterians of Scotland, or the Unitarians of Massachusetts.   But doctrinal differences, differences in manner of worship, divergencies in church government, are losing much of the acerbity of former ages. Roman Catholics, after three centuries of separation, can hardly expect that Lutherans and Presbyterians will return to the ancient fold, nor can they in charity continue to pronounce the eternal perdition of all who protest against their Church.   Calvinists on their side are losing the stern fidelity with which they once followed the institutes of their master, and in England, Switzerland, and parts of Scotland, are mitigating, if not openly abandoning, the harsher doctrines of election and predestination.   Dogma has no longer the sway it once had ; St. Thomas Aquinas, St. Dominic, and John Knox, are no longer obeyed with unhesitating faith. Instead of preaching unity of doctrine, men are told to hold the faith in unity of spirit, in the bond of peace, and in righteousness of life. May this bond of peace one day unite all Christians in brotherly love, forgiveness of trespasses, and universal charity.

But let us return to the first effects of the Reformation.

While, during and after the Reformation, the disappointment caused to the friends of religious liberty by the measures of intolerance sanctioned by the governments of France, Austria, Spain, Italy and Russia, was painful, there was likewise a failure on the part of the Reformers in their attempts to reform effectually the abuses of the Church of Rome, or to substitute a new Church founded expressly and entirely on the doctrines contained in the Gospel. The laws maintained by the different countries of Europe left the Church of Rome in possession of the theory of infallibility, whether exercised by the Pope in person, or by a council of bishops.

On the opposite side, Luther and Calvin had failed to erect a new superstructure founded on the Gospel. Neither the dogma of salvation by faith alone, nor the still more arbitrary dogma of predestination, the favourite dogma of the Calvinists, could be said to have their foundations fixed on the words of Scripture. The cardinals and bishops, who denounced at Trent the heresy of Luther and the Protestant divines, who opposed at Lambeth the theory of Calvin, both prevailed in reasoning over their adversaries.

But while neither the Romanists nor the Reformers succeeded in founding a new scriptural and impregnable Church, there is no reason to despair that

such a Church, immortal and unchanged, may be
founded in the age yet to come. M. Merle D'Aubigné
says of Farel, one of the most fervid of the
Reformers, who hoped for the reign of peace and
concord, 'Christian union thus found, in the first
moments of the Reformation, a fervent apostle. The
nineteenth century is called upon to take up this
work, which the sixteenth was not able to accomplish.' [1]
But whatever might be the failures of the Papal Church
of Rome or of the Reformed Churches of the sixteenth
century, there was one immense service rendered to
the cause of true religion and to the hopes of peace
and goodwill among men, which nothing can destroy.
In the sixteenth century, by the efforts of Erasmus, of
Luther, of Zuinglius, and of Calvin, the Bible was
opened to all Protestants, and the doctrines of love and
mercy which it contains were spread among all nations.
Chillingworth declares that the Bible is the religion of
Protestants. It is the Bible which, making its way
with the progress of civilisation among all Christians,
has abolished the abominable crime of the slave-trade
and the sin of slavery in England and in America. It
is by the force of Christianity and civilisation that
respect for the rights of conscience has gradually
prevailed over persecution, and that, except in Russia,
all the nations of Europe permit men to worship
according to the dictates of their own consciences. It
is by the same operation of the lessons of the Bible,
and the increased and increasing mildness of succeeding

[1] *Hist. de la Réformation du 16me Siècle*, vol. iv. p. 302. Ed.
Paris, 1860.

ages, that penal laws have lost much of their cruelty, and governments much of their intolerance. It may be hoped that capital punishments will be abolished, and toleration be sovereign even in social intercourse.

While we acknowledge these benefits as owing to the influence of Christianity, and while we boast that the shows of gladiators, which made the Roman holiday, would be viewed with abhorrence by the spectators of modern theatres, let us take care to pay due homage to the Reformation, and admit that the spirit it produced has been favourable to political liberty and to the propagation of spiritual truth. We may lament that learning and wisdom did not preside over all the events of the Reformation; we may wish that Erasmus had been endowed with the energy and perseverance of Luther; or that Luther and Calvin had shared the temper and discretion of Erasmus. But these wishes are vain, the Reformation went on its way, as a torrent bearing along all that it caught up in its impetuous career; and we have inherited the marks of its destructive course, as well as the fertility which it spread around, like the inundations of the Nile..

But, while thus rejoicing over the victories of the Reformation, let us not suppose that the Roman Church can be extinguished by anything less than a revolution which would destroy Christianity, or a change in the nature of man which would deprive him of feeling and imagination.

A young lady endowed with beauty and talents was deeply attached to a Frenchman of noble family and eminent qualities. Her lover gained her affections, and earnestly exhorted her to join the Roman Church. But such a concession would have deeply afflicted her mother, and she refused. After their marriage the husband suffered seriously from illness. The wife bore patiently the calamity; but when the illness became severe and dangerous, she exclaimed on a sudden, ' I am a Catholic !' She had seen no priest; she had heard no arguments. Her heart had retained her a Protestant; her heart had made her a Catholic.

Every age gives an Italian of genius to the world. Manzoni, the author of the ' Promessi Sposi,' has been the genius given by Italy to this age. In his ode on the death of Napoleon, he poetically exclaims—

> Bella, Immortal, benefica,
> Fede ai trionfi avvezza,
> Scrivi ancor questo : Allegrati
> Che più superba altezza,
> Al disonor del Golgota,
> Giammai non si chimo.[1]

To the same effect, portraying admirably the Roman Church, Abbondio, in the ' Promessi Sposi,' complains that while he is sharply rebuked for marrying irregularly a virtuous young couple, the Innominato, who had pursued a career of crimes of the most atrocious nature, is received by the cardinal with forgiveness and benedictions.

Such is the influence of the heart and the imagination in guiding to conversion and depth of devotion. The Roman priesthood know it well. They know that the influence they exercise is founded securely on the faculties of imagination and on the heart planted in man by his Creator.

[1] Cinque Maggio.

ESSAY XVIII.

PRESENT STATE AND FUTURE PROSPECTS OF CHRISTIANITY.

IN writing an essay on the state and prospects of Christianity, I propose to treat, not of the Christianity of Athanasius or Thomas Aquinas, not of the Emperor Constantine or of the Emperor Theodosius, not of Pope Gregory VII. or of Pope Julius II., not of Luther or of Calvin, but of Christ and His Apostles, of St. Peter, of St. John, and St. Paul. It is needful to point out that Christianity thus defined rests on the various declarations of Christ, pointing out that not those who called 'Lord, Lord,' should be acknowledged by Him as His followers, but those who did the will of God. In the same spirit He declared that those would be truly blessed who did what His Father in heaven had commanded. In the Sermon on the Mount the meek and the humble, the peace-makers, and the poor in spirit are commended. At all times He called upon men to love God with all their heart, mind, and soul, and to love their neighbours as themselves. He never suggested that there could be any dispensation from these two great duties. To the same effect Paul taught that love, which worketh no ill, is to be cherished, and while he commends to us 'faith, hope, and love,

these three,' he adds, ' the greatest of these is love.'
It has been shown by a living author how much mistaken those are who place love, goodwill, harmony,
purity of life, in the second rank of Paul's lessons to
Christians. Indeed, it would be absurd to suppose that
Christ spent His life in teaching what were merely
secondary lessons without bearing on life and immortality, which He is declared to have brought to light,
or that Paul gave the labour of his days and nights
to a work which the death of Christ had made subordinate and almost superfluous.[1] There have indeed been
found persons in these days who maintain that their
salvation is already secured by the death of Christ,
and that they have nothing to do but to forbear from
all action and exertion. They expect the fulfilment of
the promises which they deem to have been made by
a God incapable of breaking His word, or of depart-
ing in any way from His decree.[2] Hence there has
arisen, on the part of the Calvinistic Reformers, a state
of mind at total variance with the solemn lessons and
positive precepts of Christ.

The Church of England in her Articles has carefully
avoided two sources of error—the superstitions of the
Church of Rome, and the fanaticism of the Church of
Calvin. The Articles of the Church of England, after
declaring ' There is but one living and true God, ever-

---

[1] Lord Macaulay found on a book-stall in London this couplet, as
part of a poetical sermon:—

> Your ticket, Faith, to heaven will attain;
> Your works will follow by the luggage train.

[2] See *Short Essays on Great Subjects*, by Mr. Froude.

lasting, without body, parts, or passions, of infinite
power, wisdom, and goodness, the Maker and Pre-
server of all things, both visible and invisible,' goes
on to make the following declarations : ' Transubstantiation (or the change of the substance of bread and wine
in the Supper of the Lord cannot be proved by Holy
Writ, but is repugnant to the plain words of Scripture
overthroweth the nature of a sacrament, and hath
given occasion to many superstitions. The body o
Christ is given, taken, and eaten in the Supper only
after an heavenly and spiritual manner. And the
mean whereby the body of Christ is received and
eaten in the Supper is Faith. The Sacrament of the
Lord's Supper was not by Christ's ordinance reserved
carried about, lifted up, or worshipped.' As to Cal
vinism, it is said, ' As the godly consideration of pre
destination, and our election in Christ, is full of sweet
pleasant, and unspeakable comfort to godly persons
and such as feel in themselves the working of the
Spirit of Christ, mortifying the works of the flesh and
their earthly members, and drawing up their mind to
high and heavenly things, as well because it doth
greatly establish and confirm their faith of eterna
salvation to be enjoyed through Christ, as because i
doth fervently kindle their love towards God ; so, fo
curious and carnal persons, lacking the Spirit of Christ
to have continually before their eyes the sentence o
God's predestination is a most dangerous downfall
whereby the devil doth thrust them either into despera
tion or into wretchlessness of most unclean living, no

less perilous than desperation. Furthermore, we must receive God's promises in such wise as they be generally set forth to us in Holy Scripture : and, in our doings, that will of God is to be followed which we have expressly declared unto us in the Word of God.' There is another declaration at the end of the service of the Holy Communion in the Book of Common Prayer, which shows still more strongly how far the Church of England has been from recognising the doctrine of Transubstantiation. It is in the following terms : ' Whereas it is ordained in this office for the administration of the Lord's Supper that the communicants should receive the same kneeling (which order is well meant for a signification of our humble and grateful acknowledgment of the benefits of Christ therein given to all worthy receivers, and for the avoiding of such profanation and disorder in the Holy Communion as might otherwise ensue); yet, lest the same kneeling should by any persons, either out of ignorance or infirmity, or out of malice and obstinacy, be misconstrued and depraved, it is hereby declared that thereby no adoration is intended, or ought to be done, either unto the sacramental bread or wine there bodily received, or unto any corporal presence of Christ's natural flesh and blood. For the sacramental bread and wine remain still in their very natural substances, and therefore may not be adored (for that were idolatry, to be abhorred of all faithful Christians); and the natural body and blood of our Saviour Christ are in heaven, and not here ; it being against the truth

of Christ's natural body to be at one time in more
places than one.'[1]

It was decided, at the beginning of the English
Reformation, that the power of deciding upon all
controversies of faith, which had hitherto belonged to
the Pope, should be transferred to judges appointed by
the king. The stability of the Church of England
depends upon this enactment; and, although many
churchmen have complained of it, as a rein upon
their necks and a curb in their mouths, the decisions
of recent years have shown how valuable the in-
terposition of the judges has been to the security of
the Church itself. Upon three great questions three
decisions have preserved at once the authority of
the law and the harmony of contending ecclesiastical
parties :—1. The question of baptism, contended between the High and Low Church, decided in favour
of the liberty of the Low Church. 2. The question
of 'Essays and Reviews,' contended between the High
Church and the Broad Church, decided in favour of
the liberty of the Broad Church. 3. The question of
liberty of speculation regarding the Eucharist within
the limits of the Articles of the Church of England,
contended between the High Church and its enemies,
decided in favour of liberty of speculation on the part
of the High Church.

The 'Edinburgh Review,' in the number for July 1872,
records the following remarks on a late judgment regarding Mr. Bennett :—'There are, however, other aspects of
the judgment which are more than sufficient to compen-

[1] Book of Common Prayer.

sate for any temporary defeat of one party, or temporary exaltation of the other. The decision in the case
of Mr. Bennett is but a signal carrying out of those principles of law and equity, which have characterised the
greater judgments of the Supreme Court of Appeal for
the last twenty years, which we in these pages have
earnestly and constantly defended, and against which
the High Church party have hitherto vehemently protested. It was they who began the series of ecclesiastical litigations in the case of Mr. Gorham, and who
continued it in the cases of Mr. Wilson and Dr. Williams. In both instances they were foiled by the
determination of the Supreme Tribunal to view the statements sought to be assailed, not in the heated atmosphere of partisan theologians, but by the dry daylight
of English law, not with the intention of excluding
everything which could possibly be excluded, but
of including everything that could possibly be included.
Of these principles the Evangelical party reaped the
fruits in 1850, and the Liberal Theologians in 1864.
And now the wheel of theological prosecution had
turned round its whole cycle, and the defeated assailants
of 1850 and 1864 found themselves the endangered
defendants in 1872. Had the policy which they so
vehemently, we may say so fiercely, urged on the two
former occasions been applied to themselves on this
occasion, there cannot be a doubt of the result.
Mr. Bennett must have been condemned, and his
admirers must have sustained at least an ignominious
discomfiture, if not a rigid exclusion from the Church.
But the Supreme Court of Appeal held on its even

x

course, undeterred by intimidations or recriminations
on one side or the other, and the result has been that
the same measure that was meted, in spite of the furious
protestations from the High Church School, to the Vicar
of Bramford Speke and the Vicar of Broad Chalk has
been now meted out to the Vicar of Frome Selwood.
Again and again, in the course of the recent decision,
the toleration of the Lutheran or Roman doctrine of
the Eucharist is based on the maxims laid down for
the toleration of the Calvinistic doctrine of baptism, of
the free critical interpretation of the Scriptures, and of
the Origenist doctrine of future punishment. It is the
last and crowning triumph of the Christian Latitudi-
narianism of the Church of England. And the very
extravagance of Mr. Bennett's positions, by offering
the most crucial test for the application of these just
and wise principles, signalises the extent of the victory
thus obtained in the cause of freedom. Even had his
original statement been preserved intact, it seems to us
that the breadth of the principles here laid down would
have been sufficient to have covered it. A " visible presence " of that which on all hands is allowed to be
invisible, might fairly have been declared to be itself
unmeaning ; and, if unmeaning, then capable of the
same charitable construction which, under like circumstances, the judgment has placed on the words " adoration," " sacrifice," and " objective presence." In fact,
there are very few deviations from the formularies which
this decision would not cover ; and if, in the case of
Mr. Heath and Mr. Voysey, an acquittal was not found
possible, it is enough (without referring to the more

special peculiarities of those two prosecutions) to point
out that the principles which guided the Gorham
judgment were not on those occasions, as on this, expressly invoked. It is to be hoped that all parties may
learn some lessons of moderation from this striking
failure of the attempt to convict one who had, even
in the favourable judgment of the Dean of the Court
of Arches and of his own party, been guilty of crude,
rash, and inconsiderate expressions, and whose own
exposition of his opinions had been condemned as
" erroneous by the very divine whose opinions Mr.
Bennett seems to have sought to represent." The
theological disputants of all the various schools within
the Church may see that there is a more excellent way
of silencing their opponents than by bringing them
before a Court of Law, which is, by the very nature
of the case, precluded from discussing the tendencies
and pretensions which are really, or would be deemed
by the combatants, the most dangerous. All may
learn the wisdom and charity of abstaining from wild
defiances and coarse exaggerations, which, though
they happily fail in most cases to disturb the unim-
passioned atmosphere of a legal tribunal, are needlessly
irritating and inflaming to the mass of minds, which
constitute the public opinion of the Church at large.' [1]

In this manner, as far as the legal position of the
Church is concerned, the Church of England has
become more of a National Church than it had
ever been before ; it comprehends those diversities of
opinion which are sure to arise in a free country, and

[1] *Edin. Review*, July 1872.

x 2

which are happily found by the keenest lawyers compatible with the Articles and the Liturgy. It remains to be asked, what is the general state of opinion in the nation with regard to the Church of England?

But before I enter on this question, it will be well to give the judgment of Macaulay upon the attempt of the Commissioners of King William to rewrite a great part of the Liturgy :—' It was determined to remove some obvious blemishes. And it would have been wise in the Commissioners to stop here. Unfortunately they determined to rewrite a great part of the Prayer Book. It was a bold undertaking, for in general the style of that volume is such as cannot be improved. The English Liturgy, indeed, gains by being compared even with those fine ancient liturgies from which it is to a great extent taken. The essential qualities of devotional eloquence, conciseness, majestic simplicity, pathetic earnestness of supplication, sobered by a profound reverence, are common between the translations and the original. But in the subordinate graces of diction the originals must be allowed to be far inferior to the translations. And the reason is obvious. The technical phraseology of Christianity did not become a part of the Latin language till that language had passed the age of maturity and was sinking into barbarism. But the technical phraseology of Christianity was found in the Anglo-Saxon and in the Norman French, long before the union of those two dialects had produced a third dialect superior to either. The Latin of the Roman Catholic services, therefore, is Latin in the last stage of decay. The English of our services is English in all the vigour and suppleness of early youth.'

Returning to the question of public opinion in England, the decisions of the School-Boards formed under the Education Act of 1870, shows the use which those boards have made of the discretion vested in them to adopt or to reject religious instruction in the education to be given in schools under their control. On March 6, 1872, Mr. Forster made the following statement in the House of Commons :—' I have not gathered from either the addresses or the actions of the School-Boards that they are in favour of a secular system. Having felt it to be my duty to go through the statistics on the subject, I find that eight only, representing a population of less than *two hundred thousand*, have so far agreed with the honorable member as to recommend that the Bible should be read in the schools without note or comment; whereas thirty-eight, representing a population of more than *six millions*, have decided that the Bible shall be read, with explanations such as a child can easily understand. But not one of these School-Boards has adopted the secular system, which they have a perfect right to do under the provisions of the Act.'[1]

If this account be correct, it confirms very fully the account of the religion of the people of England given by Dr. Newman in the ' Grammar of Assent.'

Considering the Church of England in as flourishing a state as it has ever reached, we must now take

[1] Sixty-seventh Report of the British and Foreign School Society, May 1872.

into our view the position of the Roman Church.
If we reflect on the relation of the Church of Rome
with France, Austria, Italy, and Spain, we shall be able ·
to judge how far that Church has declined in power.
She can no longer point to Rome and the grand
Cathedral of St. Peter's as 'caput urbis et orbis;'
the Pope can no longer expect the sovereigns of Germany and France to vie with each other in acts of profound homage ; nor can he assume for the Holy See,
with faint contradiction, the temporal as well as the
spiritual sovereignty of the world. The treaties made
with the Pope under the name of ' Concordats ' are
falling into disuse, the oath of obedience to the Pope,
added by the Jesuits to their monastic vows, raises only
a smile, or at best a contradiction. The temporal power
assumed is matter of scorn in England and in Germany,
and is little regarded in France, Italy, or Spain. Yet,
with all this decline of visible power, there remains to
the Roman Church one of the great elements of her
former sway, the devotion of millions of hearts. In
my opinion, and that of Protestants in general, it was a
great mistake of the Roman Church, when the revival
of letters induced men to resort to the works of-
philosophy and of oratory, derived from Greece and
Rome, not to acknowledge the progress of reason in
Europe, and abandon those appeals to the senses, which
enabled her to teach that bread and wine were
converted into flesh and blood, and to permit a
kind of homage to images of the Virgin Mary
and the Saints, which resembled, but too nearly,
acts of worship and adoration which are due only to

God, the Father, the Son, and the Holy Ghost. A very able French philosopher, the late M. Cousin, gave me his opinion, that if the Roman Catholic Church had spread the Bible everywhere, in her own version, she would have maintained a supremacy over the world. The Roman Church might then have partaken of the general movement of mind in the cultivated nations of Europe. Vittoria Colonna might then have been allowed to make her appeal to God, without the intercession of any Saint, and Galileo might then have been allowed to prove the motion of the earth without being subjected to torture. But it is to be said, on the other hand, that the hearts of multitudes of the poorer classes are attracted by those very appeals to the senses. How many women pour out their griefs before an image of the Virgin Mary, and believe that they derive from the sympathy of the Mother of God, relief and consolation.

Lord Macaulay, in one of the most powerful of his Essays, has described the Jesuit Confessor as conniving at the infidelity to their husbands of the wives of the higher classes, and as teaching that it was better to be an unfaithful wife and a true member of the Church, than a faithful wife and a heretic. But there is no reason to suppose that the Jesuits, or any other spiritual confessors, were parties to so sinful a compromise. It is rather to be presumed that the clergy, regular and secular, always taught virtuous behaviour, or repentance for sin committed, but of course they were unable to control the passions of their fair penitents. These unlawful bonds were often stronger than the holy ties of marriage. At one time, Madame de

Montespan had fully resolved to relinquish her intimate relations with Louis XIV. The cessation of
this notorious scandal was to be treated as a solemnity;
but when the courtiers expected a sad and affecting
parting, they were surprised to see that the lovers had
resolved upon reconciliation instead of repentance.
The courtiers were all dismissed, and three children
were added to the list of legitimatised offspring as the
result of this solemn scene. But when the proud
Vashti was really discarded, and the widow of Scarron,
the buffoon author, had triumphed over her, a marriage
which astounded the whole Court, reconciled the precepts of the priests with the society of the lady preferred, and she was left to amuse a king who was no
longer amusable.

It is to be said, however, that the sins of Louis XIV.
might always be absolved in virtue of the persecution
of the Protestants, and that a regiment of dragoons,
cutting to pieces a congregation in the Cevennes, and
putting to death husbands and wives, mothers and
children, for the crime of praying to God in a Huguenot
version of the Psalms, atoned for years of sin on the
part of the pious monarch.

It is no wonder if the Church of Rome—possessed
of this strength, and filled with the pride arising from
the recovery of the Papal power after the shock of
the Reformation, and the restoration of the Pope to his
seat in the Vatican after the storm of the French
Revolution, and the squall of his deposition by Napoleon
—should adhere to her ancient rules, and fondly
trust to see the Powers of Europe again in subjection

to her throne. Yet I cannot forbear from pointing out two circumstances, the one a source of weakness to the Church of Rome, the other a cause of enmity and opposition on the part of all the friends of progress and the leaders of civilization in this advanced stage of the world.

1. The element of weakness is the constant appeal to the senses, in a period when the great diffusion of knowledge and the spread of education over the greater part of the nations of Europe have accustomed men to attend to the facts of physical science, and when the habit of reading popular works of the greatest authors of England, France, Italy, and Germany has prepared men to doubt the truth of dogmas, which seem addressed rather to the blindness of superstition than to the reasoning of a critical age. Gibbon, referring to the conversion of Constantine, and the force of the evidence to which he yielded, says, ' Nor can it be deemed incredible that the mind of an unlettered soldier should have yielded to the weight of evidence which in a more enlightened age has satisfied or subdued the reason of a Grotius, a Pascal, or a Locke.' [1] Such a reference, and the authority of men endowed with ' the reason of a Grotius, a Pascal, and a Locke,' may well make persons of less power of understanding pause, and, ' looking before and after,' hesitate before they use their ' capability and godlike reason ' to reject narratives thus vouched, and arguments thus fortified. Those who have studied the writings of these celebrated men must have perceived

[1] Gibbon's *Decline and Fall*, chap. xx.

with how much care and reflection they sought to weigh and examine the proofs of a miraculous inter-ference in the affairs of the world.

It was long after the introduction of Christianity that an obscure theologian invented the dogma of Transubstantiation, and many a priest in the celebra-tion of the Mass will be disposed to address the bread and wine in the language which Luther heard from the dignified priesthood of Rome—

Panis es et panis manebis, vinum es et vinum manebis.

In the same manner, the veneration paid, although without professed adoration, to the images of the Virgin Mary and the Saints, the frequent miracles attributed to them, and the respect which the Church shows in preserving relics, are apt to excite ridicule rather than reverence in a cultivated mind. Boccaccio describes the trick played by some mischievous boys upon a friar, by placing cinders in a box, in which he kept a parrot's feather, to delude the multitude by pre-tending to show them a part of the wing of the Archangel Gabriel. The friar, however, outwitted his persecutors, telling the people that by mistake he had brought some of the cinders which were used in the martyrdom of St. Lawrence. All these appeals to the senses, so well fitted to the fourteenth century, were unsuited to the period of the revival of letters, and ought to have been relinquished for the lessons of St. Athanasius, St. Augustine, St. Ambrose, and other works in which the Church of Rome is so rich and so abundant.

2. I come now to the second circumstance by which the Roman Church, if not directly weakened, is exposed to the enmity, the sarcastic irony, the free enquiry, and the witty ridicule of the surrounding world. Calvin and John Knox, in their indignant invectives, Swift and Voltaire, in their witty parodies, have exposed the hollow pretensions of a power which assumes infallibility, and displays the most deplorable weakness. It is singular to find that, in this nineteenth century, Pope Pius IX. proclaimed at Rome (on December 8th, 1864) the most astounding claims to the most humble obedience, coupled with a defiance of all that the science of three centuries had discovered and affirmed, and proclaimed the most absolute right of interference by force in the affairs of the world. The Powers of Europe have one after another been abjuring the allegiance so haughtily required. The Syllabus has been rejected by every Roman Catholic nation of Europe as utterly incompatible with civil government, subversive of the rights of every people, and breaking the bonds of that civil allegiance which every Government requires at the hands of its subjects. Yet it may be instructive to extract some out of the eighty propositions stated in the title of the Syllabus to embrace the principal errors of our times which have been censured in Consistorial Allocutions, Encyclicals, and other Apostolic Letters of our Most Holy Father, Pope Pius IX. At this very time, the Government of England is hesitating whether it may not be better to give up the education of the people of Ireland to the orders of

Cardinal Cullen and the decrees of Pope Pius IX.,
subjecting all who disobey these orders and decrees to
deprivation of their rights as freemen. I will begin
with Articles XII. and XIII. :—

XII. The decrees of the Apostolic See and of the
Roman congregations interfere with the free progress
of science.

XIII. The method and principles whereby the ancient scholastic doctors cultivated theology are not
suited to the necessities of our time, and to the progress of the sciences. It would appear that, by Article
XII. of the Syllabus, the interference of the Apostolic
See with the progress of Galileo, and even his punishment, are not to be accounted an interference with
the free progress of science, and that the assertion of Galileo, that the earth moves, is to be considered as an heretical refusal to comply with astronomical truths which the Holy See has solemnly
proclaimed. Article XVIII. of the Syllabus is to the
following effect :—' Protestantism is nothing else than
a different form of the same Christian religion, in which
it is permitted to please God equally as in the true
Catholic Church.' Unless the Ritualists of England are
prepared to abjure altogether the Church of England,
they must fall under the weight of this censure.

I will proceed to copy some more of the Articles, or
rather the doctrines, which are pointed out for condemnation as fallacies.

XXIV. The Church has no power of employing
force, nor has she any temporal power, direct or in-
direct.

XXXVII. National Churches, separated and totally disjoined from the Roman Pontiff's authority, may be instituted.

XLV. The whole government of public schools, wherein the youth of any Christian state is educated, episcopal seminaries only being in some degree excepted, may and should be given to the civil power; and in such sense be given, that no right be recognised in any other authority of mixing itself up in the management of the schools, the direction of studies, the conferring of degrees, the choice or approbation of teachers.

LXII. The principle of non-intervention (as it is called) should be proclaimed and observed.

LXIII. It is lawful to refuse obedience to legitimate princes, and even rebel against them.

LXXIII. By virtue of a purely civil contract, there may exist among Christians marriage, truly so called; and it is false that either the contract of marriage among Christians is always a Sacrament, or that there is no contract if the Sacrament be excluded.

It is well known that on the questions of education and marriage, the Roman Church claims a plenary and despotic authority. I propose here to refer to the dispute which has taken place in Ireland, with respect to the management and direction of three or four parochial schools. The parish priest of three or four parishes, Mr. O'Keeffe, gave notice of an action for slander against a Roman Catholic coadjutor bishop. As soon as his intention was known, the coadjutor bishop applied to the superior spiritual authorities with regard to the offence of appealing to the jurisdiction of the civil courts. Cardinal Cullen decided that the parish priest must be dismissed for appealing to a civil court with regard to a Roman Catholic priest. The parish priest was dismissed, and his successor asked the Education Board to recognise him as the manager of the parish schools. The Education Board has been in the habit, when a priest has been dismissed under the rules of the Roman Catholic Church, to recognise his successor as manager of the parish schools; but this was a peculiar case. The priest had not been dismissed for any moral or ecclesiastical offence. His offence was that he did not acknowledge the immunity of the Roman clergy from the civil courts. It was obvious that this immunity could not be acknowledged by the Education Board of Ireland without placing the whole education of Ireland under Cardinal Cullen. His language—that is to say, the language of Cardinal Cullen, in reference to the Bulla Cœnæ, and the bull of October 12, 1869—asserts for the clergy immunity from the jurisdiction of the civil courts, and places the money raised from the taxes, paid by the English and Scotch people, at the disposal of Cardinal Cullen and his sovereign the Pope. In the Gospel of St. Mark, it is written of Christ's enemies :—

'And they sought to lay hold on Him, but feared the people: for they knew that He had spoken the parable against them : and they left Him and went their way. And they sent unto Him certain of the Pharisees and Herodians to catch Him in His words. And when they were come, they say unto Him, Master, we know that thou art true, and carest for no man, for thou regardest not the person of men, but teachest the way of God in truth : Is it lawful to give tribute to Cæsar or not? But He, knowing their hypocrisy, said unto them, Why tempt ye Me? Bring Me a penny, that I may see it : and they brought it. And He saith unto them, Whose is this image and super-scription? And they said unto Him, Cæsar's. And Jesus answering said unto them, RENDER TO CÆSAR THE THINGS THAT ARE CÆSAR'S, AND TO GOD THE THINGS THAT ARE GOD'S.'[1] If the schoolmaster of Callan, when he saw the coined sovereigns contributed by the State to assist the school, had asked, 'Whose image and superscription is this?' he would have been told 'Queen Victoria's.' It is to be hoped that, as the Board of Education seem to have been misled by the precedents which they had before them, some means will be taken in a future session to remedy the wrongs inflicted upon the people of Great Britain.

But who is to define the things that are Cæsar's, and the things that are God's? Is it to be the sacerdotal power? In answer to this question,

Cardinal Cullen maintains that education belongs to the spiritual power. He must argue, that if a Roman Catholic boy learn the multiplication table with a Protestant companion, his faith and morals are en-dangered ; that if a Roman Catholic professor be not allowed to teach the Syllabus approved by the Pope, the faith and morals of Ireland—of Roman Catholic Ireland, at least—are endangered. Against all this I

[1] St. Mark, chap. xii.

protest. I know that if the Papal doctrines of the Syllabus are taught to the educated youth of Ireland, high treason, under a covert form, will be the daily food of the Irish mind.

The issue is serious, and far more important than the continuance of any Cabinet. The laws of Henry VIII. and of William III. must be maintained, or the kingdom of Ireland transferred to the Pope.

The Roman Catholic parish priest of Callan, in Ireland, had made known his intention of prosecuting for slander the coadjutor Bishop of Ossory. It appears to be a rule of the Roman Church that no ecclesiastic of that Church shall bring any ecclesiastic of the same Church into a court of law. The coadjutor bishop was supported by Cardinal Cullen, Archbishop of Dublin ; the cardinal was supported by the Pope ; the parish priest of Callan was displaced, and was also dismissed from the office of manager of the parish schools of Callan in a majority of one of the National Board of Education, led by the Lord Chancellor of Ireland against Chief Justice Monahan, both being Roman Catholics. It is obvious that a grievous wrong has been done. The Pope, as the head of the Roman Church, had the right to appoint and to displace the parish priest of Callan, but he had no right to appoint or displace the manager of the parish schools of Callan, nor had the Lord Chancellor of Ireland any right to interfere in any way to influence, directly or indirectly, the decision of a court of justice. The Sovereign of this country has declared by Magna Charta—' To no one will we sell, to no one will we deny, to no one will we delay right or justice.'

Thus the Board of Education in Ireland disobeyed the precept of Christ, and violated the spirit of Magna Charta. In 1215, a Roman Catholic Archbishop of Canterbury vindicated the laws, the liberties, and the independence of England. In 1872, upwards of six hundred years afterwards, an Irish Archbishop of Dublin was allowed to proclaim the jurisdiction of the Pope, a foreign prince, over the Queen's kingdom of Ireland.

It is clear that, in some way or other, this flagrant violation of Divine and human law must be reviewed, reconsidered, and reversed.

ESSAY XIX.

THE ROMAN CATHOLIC CHURCH AND THE CON-STITUTION OF THE UNITED KINGDOM.

IT is important to consider in what manner a country like England, which accepted the Bible as its rule of faith, made terms of amity with one of the three parts of the United Kingdom, which professed, by the voice of a great majority of its people, attachment to the Roman Catholic Church, and obedience to its spiritual authority. In 1829 Roman Catholics were admitted, when duly elected, to seats in the House of Commons, Irish peers, duly elected, were included in the roll of the House of Lords, and Roman Catholics were made capable of holding offices under the Crown, not excepting those of Secretary of State, First Lord of the Treasury, and other Cabinet offices. But in the bill introduced by Mr. Peel, it was enacted, 'that from and after the commencement of this Act, it shall and may be lawful for any person professing the Roman Catholic religion, being a peer, or who shall after the commencement of this Act be returned as a member of the House of Commons, to sit and vote in either House of Parliament respectively, being in all other respects duly qualified to sit and vote therein, upon taking and subscribing an oath, instead of the oaths of allegiance, abjuration, and supremacy, and instead of making and subscribing the declaration against transubstantiation and the invocation of saints, and the sacrifice of the mass as practised in the Church of Rome.'

In the oath prescribed in the Roman Catholic Relief Bill, introduced by Mr. Peel, there are contained, besides the disavowal of many obsolete or imaginary tenets, the following words: 'And I do declare, that I do not believe that the Pope of Rome, or. any other foreign prince, prelate, person, state, or potentate, hath or ought to have any temporal or civil jurisdiction, power, superiority, or pre-eminence, directly or indirectly, within this realm.'

The question hereupon arises, what is temporal or civil jurisdiction, and what subjects properly belong to spiritual jurisdiction? The laws relating to marriage and education are asserted by the Pope to be subjects pertaining to spiritual jurisdiction. In France and Italy the laws relating to marriage and education are declared by the laws of those countries to belong to the civil law. In France and· Italy the civil marriage is the only form of marriage binding upon those nations. In England the form of marriage enacted by the canon law of Rome is, with certain conditions of registration, allowed to be valid. But on the question of education a contest is evidently impending. Will England assume for herself, as she has hitherto done, the power of laying down, by her own Parliamentary authority, the conditions according to which the education of the young must be carried on, or will Pope Pius IX. be allowed to assume, by himself and his legates, by Cardinal Cullen and the Irish Roman Catholic bishops, the supreme direction of education?

This question · is one of those which our French neighbours, by an expressive phrase, call 'burning.' In 1830 or 1831, the late Lord Derby, then Lord Stanley, Archbishop Whately, and Earl Grey, established a new system of national education for Ireland; and on the faith of the equity and efficiency of that system, the Government, for many years, proposed and carried the grant of large sums of money by the House of Commons. I have often had to defend that system in company with Mr. Chichester Fortescue.

The principle of that system of national education was, that secular instruction should be in common, but that religious instruction should be separate. Accordingly a placard is exhibited· in the schools, with the words *secular instruction* or *religious instruction* printed in large letters, according to the hours of local regulation. This is no theoretical distinction. The Roman Church has declared in effect that faith and morals will be endangered, if a Roman Catholic child is found learning the multiplication table side by side with a Protestant boy, or if the two are found playing at trap-ball together in the playground. Father O'Keeffe, a Roman Catholic priest, has been caught in one of the many snares which the Jesuits of Rome have prepared, and he has lost upwards of 300*l.* a year, by being deprived of the management of the schools of Callan. No doubt upon each of the coins which he has lost, the image and superscription of Victoria, that is the image and superscription of Cæsar,

were inscribed. Every Englishman and every Scotch-
man, by submitting to the decree of the National Board
of Education in Ireland, has virtually consented to the
supremacy of Pope Pius IX., and has thereby departed from the precedent set long before the Reformation, when Stephen Langton, the Popish Archbishop
of Canterbury, boldly asserted the independence of
England on the plain of Runnymede.

That this is no trifling matter may be illustrated by
the solemn warning which Sir Robert Peel, in con-
cluding his speech in favour of the admission of Roman
Catholics to Parliament and to office, gave to the House
of Commons.   He then said :

'In the course I have taken, I have been mainly
influenced by the anxious desire to provide for the
maintenance of Protestant interests, and for the security
of Protestant establishments.   This is my defence—
this is my consolation—this shall be my revenge.

'Sir, I will hope for the best.   God grant that the
moral storm may be appeased, that the turbid waters
of strife may be settled and composed, and that, having
found their just level, they may be mingled, with equal
flow, in one clear and common stream.   But if these
expectations are to be disappointed, if unhappily civil
strife and contention shall survive the restoration of
political privilege ; if there be something inherent in
the spirit of the Roman Catholic religion which dis-
dains equality, and will be satisfied with nothing but
ascendency—still, I am content to run the hazard of
the change.   The contest, if inevitable, will be fought
for other objects, and with other arms.   The struggle

will be not for the abolition of civil distinctions, but for the predominance of an intolerant religion.

'Sir, I contemplate the progress of that struggle with pain ; but I look forward to its issue with perfect composure and confidence. We shall have dissolved the great moral alliance that has hitherto given strength to the cause of the Roman Catholics. We shall range on our side the illustrious authorities which have heretofore been enlisted upon theirs; the rallying cry of " Civil Liberty " will then be all our own. We shall enter the field with the full assurance of victory, armed with the consciousness of having done justice, and of being in the right; backed by the unanimous feeling of England, by the firm union of orthodoxy and dissent, by the applauding voice of Scotland ; and, if other aid be requisite, cheered by the sympathies of every free state in either hemisphere, and by the wishes and the prayers of every free man, in whatever clime or under whatever form of government his lot may have been cast.'

These are solemn words, not to be forgotten by the members for England, for Scotland, and for Ulster in the House of Commons ; they will not be forgiven if they transfer the sovereignty of Ireland from Queen Victoria to Pope Pius IX.

Unhappily a change has taken place in Ireland which is unfavourable to the prospects of peace and conciliation.

Dr. Murray *was* the Roman Catholic Archbishop of Dublin ; Cardinal Cullen *is* the Roman Catholic Archbishop of Dublin. It may be said there is no difference : Dr. Murray was a Roman Catholic archbishop ; Cardinal Cullen is a Roman Catholic archbishop. The difference is this : Dr. Murray was more Catholic than Roman ; Cardinal Cullen is more Roman than Catholic.

Dr. Murray agreed with Archbishop Whately ; Cardinal Cullen has accepted the Syllabus, and looks to force as the true mode of restoring the Roman supremacy as *caput urbis et orbis*. We must either take up the gauntlet or admit that the Pope has, and ought to have, temporal jurisdiction in Ireland.

The policy pursued towards Scotland has been since the Revolution of 1688 wise, both in its enlarged spirit and its practical effect. When King William obtained the Crown of England, he consulted the wishes of the Scotch nation as to the nature of the Church establishment. The Stuarts had endeavoured, by force, by persecution, and by torture, to plant the Church of England, its bishops, and its Liturgy in Scot- land. William saw how completely their efforts had failed, and he consented at once to a form of Presby- terian Church government in Scotland. When William was succeeded by Anne, and a union of the two par- liaments was contemplated, Lord Somers, with wisdom akin to that of William, gave the strongest pledges to Scotland that her Church should be maintained by all the succeeding kings and queens of England.

We have seen in the last Essay that the Pope in his Syllabus has condemned the error of those who say ' the Church not only ought never to animadvert on philosophy, but ought to tolerate the errors of philosophy, and leave it to her to correct herself.

Now we know that the Church of Rome, so far from tolerating the errors of Galileo, who believed that the earth moved, endeavoured to persuade him of his mistake by torture, and was unable to convince that obstinate heretic even by so cogent an argument. We know also that the Church of Rome denounced a similar error put forth by one Isaac Newton, who was not only an arch-heretic, but a Whig member of Parliament into the bargain. But we are now told that teachers of the Roman Catholic Church will be supplied in Dublin, who, no doubt, will accept the Syllabus of Pope Pius IX., given at Rome in December 1864, and who, if they ·admit the possibility of the earth moving at all, will no doubt do so with the qualification prefixed to Newton's works by two of his able editors. In the edition of Newton's ' Principia,' by Le Seur and Jacquier, 1760, is the following declaration :—

DECLARATIO.

Nevtonus in hoc tertio libro telluris motæ hypothesem assumit, auctoris propositiones aliter explicari non poterant, nisi eâdem quoque justâ hypothesi. Hinc alienam coacti sumus gerere personam, cæterum latis a summis Pontificibus contra telluris motum decretis nos obsequi profitemur.[1]

But I have better hopes for Ireland and for the present House of Commons. There are in Ireland, as we well know, many Roman Catholics, some judges, some

---

[1] *Philosophiæ Naturalis Principia Mathematica*, 1760, vol. iii.

priests, many lawyers, and many country gentlemen, who, with a profound veneration for the Roman Catholic Church, mingle a large and liberal understanding of the great truths of science, and of the great facts of history, who do not applaud the Massacre of St. Bartholomew, or recoil from the manly assertion of the principles upon which the constitutional monarchy of England and the republic of the United States found their laws and vindicate their liberties.

Let me add one reflection on the policy of great English and Irish statesmen.   Mr. Pitt, Lord Grenville, Lord Spencer, Lord Melville, Mr. Windham, and, I believe, Mr. Grattan, were agreed to recommend a grant in money to the Roman Catholic Church, but not to adopt by the State any part of the Roman Catholic religion.   The Duke of Wellington was desirous in opening the door of Parliament and of office to Roman Catholics to provide by parliamentary grant 300,000*l.* a year for the subsistence of the clergy of the Roman Catholic communion.   Mr. Grattan concurred in and advised the parliamentary grants to Maynooth, on the ground that as the majority of the people of Ireland would certainly receive their instruction in religion from Roman Catholic priests, it was the interest of the State that those priests should be well and not ill educated.   Even this moderate grant, given on those reasonable grounds, has been abolished of late years.

Indeed it seems that the whole policy of the State is to be rested on grounds of a totally different nature from those approved by Mr. Pitt, Lord Grenville, and the Duke of Wellington. Instead of a grant of money, and a refusal to sanction any part of the Roman Catholic creed, all money grants are to be refused, but the Pope's Syllabus, and the teaching of young men by Papal professors, are to receive the recognition and the sanction of the Parliament of the United Kingdom !

So that Parliament will only have to choose between Mr. Butt and Home Rule, or Cardinal Cullen and Foreign Rule! As Mr. Burke said on another occasion, ' An ugly alternative.'

But a great question remains for solution. If, according to the opinion of Butler, Bishop of Durham, Milman, Dean of St. Paul's, and Dr. Newman, of the Roman Church, Christianity is to have a new development, the question remains, in what direction is it to be developed ? Shall it be developed in the direction of the Church of England, of the Church of Rome, of the Lutherans, the Calvinists, the Baptists, the Independents, or the Unitarians? This question shall be partially, if not fully, examined.

ESSAY XX.

ON THE DEVELOPMENT OF CHRISTIANITY.

LET us now recur to the general belief in Christianity, as entertained by the people of England and Scotland, and of the continent of Europe. I have already stated the view of Dr. Newman of the Church of Rome, and of Dean Milman of thé Church of England, upon this subject.

A question of very great importance remains for the future—What changes are the chief Churches of Christendom likely to make for themselves, and what has been the tendency of men of the greatest minds, and the most enlightened faculties, belonging to the Church of England, the Church of Rome, and the Lutheran Church of Germany?

I. With respect to the Church of England, we may take as samples Archbishop Tillotson, Bishop Butler, and the late Dean of St. Paul's. It will be found that each of these enlightened men, without wishing to alter the letter, is of opinion that the whole spirit of the Scripture was imperfectly understood, and required to be revised by the progress of learning and of liberty. We know that Archbishop Tillotson objected to the Athanasian Creed, and wished that the Church were well rid of it. In this sense, therefore, must be understood the second article of his proposals for comprehension drawn up in 1689—'That the Liturgy be carefully reviewed, and such alterations and changes be therein made as may supply the defects, and re- move as much as possible all ground of exception to any part of it, by leaving out the apocryphal lessons, and correcting the translation of the Psalms used in the public service where there is need of it, and in many other particulars.'[1]

Such also was the opinion of Bishop Butler, when he wrote in his Analogy that 'the Bible contains many truths as yet undiscovered.'

'And as,' he says, 'the whole scheme of Scripture is not yet understood, so, if it ever comes to be under- stood, before the restitution of all things, and without miraculous interpositions, it must be in the same way as natural knowledge is come at, by the continuance and progress of learning and of liberty, and by par- ticular persons attending to, comparing, and pursuing intimations scattered up and down it, which are over- looked and disregarded by the generality of the world. For this is the way in which all improvements are made; by thoughtful men's tracing on obscure hints, as it were, dropped as by nature accidentally, or which seem to come into our minds by chance.' And again: 'Our existence is not only successive, as it must be of necessity, but one state of our life and being is ap- pointed by God to be a preparation for another, and

---

[1] *St. Paul and Protestantism*, p. 180.

that to be the means of attaining to another succeeding one ; infancy to childhood, childhood to youth,
youth to mature age. Men are impatient, and for
precipitating things ; but the Author of Nature appears
deliberate throughout His operations, accomplishing His
natural ends by slow successive steps. Thus, in the
daily course of natural providence, God operates in
the very same manner as in the dispensation of Christianity, making one thing subservient to another, this
to somewhat further, and so on through a progressive
series of means which extend both backward and forward beyond our utmost view. Of this manner of
operation, everything we see in the course of nature
is as much an instance as any part of the Christian
dispensation.' [1]

The late Dean of St. Paul's has said : ' What distinct-
ness of conception, what precision of language, may be
indispensable to true faith ; what part of the ancient
dogmatic system may be allowed silently to fall into
disuse, as at least superfluous, and as beyond the proper
range of human thought and human language ; how
far the sacred records may, without real peril to their
truth, be subjected to closer investigation ; to what
wider interpretation, especially of the Semitic portion,
those records may submit, and wisely submit, in order
to harmonize them with the irrefutable conclusions of
science ; how far the Eastern veil of allegory which
hangs over their truth may be lifted or torn away to
show their unshadowed essence ; how far the poetic

[1] Butler, *Analogy of Natural and Revealed Religion.*

vehicle through which truth is conveyed may be gently severed from the truth—all this must be left to the future historian of our religion. As it is my own confident belief that the words of Christ, and His words alone (the primal, indefeasible truths of Christianity), shall not pass away; so I cannot presume to say that men may not attain to a clearer, at the same time more full and comprehensive and balanced sense of those words, than has as yet been generally received in the Christian world. As all else is transient and mutable, these only eternal and universal, assuredly whatever light may be thrown on the mental constitution of man, even on the constitution of nature, and the laws which govern the world, will be concentrated so as to give a more penetrating vision of those undying truths. Teutonic Christianity (and this seems to be its mission and privilege), however nearly in its more perfect form it may already have approximated, may approximate still more closely to the absolute and perfect faith of Christ; it may discover and establish the sublime unison of religion and reason; keep in tone the triple-chorded harmony of faith, holiness, and charity; assert its own full freedom, know the bounds of that freedom in others. Christianity may yet have to exercise a far wider, even if more silent and untraceable influence, through its primary, all-penetrating, all-pervading principles, on the civilization of mankind.'[1]

We must now proceed to notice the views of one of the most able and one of the most plausible of the

---

[1] *Hist. of Latin Christianity*, vol. vi. p. 633.

advocates of the Roman Church. Dr. Newman, in his 'Grammar of Assent,' has pointed out, that as there are many kinds of minds, so there are various dispositions and tendencies which affect religious as well as civil questions. Thus, he says most truly, tradition, which may produce conviction in one man, may only produce scorn and disdain in another. The early legends of Rome might be accepted by Colonel Mure, to whom tradition is a welcome ground of belief, while they are rejected, in virtue of an inexorable rule, by the mind of Sir George Lewis.

Yet Dr. Newman accepts as a law of history, and of human nature, the postulate, that the progress of knowledge, the necessity of the times, and the intuitive sagacity of man, may produce great changes of opinion.

'We have to account,' says Dr. Newman, in his Essay on Development, 'for that apparent variation and growth of doctrine which embarrasses us when we would consult history for the true idea of Christianity. The increase and expansion of the Christian creed and ritual, and the variations which have attended the process in the case of individual writers and churches, are the necessary attendants on any philosophy or polity which takes possession of the intellect and heart, and has had any wide or extended dominion. From the nature of the human mind, time is necessary for the full comprehension and perfection of great ideas. The highest and most wonderful truths, though communicated to the world once for all by inspired teachers, could not be comprehended all at once by the recipients; but, as admitted and transmitted by minds not inspired, and through media which were human, have required only the longer time and deeper thought for their full elucidation.' And again : ' Ideas may remain when the expression of them is indefinitely varied. Nay, one cause of corruption in religion is the refusal to follow the course of doctrine as it moves on, and an obstinacy in the notions of the past. So Our Lord found His people precisians in their obedience to the letter ; He condemned them for not being led on to its spirit—that is, its development. The Gospel is the development of the Law ; yet what difference seems wider than that which separates the unbending rule of Moses from the grace and truth which came by Jesus Christ ? The more claim an idea has to be considered living, the more various will be its aspects ; and the more social and political is its nature, the more complicated and subtle will be its developments, and the longer and more eventful will be its course. Such is Christianity.' And once more : ' It may be objected that inspired documents, such as the Holy Scriptures, at once determine doctrine without further trouble. But they were intended to create *an idea*, and that idea is not in the sacred text, but in the mind of the reader ; and the question is, whether that idea is communicated to him in its completeness and minute accuracy on its first apprehension, or expands in his heart and intellect, and comes to perfection in the course of time. If it is said that inspiration supplied the place of this development in the first recipients of Christianity, *still the time at length came when its recipients ceased to be inspired ;* and on these recipients the revealed truths

would fall as in other cases, at first vaguely and generally, and would afterwards be completed by developments.' Again: ' Development is not an effect of
wishing and resolving, or of forced enthusiasm, or of
any mechanism of reasoning, or of any mere subtlety
of intellect; but comes of its own innate power of
expansion within the mind in its season, though with
the use of reflection and argument and original thought,
more or less as it may happen, with a dependence on
the ethical growth of the mind itself, and with a reflex
influence upon it.' [1]

We may accept the general reasoning of Dr. Newman, but we must take care not to be entangled in the
consequences in which he would involve us. Like a
skilful advocate, he draws from the premisses, which he
has so well laid down, the prodigious inference, that
the decrees, bulls, and organization of the Church of
Rome are the very development of which we are in
search. Admitting with Bishop Butler and Dr. Newman, that the words of Scripture give us ideas, and
that it is for men to whom those words were uttered
or written to fill up the full meaning, we have a right
to examine and investigate whether the Church of Rome
fulfils the expectations we have a right to entertain of
a holy, pure, and benevolent Church. The words sung
by the Angels, ' Glory to God in the highest, and on
earth peace and goodwill toward men,' contain the
promise given by God to mankind, as the substance of
His revelation.

[1] *Essay on Development*, by Dr. Newman.

Z

Examining the history of the Church of Rome by this test, I find—

1. Admitting the chronology of learned men, that St. Peter was crucified and St. Paul beheaded at Rome ; [1] I can find no authority for the assumption, that a perpetual succession of a Head as Pope was to take place; and still less that any body of cardinals or princes were authorised to express an affirmative or negative voice in the choice of the Pope.

2. It appears clear from history that the words adopted by the Council of Nice, 'being of the same substance,' are words not authorised by Scripture, and were inserted solely for the purpose of confuting, destroying, and putting to death the abettors of the Arian heresy.

3. That the articles adopted at Paris of what is called the Athanasian Creed, were articles derived from Arabic translations of the theories of Aristotle, and, however they may agree with Aristotelian logic, are repugnant to the words of Christ.

4. That the doctrine of the Transubstantiation of the bread and wine of the Holy Communion into the Body and Blood of Christ is not to be found in Scripture, and affirms the presence on earth of Christ, who is in Heaven.

5. The Roman Church has adopted many superstitious practices, prayers to Saints, of whom we know not whether they be saints or no, and supplications for the intercession of fallible and sinful men and women,

---

[1] See *Art de Vérifier les Dates.*

instead of humble supplications to the throne of Almighty God.

6. That some of the most vicious men living at the time, known for the most scandalous and horrible crimes, have been placed on the throne of Peter from age to age, and worshipped as infallible guides.

7. That the most cruel wars, the most bloody executions, and the most destructive ravages of civilised countries have, in the case of the Albigenses, of the Arians, of the Lutherans, of John Huss, of Jerome of Prague, and of many others in Italy and in Spain, in France and in England, in Germany and the Low Countries, been sanctioned by those who ought to have been the examples of mercy and of forgiveness.

8. That the errors and crimes, the forgery of decretals, the usurpation of secular power, the blessings bestowed upon St. Bartholomew's Day and other massacres, the assumption of a control over science and over a knowledge of astronomy and physics, have not yet been abandoned as errors due to human infirmity or casual inadvertence, but are held up in the Papal Syllabus of 1870 as the unerring judgments of a sovereign lord, who claims both spiritual and temporal supremacy.

These appear to me sufficient grounds for not bowing to the claim of infallibility put forth by the last Council of the Vatican, for not yielding to the control of the Roman Church over the relations of marriage and education, asserted by the Pope and assented to by Roman Catholic bishops of Germany and of Ireland as the proper domain of spiritual and ecclesiastical power.

Convinced, as I am, that the Protestants of Europe and America will never bend their necks beneath a yoke which could only be imposed upon mankind by risking the loss of all progress, of all advance in freedom, and of all national independence, I put aside this claim as one that can never be admitted.

We must, therefore, have recourse to the Protestant communities of the world, with the hope of finding among them some firm ground upon which the future religion of Christians may take the shape of a permanent and progressive institution. Let us pass over some of these various sects and communities, not with a view of fixing the boundaries of truth or developing the hidden meaning of Divine lessons, but rather in the hope of pointing out errors which have been prevailing, efforts of which the direction has been mistaken, and the spirit in which progress may be made rather than creeds which may safely be adopted.

Let us first say that neither Luther nor Calvin, the one a monk and the other a priest, contending three centuries ago, in the midst of the most violent conflicts between old institutions and new speculations, can be looked to as having arrived at conclusions upon which mankind or even the educated part of Christendom can be contented to rest.

Let us next observe that in these times there is a wide distinction between the professions of different sects and the opinions really entertained by the majority of those who profess themselves members of certain established Churches or adherents of voluntary sects. Men of the highest education in France and

Italy are professed members of the Roman Catholic Church, but if any one enquires as to the prevailing opinions he will find that the greater part of them are what is called Voltairians, who, while they worship God as Roman Catholics, are Deists, and not really Christians.

An error of an opposite kind is made with regard to the higher classes of England. It is presumed or taken for granted, that a man who has learned political economy, and has adopted the policy of the enlightened classes, disregards or disbelieves the Christian religion. Yet this would be an absurd mistake. It is not because a man is so far a free-trader as to admit that corn and cotton, wool and silk may pass freely from one country to another, that he loses sight of religious obligations. On the contrary, if a statesman says, it shall be free to him who raises a bushel of corn in Michigan or Ohio to exchange it at a fair price with the weaver of a yard of cotton or woollen-cloth in Lancashire, it is no proof that he has no faith in Christ, it proves rather that where there is no paramount political objection, he is willing that the various nations of the world should be free to help one another. Still more, if the Parliaments and Assemblies of England and the United States agree, first to prohibit slave-trade, and after a course of years to abolish slavery, so far from proving that they disregard the Christian religion, the facts imply, although they may not make a boast of their motives, that the spirit of Christ's commandments has entered into their speeches and guided their acts.

Lord Althorp, when asked by Lord Melbourne to

accept the office of Governor of Canada, told me that if
he had been able to ascertain that it was the will of
God that he should go to Canada, he would have gone.
As he could not convince himself it was the will of God,
he declined the office.

Much has been made of the differences said to exist
among the clergy of the Church of England; but these
differences amount to tendencies rather than to broad
distinctions.   The High Church tend towards the
Church of Rome, or, as Bishop Pearce expressed it,
' Tendimus in Latium.'   The Low Church tend towards
the teaching of Calvin.   The Broad Church are content
with the letter and the spirit of the words of Christ.
But these differences, not being of vital importance, will
change from time to time.   It little matters whether
what is called the Athanasian Creed is omitted in the
Liturgy or whether the congregation, imitating what
King George III. is said to have done, shut up their
Prayer-books when that Creed· is read.   The great
matter is, that the people of England should do, as Dr.
Newman says they do, namely, read their Bibles and
be sensibly alive to the superintending providence of
God.   If such is the religion of the people of England
and of Scotland, we need not be very uneasy as to the
result.

For my part I believe that such is the state of the
case.   In the prayer for ' all conditions of men,' inserted in the Book of Common Prayer, the Church of
·England prays that ' the Catholic Church may be so
guided and governed by thy good Spirit, that all who
profess and call themselves Christians, may be led into

the way of truth, and hold the faith, in unity of spirit, in the bond of peace, and in righteousness of life.'

It will be observed that the Church of England, in this prayer, does not ask that all who profess and call themselves Christians may hold the faith in unity of dogma. Every English clergyman knows full well that in 1768 Lord Mansfield, in one of the most elaborate and enlightened judgments ever delivered in the House of Lords, declared that the Protestant dissenters were by Act of Parliament not tolerated, but established. In attending their own chapels, in using their own forms of worship and their own language of prayer, the Protestant dissenters are not making use of an indulgence, but exercising a right. By Acts passed in 1778, in 1792, in 1828, and in subsequent years, Roman Catholics enjoy the same rights, and are entitled to similar political privileges. The Unitarians have been admitted to worship God in their own chapels, the Jews in their synagogues, and to participate in all civil privileges.

It is clear, therefore, that at the present time, all who profess and call themselves Christians and the Jews are in the full enjoyment of religious liberty. It is true that the members of the Established Church have some advantages, not in point of income, but in point of the source from which that income is derived. The clergyman of the Established Church, who conducts public worship in the borough of Southwark, receives his income as a commutation for tithe rent-charge. The dissenting minister who receives an equal or probably a greater income in Camberwell, derives that income from voluntary contributions. The chief effect of this distinction between the different sources of income is that the extremes of superstition and fanaticism are kept in check by the intervention of the Crown, and of lay proprietors who have received all the advantages of a liberal education without imbibing sacerdotal prejudices. Those who wish to promote the ascendancy of Roman Catholic superstitions, or of Calvinistic enthusiasm, are more restrained than they would be if the Church of England were disestablished. In like manner, if no religious lessons derived from the Bible were read in the primary schools, the various sects would enforce their own peculiar views in their own chapels with increased emphasis, with augmented bitterness, with war and ill-will upon earth. There are many who desire this change; for my part I shall deprecate and oppose it as long as my life remains.

The word progress is often used in these times, and there are few educated men who will not be ready to promote the cause of true and rational progress. But there exists in these times too great a disposition to be satisfied with the word, and to apply it to any measure of which the writer or speaker has a favourable opinion. Yet there is a vast and necessary distinction, which I can best explain by an illustration.

Since the beginning of the present century, the science of agriculture has made great progress, and the effects of that progress are to be seen in the great increase in food for man and beast, the great extension of tillage, and the improvement in the means of increasing our green crops. For instance, since the time of Charles I., great sums have been applied in Cambridgeshire, Lincolnshire, and adjoining counties in the erection of dykes, and making new channels to the sea for the lazy rivers that pass through what is called the Bedford Level. But it is only of late years that a skilful engineer, acting in conjunction with Mr. Brassey, has transformed a shallow lake, which I had known for many years as Whittlesea Mere, into fertile fields, producing barley and oats, turnips and clover. Such is true progress. I will take an instance of false progress from the author of two of the cleverest books in our language, 'The Tale of a Tub' and 'Gulliver's Travels.' In the latter of these works Swift relates that an ingenious philosopher of Laputa taught that the germinal principle of corn was really to be found in chaff. He had tried the experiment for many years, but had never succeeded in producing a good crop of wheat.

Such are some of the projects to which our philosophers and advanced Liberals, emulating the philosopher of Laputa, give the name of progress. But they are no more successful than their unhappy predecessor. Secrecy and falsehood, evasions and misrepresentations are tried in vain, and the teachers of those arts are obliged to confess that true progress is not to be attained by a thousand bushels of chaff, and that no harvest is gathered from their mistaken industry.

Before I ask the reader to consider the state of Christianity in the established communities of Europe and of America, I will ask him to cast his eye upon a table formed by a society of Nonconformists containing the number of sittings in places of worship in sixty-

four towns frequented by members of the Established
Church, and by adherents to the voluntary principle :—

SITTINGS 1872.

In sixty-four towns.

Church of England	881,937
Wesleyans	283,440
Congregationalists	265,053
Baptists	189,247
Roman Catholics	117,976
Primitive Methodists	100,591
United Methodists	93,534
New Connexion Methodists	54,112
Presbyterians	66,532
Unitarians	35,244
Society of Friends	23,981

In looking at the present state of Christianity in
Europe, and the progress of opinion among the Christian communities of America, Asia, and Africa, there
is much to encourage Christianity ; great reason
for hope, and no ground for despair. In France
and Italy civil marriage has been established, and no
other marriage is legal. In France and Italy education is in the hands of the State, and is making great
progress. In Austria there existed a few years ago by
a *concordatum*, or treaty made with the Pope, a complete
control over education in the hands of the bishops.
But the authority of this treaty has been entirely over-
thrown, and by recent legislation the State is fully
empowered to deal with education as it thinks fit. In
Russia religious liberty is subject to violent interference
authorised by the Emperor. By the laws of England
the religious rites sanctioned by different denomina-
tions for marriage are protected and registered ; civil

marriages also are sanctioned by-law. In Ireland the Roman Catholic Church has of late years interfered with religious liberty on the subject of education, but it is to be hoped that this interference will not be much longer permitted. Nearly two centuries ago the Parliament of England proclaimed religious liberty by the Toleration Act. Forty years ago Sir Robert Peel, while proposing the admission of Roman Catholics to Parliament, and to political office, bound them to take an oath, that neither the Pope nor any other foreign prince could claim any temporal jurisdiction in the United Kingdom. In the United States of America religious liberty is permanently and universally established. British subjects in India and in the colonies enjoy the same rights as the Queen's subjects in England.

The intolerance which used to prevail to the injury of Roman Catholics in Sweden has been greatly mitigated of late years, but I fear that religious liberty is not fully established.

Thus, upon the whole, the prospects of religious liberty among the Christian communities of the world have of late years become far brighter than they had been during the whole period which has elapsed from the reign of Tiberius to the present time. It was of little advantage to a Christian subject of a Roman Emperor that a Gallio should take no heed of his religion, if a Pliny could put him to death because he would neither adore the Emperor nor abjure Christ. Let us hope that before long a boy of Irish parents may not be separated from the children of Protestant

parents from a fear lest his faith and morals should be
endangered by their learning together the mysteries of
the multiplication table, and that in the German provinces of Russia a young girl of fourteen years old
may not be kept twelve hours of the night without
food in order to compel her to embrace the orthodoxy of
the Greek Church.   I trust the time is coming when in
regard to moral as to physical darkness the Divine
command will issue, ' LET THERE BE LIGHT, AND THERE
WAS LIGHT.'

LONDON : PRINTED BY
SPOTTISWOODE AND CO., NEW-STREET SQUARE
AND PARLIAMENT STREET

39 PATERNOSTER ROW, E.C.

LONDON: *November* 1872.

GENERAL LIST OF WORKS

PUBLISHED BY

Messrs. LONGMANS, GREEN, READER, and DYER.

History, Politics, Historical Memoirs, &c.

Estimates of the English Kings from William the Conqueror to George III. By J. LANGTON SANFORD, Author of 'Studies and Illustrations of the Great Rebellion' &c. Crown 8vo. price 12s. 6d.

The History of England from the Fall of Wolsey to the Defeat of the Spanish Armada. By JAMES ANTHONY FROUDE, M.A.

CABINET EDITION, 12 vols. cr. 8vo. £3 12s.
LIBRARY EDITION, 12 vols. 8vo. £8 18s.

The English in Ireland in the Eighteenth Century. By JAMES ANTHONY FROUDE, M.A. late Fellow of Exeter College, Oxford. In Two Volumes. VOL. I., 8vo. price 16s.

The History of England from the Accession of James II. By Lord MACAULAY :—

STUDENT'S EDITION, 2 vols. crown 8vo. 12s.
PEOPLE'S EDITION, 4 vols. crown 8vo. 16s.
CABINET EDITION, 8 vols. post 8vo. 48s.
LIBRARY EDITION, 5 vols. 8vo. £4.

Lord Macaulay's Works. Complete and uniform Library Edition. Edited by his Sister, Lady TREVELYAN. 8 vols. 8vo. with Portrait, price £5. 5s. cloth, or £8. 8s. bound in tree-calf by Rivière.

Memoirs of Baron Stockmar. By his Son, Baron E. VON STOCKMAR. Translated from the German by G. A. M. Edited by MAX MÜLLER, M.A. 2 vols. crown 8vo. price 21s.

Varieties of Vice-Regal Life. By Major-General Sir WILLIAM DENISON, K.C.B. late Governor-General of the Australian Colonies, and Governor of Madras. With Two Maps. 2 vols. 8vo. 28s.

On Parliamentary Government in England : its Origin, Development, and Practical Operation. By ALPHEUS TODD, Librarian of the Legislative Assembly of Canada. 2 vols. 8vo. price £1. 17s.

The Constitutional History of England since the Accession of George III. 1760—1860. By Sir THOMAS ERSKINE MAY, K.C.B. Cabinet Edition (the Third), thoroughly revised. 3 vols. crown 8vo. price 18s.

A Historical Account of the Neu- trality of Great Britain during the American Civil War. By MOUNTAGUE BERNARD, M.A. Royal 8vo. price 16s.

The History of England, from the Earliest Times to the Year 1865. By C. D. YONGE, Regius Professor of Modern History in Queen's College, Belfast. New Edition. Crown 8vo. 7s. 6d.

A

Lectures on the History of England, from the Earliest Times to the Death of King Edward II. By WILLIAM LONGMAN. With Maps and Illustrations. 8vo. 15s.

The History of the Life and Times of Edward the Third. By WILLIAM LONGMAN. With 9 Maps, 8 Plates, and 16 Woodcuts. 2 vols. 8vo. 28s.

History of Civilization in England and France, Spain and Scotland. By HENRY THOMAS BUCKLE. New Edition of the entire work, with a complete INDEX. 3 vols. crown 8vo. 24s.

Realities of Irish Life. By W. STEUART TRENCH, Land Agent in Ireland to the Marquess of Lansdowne, the Marquess of Bath, and Lord Digby. Fifth Edition. Crown 8vo. 6s.

The Student's Manual of the History of Ireland. By M. F. CUSACK, Authoress of 'The Illustrated History of Ireland.' Crown 8vo. price 6s.

A Student's Manual of the History of India, from the Earliest Period to the Present. By Colonel MEADOWS TAYLOR, M.R.A.S. M.R.I.A. Crown 8vo. with Maps, 7s. 6d.

The History of India, from the Earliest Period to the close of Lord Dalhousie's Administration. By JOHN CLARK MARSHMAN. 3 vols. crown 8vo. 22s. 6d.

Indian Polity; a View of the System of Administration in India. By Lieut.-Col. GEORGE CHESNEY. Second Edition, revised, with Map. 8vo. 21s.

A Colonist on the Colonial Question. By JEHU MATHEWS, of Toronto, Canada. Post 8vo. price 6s.

An Historical View of Literature and Art in Great Britain from the Accession of the House of Hanover to the Reign of Queen Victoria. By J. MURRAY GRAHAM, M.A. 8vo. price 14s.

Waterloo Lectures: a Study of the Campaign of 1815. By Colonel CHARLES C. CHESNEY, R.E. late Professor of Military Art and History in the Staff College. Second Edition. 8vo. with Map, 10s. 6d.

Memoir and Correspondence relating to Political Occurrences in June and July 1834. By EDWARD JOHN LITTLETON, First Lord Hatherton. Edited, from the Original Manuscript, by HENRY REEVE, C.B. D.C.L. 8vo. price 7s. 6d.

Chapters from French History; St. Louis, Joan of Arc, Henri IV. with Sketches of the Intermediate Periods. By J. H. GURNEY, M.A. New Edition. Fcp. 8vo. 6s. 6d.

History of the Reformation in Europe in the Time of Calvin. By J. H. MERLE D'AUBIGNÉ, D.D. VOLS. I. and II. 8vo. 28s. VOL. III. 12s. VOL. IV. price 16s. and VOL. V. price 16s.

Royal and Republican France. A Series of Essays reprinted from the 'Edinburgh,' 'Quarterly,' and 'British and Foreign' Reviews. By HENRY REEVE, C.B. D.C.L. 2 vols. 8vo. price 21s.

The Imperial and Colonial Constitutions of the Britannic Empire, including Indian Institutions. By Sir EDWARD CREASY, M.A. &c. With Six Maps. 8vo. price 15s.

Home Politics: being a Consideration of the Causes of the Growth of Trade in relation to Labour, Pauperism, and Emigration. By DANIEL GRANT. 8vo. 7s.

The Oxford Reformers—John Colet, Erasmus, and Thomas More; being a History of their Fellow-Work. By FREDERIC SEEBOHM. Second Edition. 8vo. 14s.

The History of Greece. By C. THIRLWALL, D.D. Lord Bishop of St. David's. 8 vols. fcp. 28s.

The Tale of the Great Persian War, from the Histories of Herodotus. By GEORGE W. COX, M.A. late Scholar of Trin. Coll. Oxon. Fcp. 3s. 6d.

The Sixth Oriental Monarchy; or, the History, Geography, and Antiquities of Parthia. Collected and Illustrated from Ancient and Modern sources. By GEORGE RAWLINSON, M.A. Camden Professor of Ancient History in the University of Oxford, and Canon of Canterbury. 8vo. with Maps and Illustrations. [*Nearly ready.*

Greek History from Themistocles to Alexander, in a Series of Lives from Plutarch. Revised and arranged by A. H. CLOUGH. Fcp. with 44 Woodcuts, 6s.

Critical History of the Language and Literature of Ancient Greece. By WILLIAM MURE, of Caldwell. 5 vols. 8vo. £3 9s.

History of the Literature of Ancient Greece. By Professor K. O. MÜLLER. Translated by LEWIS and DONALDSON. 3 vols. 8vo. 21s.

Biographical Works.

Life of Alexander von Humboldt. Compiled, in Commemoration of the Centenary of his Birth, by JULIUS LÖWENBERG, ROBERT AVÉ-LALLEMANT, and ALFRED DOVE. Edited by Professor KARL BRUHNS, Director of the Observatory at Leipzig. Translated from the German by JANE and CAROLINE LASSELL. 2 vols. 8vo. with Three Portraits.   [*Nearly ready.*

Autobiography of John Milton; or, Milton's Life in his own Words. By the Rev. JAMES J. G. GRAHAM, M.A. Crown 8vo. with Vignette-Portrait, price 5s.

Recollections of Past Life. By Sir HENRY HOLLAND, Bart. M.D. F.R.S., &c. Physician-in-Ordinary to the Queen. Second Edition. Post 8vo. 10s. 6d.

Biographical and Critical Essays. By A. HAYWARD, Esq., Q.C. A New Series. 2 vols. 8vo.   [*In the press.*

The Life of Isambard Kingdom Brunel, Civil Engineer. By ISAMBARD BRUNEL, B.C.L. of Lincoln's Inn, Chancellor of the Diocese of Ely. With Portrait, Plates, and Woodcuts. 8vo. 21s.

Lord George Bentinck; a Political Biography. By the Right Hon. B. DISRAELI, M.P. Eighth Edition, revised, with a new Preface. Crown 8vo. 6s.

The Life and Letters of the Rev. Sydney Smith. Edited by his Daughter, Lady HOLLAND, and Mrs. AUSTIN. New Edition, complete in One Volume. Crown 8vo. price 6s.

Memoir of George Edward Lynch Cotton, D.D. Bishop of Calcutta, and Metropolitan. With Selections from his Journals and Correspondence. Edited by Mrs. COTTON. New Edition. Crown 8vo.   [*Just ready.*

The Life and Travels of George Whitefield, M.A. By JAMES PATERSON GLEDSTONE. 8vo. price 14s.

The Life and Times of Sixtus the Fifth. By Baron HÜBNER. Translated from the Original French, with the Author's sanction, by HUBERT E. H. JERNINGHAM. 2 vols. 8vo. 24s.

Essays in Ecclesiastical Biogra-phy. By the Right Hon. Sir J. STEPHEN, LL.D. Cabinet Edition. Crown 8vo. 7s. 6d.

Father Mathew; a Biography. By JOHN FRANCIS MAGUIRE, M.P. Popular Edition, with Portrait. Crown 8vo. 3s. 6d.

The Life and Letters of Faraday By Dr. BENCE JONES, Secretary of the Royal Institution. Second Edition, with Portrait and Woodcuts. 2 vols. 8vo. 28s.

Faraday as a Discoverer. BY JOHN TYNDALL, LL.D. F.R.S. New and Cheap Edition, with Two Portraits. Fcp. 8vo price 3s. 6d.

The Royal Institution: its Found and its First Professors. By Dr. BENCE JONES, Honorary Secretary. Post 8vo price 12s. 6d.

Leaders of Public Opinion in Irland; Swift, Flood, Grattan, O'Connell By W. E. H. LECKY, M.A. New Edition revised and enlarged. Crown 8vo. 7s. 6d.

A Group of Englishmen (1795 1815); Records of the Younger Wedgwoods and their Friends, embracing the History the Discovery of Photography. By ELIZA METEYARD. 8vo. 16s.

Life of the Duke of Wellington By the Rev. G. R. GLEIG, M.A. Popular Edition, carefully revised; with copious Additions. Crown 8vo. with Portrait, 5s.

Dictionary of General Biography containing Concise Memoirs and Notices the most Eminent Persons of all Countries from the Earliest Ages to the Present Time. Edited by WILLIAM L. R. CATES. 8vo price 21s.

Letters and Life of Francis Bacon, including all his Occasional Works. Collected and edited, with a Commentary by J. SPEDDING. VOLS. I. to VI. 8vo price £3. 12s. To be completed in One more Volume.

Felix Mendelssohn's Letters from *Italy and Switzerland*, and *Letters* from 1833 to 1847, translated by Lady WALLACE. With Portrait. 2 vols. crown 8vo. 5s. each.

Musical Criticism and Biography Selected from the Published and Unpublished Writings of THOMAS DAMANT EATON, late President of the Norwich Choral Society. Edited by his SONS. Crown 8vo.

Lives of the Queens of England By AGNES STRICKLAND. Library Edition newly revised; with Portraits of every Queen, Autographs, and Vignettes. 8 vols post 8vo. 7s. 6d. each.

History of my Religious Opinions. By J. H. NEWMAN, D.D. Being the Substance of Apologia pro Vitâ Suâ. Post 8vo. price 6s.

Memoirs of Sir Henry Havelock, K.C.B. By JOHN CLARK MARSHMAN. People's Edition, with Portrait. Crown 8vo. price 3s. 6d.

Vicissitudes of Families. By Sir J. BERNARD BURKE, C.B. Ulster King of Arms. New Edition, remodelled and enlarged. 2 vols. crown 8vo. 21s.

Maunder's Biographical Treasury. Thirteenth Edition, reconstructed and partly re-written, with above 1,000 additional Memoirs, by W. L. R. CATES. Fcp. 8vo.6s.

Criticism, Philosophy, Polity, &c.

On Representative Government. By JOHN STUART MILL. Third Edition. 8vo. 9s. crown 8vo. 2s.

On Liberty. By the same Author. Fourth Edition. Post 8vo. 7s. 6d. Crown 8vo. 1s. 4d.

Principles of Political Economy. By the same. Seventh Edition. 2 vols. 8vo. 30s. or in 1 vol. crown 8vo. 5s.

Utilitarianism. By the same. 4th Edit.8vo.5s.

Dissertations and Discussions. By the same Author. Second Edition. 3 vols. 8vo. price 36s.

Examination of Sir W. Hamilton's Philosophy, and of the principal Philosophical Questions discussed in his Writings. By the same. Third Edition. 8vo. 16s.

The Subjection of Women. By JOHN STUART MILL. New Edition. Post 8vo. 5s.

Analysis of the Phenomena of the Human Mind. By JAMES MILL. A New Edition, with Notes, Illustrative and Critical, by ALEXANDER BAIN, ANDREW FINDLATER, and GEORGE GROTE. Edited, with additional Notes, by JOHN STUART MILL. 2 vols. 8vo. price 28s.

Principles of Political Philosophy; being the Second Edition, revised and extended, of 'The Elements of Political Economy.' By H. D. MACLEOD, M.A., Barrister-at-Law. In Two Volumes. VOL. I. 8vo. price 15s.

A Dictionary of Political Economy; Biographical, Bibliographical, Historical, and Practical. By the same Author. VOL. I. royal 8vo. 30s.

A Systematic View of the Science of Jurisprudence. By SHELDON AMOS, M.A. Professor of Jurisprudence, University College, London. 8vo. price 18s.

The Institutes of Justinian; with English Introduction, Translation, and Notes. By T. C. SANDARS, M.A. Barrister-at-Law. New Edition. 8vo. 15s.

Lord Bacon's Works, collected and edited by R. L. ELLIS, M.A. J. SPEDDING, M.A. and D. D. HEATH. New and Cheaper Edition. 7 vols. 8vo. price £3. 13s. 6d.

A System of Logic, Ratiocinative and Inductive. By JOHN STUART MILL. Eighth Edition. 2 vols. 8vo. 25s.

The Ethics of Aristotle; with Essays and Notes. By Sir A. GRANT, Bart. M.A. LL.D. Third Edition, revised and partly re-written. [In the press.

The Nicomachean Ethics of Aristotle. Newly translated into English. By R. WILLIAMS, B.A. Fellow and late Lecturer Merton College, Oxford. 8vo. 12s.

Bacon's Essays, with Annotations. By R. WHATELY, D.D. late Archbishop of Dublin. Sixth Edition. 8vo. 10s. 6d.

Elements of Logic. By R. WHATELY, D.D. late Archbishop of Dublin. New Edition. 8vo. 10s. 6d. crown 8vo. 4s. 6d.

Elements of Rhetoric. By the same Author. New Edition. 8vo. 10s. 6d. Crown 8vo. 4s. 6d.

English Synonymes. By E. JANEWHATELY. Edited by Archbishop WHATELY. 5th Edition. Fcp. 3s.

An Outline of the Necessary Laws of Thought: a Treatise on Pure and Applied Logic. By the Most Rev. W. THOMSON, D.D. Archbishop of York. Ninth Thousand. Crown 8vo. 5s. 6d.

Causality; or, the Philosophy of Law Investigated. By GEORGE JAMIESON, B.D. of Old Machar. Second Edition, greatly enlarged. 8vo. price 12s.

Speeches of the Right Hon. Lord MACAULAY, corrected by Himself. People's Edition, crown 8vo. 3s. 6d.

Lord Macaulay's Speeches on Parliamentary Reform in 1831 and 1832. 16mo. price ONE SHILLING.

A Dictionary of the English Language. By R. G. LATHAM, M.A. M.D. F.R.S. Founded on the Dictionary of Dr. S. JOHNSON, as edited by the Rev. H. J. TODD, with numerous Emendations and Additions. 4 vols. 4to. price £7.

Thesaurus of English Words and Phrases, classified and arranged so as to facilitate the expression of Ideas, and assist in Literary Composition. By P. M. ROGET, M.D. New Edition. Crown 8vo. 10s. 6d.

Three Centuries of English Literature. By CHARLES DUKE YONGE, Regius Professor of Modern History and English Literature in Queen's College, Belfast. Crown 8vo. 7s. 6d.

Lectures on the Science of Language. By F. MAX MÜLLER, M.A. &c. Foreign Member of the French Institute. Sixth Edition. 2 vols. crown 8vo. price 16s.

Chapters on Language. By F. W. FARRAR, M.A. F.R.S. Head Master of Marlborough College. Crown 8vo. 8s. 6d.

Southey's Doctor, complete in One Volume, edited by the Rev. J. W. WARTER, B.D. Square crown 8vo. 12s. 6d.

Manual of English Literature, Historical and Critical; with a Chapter on English Metres. By THOMAS ARNOLD, M.A. Second Edition. Crown 8vo. 7s. 6d.

A Latin-English Dictionary. By JOHN T. WHITE, D.D. Oxon. and J. E. RIDDLE, M.A. Oxon. Third Edition, revised. 2 vols. 4to. pp. 2,128, price 42s.

White's College Latin-English Dictionary (Intermediate Size), abridged from the Parent Work for the use of University Students. Medium 8vo. pp. 1,048, price 18s.

White's Junior Student's Complete Latin-English and English-Latin Dictionary. Revised Edition. Square 12mo. pp. 1,058, price 12s.

Separately { ENGLISH-LATIN, 5s. 6d. { LATIN-ENGLISH, 7s. 6d.

An English-Greek Lexicon, containing all the Greek Words used by Writers of good authority. By C. D. YONGE, B.A. New Edition. 4to. 21s.

Mr. Yonge's New Lexicon, En-glish and Greek, abridged from his larger work (as above). Square 12mo. 8s. 6d.

A Greek-English Lexicon. Compiled by H. G. LIDDELL, D.D. Dean of Christ Church, and R. SCOTT, D.D. Dean of Rochester. Sixth Edition. Crown 4to price 36s.

A Lexicon, Greek and English, abridged for Schools from LIDDELL and SCOTT's Greek-English Lexicon. Fourteenth Edition. Square 12mo. 7s. 6d.

The Mastery of Languages; or the Art of Speaking Foreign Tongues Idiomatically. By THOMAS PRENDERGAST late of the Civil Service at Madras. Second Edition. 8vo. 6s.

A Practical Dictionary of the French and English Languages. By Professor LÉON CONTANSEAU, many year French Examiner for Military and Civil Appointments, &c. New Edition, carefully revised. Post 8vo. 10s. 6d.

Contanseau's Pocket Dictionary, French and English, abridged from the Practical Dictionary, by the Author. New Edition. 18mo. price 3s. 6d.

A Sanskrit-English Dictionary. The Sanskrit words printed both in the original Devanagari and in Roman letters with References to the Best Editions of Sanskrit Authors, and with Etymologie and comparisons of Cognate Words chiefly in Greek, Latin, Gothic, and Anglo-Saxon Compiled by T. BENFEY. 8vo. 52s. 6d.

New Practical Dictionary of the German Language; German-English, and English-German. By the Rev. W. I BLACKLEY, M.A. and Dr. CARL MARTIN FRIEDLÄNDER. Post 8vo. 7s. 6d.

Historical and Critical Commentary on the Old Testament; with a New Translation. By M. M. KALISCH, Ph.D Vol. I. Genesis, 8vo. 18s. or adapted for the General Reader, 12s. Vol. II. Exodus, 15. or adapted for the General Reader, 12. Vol III. Leviticus, Part I. 15s. or adapted for the General Reader, 8s. Vol. IV. Leviticus, Part II. 15s. or adapted for the General Reader, 8s.

A Hebrew Grammar, with Exercises By the same. Part I. Outlines with Exercises, 8vo. 12s. 6d. KEY, 5s. Part II. Exceptional Forms and Constructions, 12s. 6d

---

Miscellaneous Works and Popular Metaphysics.

An Introduction to Mental Philosophy, on the Inductive Method. By J. D. MORELL, M.A. LL.D. 8vo. 12s.

Elements of Psychology, containing the Analysis of the Intellectual Powers By J. D. MORELL, LL.D. Post 8vo. 7s. 6d

Recreations of a Country Parson. By A. K. H. B. Two Series, 3s. 6d. each.

Seaside Musings on Sundays and Weekdays. By A. K. H. B. Crown 8vo. price 3s. 6d.

Present-Day Thoughts. By A. K. H. B. Crown 8vo. 3s. 6d.

Changed Aspects of Unchanged Truths; Memorials of St. Andrews Sundays. By A. K. H. B. Crown 8vo. 3s. 6d.

Counsel and Comfort from a City Pulpit. By A. K. H. B. Crown 8vo. 3s. 6d.

Lessons of Middle Age, with some Account of various Cities and Men. By A. K. H. B. Crown 8vo. 3s. 6d.

Leisure Hours in Town; Essays Consolatory, Æsthetical, Moral, Social, and Domestic. By A. K. H. B. Crown 8vo. 3s. 6d.

Sunday Afternoons at the Parish Church of a Scottish University City. By A. K. H. B. Crown 8vo. 3s. 6d.

The Commonplace Philosopher in Town and Country. By A. K. H. B. 3s. 6d.

The Autumn Holidays of a Country Parson. By A. K. H. B. Crown 8vo. 3s. 6d.

Critical Essays of a Country Parson. By A. K. H. B. Crown 8vo. 3s. 6d.

The Graver Thoughts of a Country Parson. By A. K. H. B. Two Series, 3s. 6d. each.

Miscellaneous and Posthumous Works of the late Henry Thomas Buckle. Edited, with a Biographical Notice by HELEN TAYLOR. 3 vols. 8vo. price 2l. 12s. 6d.

Short Studies on Great Subjects. By JAMES ANTHONY FROUDE, M.A. late Fellow of Exeter College, Oxford. 2 vols. crown 8vo. price 12s.

Miscellaneous Writings of John Conington, M.A. late Corpus Professor of Latin in the University of Oxford. Edited by J. A. SYMONDS, M.A. With a Memoir by H. J. S. SMITH, M.A. LL.D. F.R.S. 2 vols. 8vo. price 28s.

The Rev. Sydney Smith's Miscellaneous Works. 1 vol. crown 8vo. 6s.

The Wit and Wisdom of the Rev. SYDNEY SMITH; a Selection of the most memorable Passages in his Writings and Conversation. Crown 8vo. 3s. 6d.

The Eclipse of Faith; or, a Visit to a Religious Sceptic. By HENRY ROGERS. Twelfth Edition. Fcp. 8vo. 5s.

Defence of the Eclipse of Faith, by its Author. Third Edition. Fcp. 8vo. 3s. 6d.

Lord Macaulay's Miscellaneous Writings:— LIBRARY EDITION, 2 vols. 8vo. Portrait, 21s. PEOPLE'S EDITION, 1 vol. crown 8vo. 4s. 6d.

Lord Macaulay's Miscellaneous Writings and SPEECHES. Student's Edition, in One Volume, crown 8vo. price 6s.

Families of Speech, Four Lectures delivered at the Royal Institution of Great Britain. By the Rev. F. W. FARRAR, M.A. F.R.S. Post 8vo. with 2 Maps, 5s. 6d.

Chips from a German Workshop; being Essays on the Science of Religion, and on Mythology, Traditions, and Customs. By F. MAX MÜLLER, M.A. &c. Foreign Member of the French Institute. 3 vols. 8vo. £2.

A Budget of Paradoxes. By AUGUSTUS DE MORGAN, F.R.A.S. and C.P.S. of Trinity College, Cambridge. Reprinted, with the Author's Additions, from the Athenæum. 8vo. price 15s.

The Secret of Hegel: being the Hegelian System in Origin, Principle, Form, and Matter. By JAMES HUTCHISON STIRLING. 2 vols. 8vo. 28s.

Sir William Hamilton; being the Philosophy of Perception: an Analysis. By JAMES HUTCHISON STIRLING. 8vo. 5s.

As Regards Protoplasm. By J. H. STIRLING, LL.D. Second Edition, with Additions, in reference to Mr. Huxley's Second Issue and a new PREFACE in reply to Mr. Huxley in 'Yeast.' 8vo. price 2s.

Ueberweg's System of Logic, and History of Logical Doctrines. Translated, with Notes and Appendices, by T. M. LINDSAY, M.A. F.R.S.E. 8vo. price 16s.

The Philosophy of Necessity; or, Natural Law as applicable to Mental, Moral, and Social Science. By CHARLES BRAY. Second Edition. 8vo. 9s.

A Manual of Anthropology, or Science of Man, based on Modern Research. By the same Author. Crown 8vo. 6s.

On Force, its Mental and Moral Correlates. By the same Author. 8vo. 5s.

The Discovery of a New World of Being. By GEORGE THOMSON. Post 8vo. 6s.

Time and Space; a Metaphysical Essay. By SHADWORTH H. HODGSON. 8vo. price 16s.

The Theory of Practice; an Ethical Inquiry. By SHADWORTH H. HODGSON. 2 vols. 8vo. price 24s.

The Senses and the Intellect.
By ALEXANDER BAIN, LL.D. Prof. of Logic in the Univ. of Aberdeen. Third Edition. 8vo. 15s.

Mental and Moral Science : a
Compendium of Psychology and Ethics. By ALEXANDER BAIN, LL.D. Third Edition. Crown 8vo. 10s. 6d. Or separately : PART I. *Mental Science*, 6s. 6d. PART II. *Moral Science*, 4s. 6d.

A Treatise on Human Nature
being an Attempt to Introduce the Experimental Method of Reasoning into Moral Subjects. By DAVID HUME. Edited, with Notes, &c. by T. H. GREEN, Fellow, and T. H. GROSE, late Scholar, of Balliol College, Oxford. 2 vols. 8vo.   [*In the press.*

Essays Moral, Political, and Literary. By DAVID HUME. By the same
Editors. 2 vols. 8vo.   [*In the press.*

Astronomy, Meteorology, Popular Geography, &c.

Outlines of Astronomy. By Sir
J. F. W. HERSCHEL, Bart. M.A. Eleventh Edition, with 9 Plates and numerous Diagrams. Square crown 8vo. 12s.

Essays on Astronomy. A Series of
Papers on Planets and Meteors, the Sun and sun-surrounding Space, Stars and Star Cloudlets; and a Dissertation on the approaching Transit of Venus : preceded by a Sketch of the Life and Work of Sir J. Herschel. By R. A. PROCTOR, B.A. With 10 Plates and 24 Woodcuts. 8vo. price 12s.

Schellen's Spectrum Analysis, in
its Application to Terrestrial Substances and the Physical Constitution of the Heavenly Bodies. Translated by JANE and C. LASSELL; edited, with Notes, by W. HUGGINS, LL.D. F.R.S. With 13 Plates (6 coloured) and 223 Woodcuts. 8vo. 28s.

The Sun; Ruler, Light, Fire, and
Life of the Planetary System. By RICHARD A. PROCTOR, B.A. F.R.A.S. Second Edition; with 10 Plates (7 coloured) and 107 Woodcuts. Crown 8vo. price 14s.

Saturn and its System. By the same
Author. 8vo. with 14 Plates, 14s.

Magnetism and Deviation of the
Compass. For the use of Students in Navigation and Science Schools. By JOHN MERRIFIELD, LL.D. F.R.A.S. With Diagrams. 18mo. price 1s. 6d.

Navigation and Nautical Astronomy (Practical, Theoretical, Scientific)
for the use of Students and Practical Men. By J. MERRIFIELD, F.R.A.S. and H. EVERS. 8vo. 14s.

Air and Rain; the Beginnings of
a Chemical Climatology. By ROBERT ANGUS SMITH, Ph.D. F.R.S. F.C.S. Government Inspector of Alkali Works, with 8 Illustrations. 8vo. price 24s.

The Star Depths; or, other Suns
than Ours; a Treatise on Stars, Star-Systems, and Star-Cloudlets. By R. A. PROCTOR, B.A. Crown 8vo. with numerous Illustrations.   [*Nearly ready.*

The Orbs Around Us; a Series
of Familiar Essays on the Moon and Planets, Meteors and Comets, the Sun and Coloured Pairs of Suns. By R. A. PROCTOR, B.A. Crown 8vo. price 7s. 6d.

Other Worlds than Ours; the
Plurality of Worlds Studied under the Light of Recent Scientific Researches. By R. A. PROCTOR, B.A. Third Edition revised and corrected; with 14 Illustrations. Crown 8vo. 10s. 6d.

Celestial Objects for Common
Telescopes. By T. W. WEBB, M.A. F.R.A.S. New Edition, revised, with Map of the Moon and Woodcuts.   [*In the press.*

A General Dictionary of Geography, Descriptive, Physical, Statistical
and Historical ; forming a complete Gazetteer of the World. By A. KEITH JOHNSTON, F.R.S.E. New Edition. 8vo. price 31s. 6d.

The Public Schools Atlas of
Modern Geography. In Thirty-one Maps exhibiting clearly the more important Physical Features of the Countries delineated, and Noting all the Chief Places Historical, Commercial, and Social Interest. Edited, with an Introduction, by the Rev. G. BUTLER, M.A. Imperial quarto, price 3s. 6d. sewed; 5s. cloth.

A New Star Atlas, for the Library
the School, and the Observatory, in Twelve Circular Maps (with Two Index Plates. Intended as a Companion to ' Webb's Celestial Objects for Common Telescopes.' With a Letterpress Introduction on the Study the Stars, illustrated by 9 Diagrams. By RICHARD A. PROCTOR, B.A. Hon. Sec. R.A.S. Crown 8vo. 5s.

Nautical Surveying, an Intro- duction to the Practical and Theoretical Study of. By JOHN KNOX LAUGHTON, M.A. F.R.A.S. Small 8vo. price 6s.

Maunder's Treasury of Geogra- phy, Physical, Historical, Descriptive, and Political. Edited by W. HUGHES, F.R.G.S. With 7 Maps and 16 Plates. Fcp. 8vo. 6s.

Natural History and *Popular Science.*

Natural Philosophy for General Readers and Young Persons; a Course of Physics divested of Mathematical Formulæ and expressed in the language of daily life. Translated from Ganot's *Cours de Physique*, by E. ATKINSON, Ph.D. Crown 8vo. with 404 Woodcuts, price 7s. 6d.

Mrs. Marcet's Conversations on Natural Philosophy. Revised by the Author's SON, and augmented by Conversations on Spectrum Analysis and Solar Chemistry. With 36 Plates. Crown 8vo. price 7s. 6d.

Ganot's Elementary Treatise on Physics, Experimental and Applied, for the use of Colleges and Schools. Translated and Edited with the Author's sanction by E. ATKINSON, Ph.D. F.C.S. New Edition, revised and enlarged; with a Coloured Plate and 726 Woodcuts. Post 8vo. 15s.

Text-Books of Science, Mechanical and Physical. The following may now be had, price 3s. 6d. each :—
1. GOODEVE's Mechanism.
2. BLOXAM's Metals.
3. MILLER's Inorganic Chemistry.
4. GRIFFIN's Algebra and Trigonometry.
5. WATSON's Plane and Solid Geometry.
6. MAXWELL's Theory of Heat.
7. MERRIFIELD's Technical Arithmetic and Mensuration.
8. ANDERSON's Strength of Materials.

Dove's Law of Storms, considered in connexion with the ordinary Movements of the Atmosphere. Translated by R. H. SCOTT, M.A. T.C.D. 8vo. 10s. 6d.

The Correlation of Physical Forces. By W. R. GROVE, Q.C. V.P.R.S. Fifth Edition, revised, and Augmented by a Discourse on Continuity. 8vo. 10s. 6d. The *Discourse*, separately, price 2s. 6d.

Fragments of Science. By JOHN TYNDALL, LL.D. F.R.S. Third Edition. 8vo. price 14s.

Heat a Mode of Motion. By JOHN TYNDALL, LL.D. F.R.S. Fourth Edition. Crown 8vo. with Woodcuts, price 10s. 6d.

Sound; a Course of Eight Lectures delivered at the Royal Institution of Great Britain. By JOHN TYNDALL, LL.D. F.R.S. New Edition, with Portrait and Woodcuts. Crown 8vo. 9s.

Researches on Diamagnetism and Magne-Crystallic Action; including the Question of Diamagnetic Polarity. By JOHN TYNDALL, LL.D. F.R.S. With 6 Plates and many Woodcuts. 8vo. 14s.

Notes of a Course of Nine Lec- tures on Light, delivered at the Royal Institution, A.D. 1869. By J. TYNDALL, LL.D. F.R.S. Crown 8vo. 1s. sewed, or 1s. 6d. cloth.

Notes of a Course of Seven Lec- tures on Electrical Phenomena and Theories, delivered at the Royal Institution, A.D. 1870. By JOHN TYNDALL, LL.D. F.R.S. Crown 8vo. 1s. sewed, or 1s. 6d. cloth.

A Treatise on Electricity, in Theory and Practice. By A. DE LA RIVE, Prof. in the Academy of Geneva. Translated by C. V. WALKER, F.R.S. 3 vols 8vo. with Woodcuts, £3. 13s.

Light Science for Leisure Hours; a Series of Familiar Essays on Scientific Subjects, Natural Phenomena, &c. By R. A. PROCTOR, B.A. Crown 8vo. price 7s. 6d.

Light: its Influence on Life and Health. By FORBES WINSLOW, M.D. D.C.L. Oxon. (Hon.) Fcp. 8vo. 6s.

Professor Owen's Lectures on the Comparative Anatomy and Physiology of the Invertebrate Animals. Second Edition, with 235 Woodcuts. 8vo. 21s.

The Comparative Anatomy and Physiology of the Vertebrate Animals. By RICHARD OWEN, F.R.S. D.C.L. With 1,472 Woodcuts. 3 vols. 8vo. £3 13s. 6d.

Kirby and Spence's Introduction to Entomology, or Elements of the Natural History of Insects. Crown 8vo. 5s.

Homes without Hands; a Description of the Habitations of Animals, classed according to their Principle of Construction. By Rev. J. G. WOOD, M.A. F.L.S. With about 140 Vignettes on Wood. 8vo. 21s.

Strange Dwellings; a Description of the Habitations of Animals, abridged from 'Homes without Hands.' By J. G. WOOD, M.A. F.L.S. With a New Frontispiece and about 60 other Woodcut Illustrations. Crown 8vo. price 7s. 6d.

B

Van Der Hoeven's Handbook of ZOOLOGY. Translated from the Second Dutch Edition by the Rev. W. CLARK, M.D. F.R.S. 2 vols. 8vo. with 24 Plates of Figures, 60s.

The Harmonies of Nature and Unity of Creation. By Dr. G. HARTWIG. 8vo. with numerous Illustrations, 18s.

The Sea and its Living Wonders. By the same Author. Third Edition, enlarged. 8vo. with many Illustrations, 21s.

The Subterranean World. By the same Author. With 3 Maps and about 80 Woodcut Illustrations, including 8 full size of page. 8vo. price 21s.

The Polar World: a Popular Description of Man and Nature in the Arctic and Antarctic Regions of the Globe. By the same Author. With 8 Chromoxylographs, 3 Maps, and 85 Woodcuts. 8vo. 21s.

A Familiar History of Birds. By E. STANLEY, D.D. late Lord Bishop of Norwich. Fcp. with Woodcuts, 3s. 6d.

Insects at Home; a Popular Account of British Insects, their Structure, Habits, and Transformations. By the Rev. J. G. WOOD, M.A. F.L.S. With upwards of 700 Illustrations engraved on Wood. 8vo. price 21s.

Insects Abroad; being a Popular Account of Foreign Insects, their Structure, Habits, and Transformations. By J. G. WOOD, M.A. F.L.S. Author of 'Homes without Hands' &c. In One Volume, printed and illustrated uniformly with 'Insects at Home,' to which it will form a Sequel and Companion.   [In the press.

The Primitive Inhabitants of Scandinavia. Containing a Description of the Implements, Dwellings, Tombs, and Mode of Living of the Savages in the North of Europe during the Stone Age. By SVEN NILSSON. 8vo. Plates and Woodcuts, 18s.

The Origin of Civilisation, and the Primitive Condition of Man; Mental and Social Condition of Savages. By Sir JOHN LUBBOCK, Bart. M.P. F.R.S. Second Edition, with 25 Woodcuts. 8vo. 16s.

The Ancient Stone Implements, Weapons, and Ornaments, of Great Britain. By JOHN EVANS, F.R.S. F.S.A. 8vo. with 2 Plates and 476 Woodcuts, price 28s.

Mankind, their Origin and Des tiny. By an M.A. of Balliol College Oxford. Containing a New Translation of the First Three Chapters of Genesis; Critical Examination of the First Two Gospels; an Explanation of the Apocalypse and the Origin and Secret Meaning of the Mythological and Mystical Teaching of the Ancients. With 31 Illustrations. 8vo price 31s. 6d.

An Exposition of Fallacies in th Hypothesis of Mr. Darwin. By C. R. BREE M.D. F.Z.S. Author of 'Birds of Europe no Observed in the British Isles' &c. With 36 Woodcuts. Crown 8vo. price 14s.

Bible Animals; a Description of ever Living Creature mentioned in the Scrip tures, from the Ape to the Coral. By the Rev. J. G. WOOD, M.A. F.L.S. With about 100 Vignettes on Wood. 8vo. 21s.

Maunder's Treasury of Nature History, or Popular Dictionary of Zoolog Revised and corrected by T. S. COBBOLI M.D. Fcp. 8vo. with 900 Woodcuts, 6s.

The Elements of Botany fo Families and Schools. Tenth Edition, r vised by THOMAS MOORE, F.L.S. Fc with 154 Woodcuts, 2s. 6d.

The Treasury of Botany, o Popular Dictionary of the Vegetable King dom; with which is incorporated a Glo sary of Botanical Terms. Edited b J. LINDLEY, F.R.S. and T. MOORE, F.L.: Pp. 1,274, with 274 Woodcuts and 20 Ste Plates. TWO PARTS, fcp. 8vo. 12s.

The Rose Amateur's Guide. By THOMAS RIVERS. New Edition. Fcp. 4s

Loudon's Encyclopædia of Plant comprising the Specific Character, Descrip tion, Culture, History, &c. of all the Plan found in Great Britain. With upwards 12,000 Woodcuts. 8vo. 42s.

Maunder's Scientific and Lite rary Treasury; a Popular Encyclopædia Science, Literature, and Art. New Editio in part rewritten, with above 1,000 ne articles, by J. Y. JOHNSON. Fcp. 6s.

A Dictionary of Science, Liters ture, and Art. Fourth Edition, re-edite by the late W. T. BRANDE (the Autho and GEORGE W. COX, M.A. 3 vols. mediu 8vo. price 63s. cloth.

Chemistry, Medicine, Surgery, and the Allied Sciences.

A Dictionary of Chemistry and the Allied Branches of other Sciences. By HENRY WATTS, F.C.S. assisted by eminent Scientific and Practical Chemists. 5 vols. medium 8vo. price £7 3s.

Supplement, completing the Record of Discovery to the end of 1869.· 8vo. 31s. 6d.

Contributions to Molecular Physics in the domain of Radiant Heat; a Series of Memoirs published in the Philosophical Transactions, &c. By JOHN TYNDALL, LL.D. F.R.S. With 2 Plates and 31 Woodcuts. 8vo. price 16s.

Elements of Chemistry, Theoretical and Practical. By WILLIAM A. MILLER, M.D. LL.D. Professor of Chemistry, King's College, London. New Edition. 3 vols. 8vo. £3.

PART I. CHEMICAL PHYSICS, 15s.
PART II. INORGANIC CHEMISTRY, 21s.
PART III. ORGANIC CHEMISTRY, 24s.

A Course of Practical Chemistry, for the use of Medical Students. By W. ODLING, M.B. F.R.S. New Edition, with 70 new Woodcuts. Crown 8vo. 7s. 6d.

Outlines of Chemistry; or, Brief Notes of Chemical Facts. By the same Author. Crown 8vo. 7s. 6d.

A Manual of Chemical Physiology, including its Points of Contact with Pathology. By J. L. W. THUDICHUM, M.D. 8vo. with Woodcuts, price 7s. 6d.

Select Methods in Chemical Analysis, chiefly Inorganic. By WILLIAM ˙CROOKES, F.R.S. With 22 Woodcuts. Crown 8vo. price 12s. 6d.

Chemical Notes for the Lecture Room. By THOMAS WOOD, F.C.S. 2 vols. crown 8vo. I. on Heat, &c. price 5s. II. on the Metals, price 5s.

The Diagnosis, Pathology, and Treatment of Diseases of Women; including the Diagnosis of Pregnancy. By GRAILY HEWITT, M.D. &c. Third Edition, revised and for the most part re-written; with 132 Woodcuts. 8vo. 24s.

Lectures on the Diseases of Infancy and Childhood. By CHARLES WEST, M.D. &c. Fifth Edition. 8vo. 16s.

On Some Disorders of the Nervous System in Childhood. Being the Lumleian Lectures delivered before the Royal College of Physicians in March 1871. By CHARLES WEST, M.D. Crown 8vo. 5s.

On the Surgical Treatment of Children's Diseases. By T. HOLMES, M.A. &c. late Surgeon to the Hospital for Sick Children. Second Edition, with 9 Plates and 112 Woodcuts. 8vo. 21s.

Lectures on the Principles and Practice of Physic. By Sir THOMAS WATSON, Bart. M.D. Physician-in-Ordinary to the Queen. Fifth Edition, thoroughly revised. 2 vols. 8vo. price 36s.

Lectures on Surgical Pathology. By Sir JAMES PAGET, Bart. F.R.S. Third Edition, revised and re-edited by the Author and Professor W. TURNER, M.B. 8vo. with 131 Woodcuts, 21s.

Cooper's Dictionary of Practical Surgery and Encyclopædia of Surgical Science. New Edition, brought down to the present time. By S. A. LANE, Surgeon to St. Mary's Hospital, &c. assisted by various Eminent Surgeons. 2 vols. 8vo. price 25s. each.

Pulmonary Consumption; its Nature, Varieties, and Treatment: with an Analysis of One Thousand Cases to exemplify its Duration. By C. J. B. WILLIAMS, M.D. F.R.S. and C. T. WILLIAMS, M.A. M.D. Oxon. Post 8vo. price 10s. 6d.

Anatomy, Descriptive and Surgical. By HENRY GRAY, F.R.S. With about 410 Woodcuts from Dissections. Sixth Edition, by T. HOLMES, M.A. Cantab. With a New Introduction by the Editor. Royal 8vo. 28s.

The House I Live in; or, Popular Illustrations of the Structure and Functions of the Human Body. Edited by T. G. GIRTIN. New Edition, with 25 Woodcuts. 16mo. price 2s. 6d.

The Science and Art of Surgery; being a Treatise on Surgical Injuries, Diseases, and Operations. By JOHN ERIC ERICHSEN, Senior Surgeon to University College Hospital, and Holme Professor of Clinical Surgery in University College, London. A New Edition, being the Sixth, revised and enlarged; with 712 Woodcuts. 2 vols. 8vo. price 32s.

A System of Surgery, Theoretical and Practical, in Treatises by Various Authors. Edited by T. HOLMES, M.A. &c. Surgeon and Lecturer on Surgery at St. George's Hospital, and Surgeon-in-Chief to the Metropolitan Police. Second Edition, thoroughly revised, with numerous Illustrations. 5 vols. 8vo. £5 5s.

Clinical Lectures on Diseases of the Liver, Jaundice, and Abdominal Dropsy. By C. Murchison, M.D. Physician to the Middlesex Hospital. Post 8vo. with 25 Woodcuts, 10s. 6d.

Todd and Bowman's Physio-logical Anatomy and Physiology of Man. With numerous Illustrations. Vol. II. 8vo. price 25s.

Vol. I. New Edition by Dr. Lionel S. Beale, F.R.S. in course of publication, with numerous Illustrations. Parts I. and II. price 7s. 6d. each.

Outlines of Physiology, Human and Comparative. By John Marshall, F.R.C.S. Surgeon to the University College Hospital. 2 vols. crown 8vo. with 122 Woodcuts, 32s.

Copland's Dictionary of Practical Medicine, abridged from the larger work. and throughout brought down to the present state of Medical Science. 8vo. 36s.

Dr. Pereira's Elements of Materia Medica and Therapeutics, abridged and adapted for the use of Medical and Pharmaceutical Practitioners and Students. Edited by Professor Bentley, F.L.S. &c. and by Dr. Redwood, F.C.S. &c. With 125 Woodcut Illustrations. 8vo. price 25s.

The Essentials of Materia Medica and Therapeutics. By Alfred Baring Garrod, M.D. F.R.S. &c. Physician to King's College Hospital. Third Edition, Sixth Impression, brought up to 1870 Crown 8vo. price 12s. 6d.

The Fine Arts, and *Illustrated Editions.*

Grotesque Animals, invented, described, and portrayed by E. W. Cooke, R.A.'F.R.S. in Twenty-Four Plates, with Elucidatory Comments. Royal 4to. price 21s.

In Fairyland; Pictures from the Elf-World. By Richard Doyle. With a Poem by W. Allingham. With Sixteen Plates, containing Thirty-six Designs printed in Colours. Folio, 31s. 6d.

Albert Durer, his Life and Works; including Autobiographical Papers and Complete Catalogues. By William B. Scott. With Six Etchings by the Author and other Illustrations. 8vo. 16s.

Half-Hour Lectures on the His-tory and Practice of the Fine and Ornamental Arts. By. W. B. Scott. Second Edition. Crown 8vo. with 50 Woodcut Illustrations, 8s. 6d.

The Chorale Book for England: the Hymns Translated by Miss C. Winkworth; the Tunes arranged by Prof. W. S. Bennett and Otto Goldschmidt. Fcp. 4to. 12s. 6d.

The New Testament, illustrated with Wood Engravings after the Early Masters, chiefly of the Italian School. Crown 4to. 63s. cloth, gilt top ; or £5 5s. morocco.

The Life of Man Symbolised by the Months of the Year in their Seasons and Phases. Text selected by Richard Pigot. 25 Illustrations on Wood from Original Designs by John Leighton, F.S.A. Quarto, 42s.

Cats and Farlie's Moral Em-blems; with Aphorisms, Adages, and Proverbs of all Nations: comprising 121 Illustrations on Wood by J. Leighton, F.S.A. with an appropriate Text by R. Pigot. Imperial 8vo. 31s. 6d.

Sacred and Legendary Art. By Mrs. Jameson. 6 vols. square crown 8vo. price £5 15s. 6d. as follows :—

Legends of the Saints and Martyrs. New Edition, with 19 Etchings and 187 Woodcuts. 2 vols. price 31s. 6d.

Legends of the Monastic Orders. New Edition, with 11 Etchings and 88 Woodcuts. 1 vol. price 21s.

Legends of the Madonna. New Edition with 27 Etchings and 165 Woodcuts. 1 vol. price 21s.

The History of Our Lord, with that of His Types and Precursors. Completed by Lady Eastlake. Revised Edition, with 13 Etchings and 281 Woodcuts. 2 vols price 42s.

Lyra Germanica, the Christian Year. Translated by Catherine Winkworth with 125 Illustrations on Wood drawn by J. Leighton, F.S.A. Quarto, 21s.

Lyra Germanica, the Christian Life Translated by Catherine Winkworth ; with about 200 Woodcut Illustrations by J. Leighton, F.S.A. and other Artists. Quarto, 21s.

The Useful Arts, Manufactures, &c.

Gwilt's Encyclopædia of Architecture, with above 1,600 Woodcuts. Fifth Edition, with Alterations and considerable Additions, by WYATT PAPWORTH. 8vo. price 52s. 6d.

A Manual of Architecture : being a Concise History and Explanation of the principal Styles of European Architecture, Ancient, Mediæval, and Renaissance ; with their Chief Variations and a Glossary of Technical Terms. By THOMAS MITCHELL. With 150 Woodcuts. Crown 8vo. 10s. 6d.

History of the Gothic Revival; an Attempt to shew how far the taste for Mediæval Architecture was retained in England during the last two centuries, and has been re-developed in the present. By C. L. EASTLAKE, Architect. With 48 Illustrations (36 full size of page). Imperial 8vo. price 31s. 6d.

Hints on Household Taste in Furniture, Upholstery, and other Details. By CHARLES L. EASTLAKE, Architect. New Edition, with about 90 Illustrations. Square crown 8vo. 18s.

Lathes and Turning, Simple, Me- chanical, and Ornamental. By W. HENRY NORTHCOTT. With about 240 Illustrations on Steel and Wood. 8vo. 18s.

Perspective; or, the Art of Drawing what one Sees. Explained and adapted to the use of those Sketching from Nature. By Lieut. W. H. COLLINS, R.E. F.R.A.S. With 37 Woodcuts. Crown 8vo. price 5s.

Principles of Mechanism, designed for the use of Students in the Universities, and for Engineering Students generally. By R. WILLIS, M.A. F.R.S. &c. Jacksonian Professor in the Univ. of Cambridge. Second Edition ; with 374 Woodcuts. 8vo. 18s.

Handbook of Practical Tele- graphy. By R. S. CULLEY, Memb. Inst. C.E. Engineer-in-Chief of Telegraphs to the Post-Office. Fifth Edition, revised and enlarged ; with 118 Woodcuts and 9 Plates. 8vo. price 14s.

Ure's Dictionary of Arts, Manu- factures, and Mines. Sixth Edition, re-written and greatly enlarged by ROBERT HUNT, F.R.S. assisted by numerous Contributors. With 2,000 Woodcuts. 3 vols. medium 8vo. £4 14s. 6d.

Encyclopædia of Civil Engineer- ing, Historical, Theoretical, and Practical. By E. CRESY, C.E. With above 3,000 Woodcuts. 8vo. 42s.

Catechism of the Steam Engine, in its various Applications to Mines, Mills, Steam Navigation, Railways, and Agriculture. By JOHN BOURNE, C.E. New Edition, with 89 Woodcuts. Fcp. 8vo. 6s.

Handbook of the Steam Engine. By JOHN BOURNE, C.E. forming a KEY to the Author's Catechism of the Steam Engine. With 67 Woodcuts. Fcp. 8vo. price 9s.

Recent Improvements in the Steam-Engine. By JOHN BOURNE, C.E. New Edition, including many New Examples, with 124 Woodcuts. Fcp. 8vo. 6s.

A Treatise on the Steam Engine, in its various Applications to Mines, Mills, Steam Navigation, Railways, and Agriculture. By J. BOURNE, C.E. New Edition ; with Portrait, 37 Plates, and 546 Woodcuts. 4to. 42s.

A Treatise on the Screw Pro- peller, Screw Vessels, and Screw Engines, as adapted for purposes of Peace and War. By JOHN BOURNE, C.E. Third Edition, with 54 Plates and 287 Woodcuts. Quarto, price 63s.

Bourne's Examples of Modern Steam, Air, and Gas Engines of the most Approved Types, as employed for Pumping, for Driving Machinery, for Locomotion, and for Agriculture, minutely and practically described. In course of publication, to be completed in Twenty-four Parts, price 2s. 6d. each, forming One Volume, with about 50 Plates and 400 Woodcuts.

Treatise on Mills and Millwork. By Sir W. FAIRBAIRN, Bart. F.R.S. New Edition, with 18 Plates and 322 Woodcuts. 2 vols. 8vo. 32s.

Useful Information for Engineers. By the same Author. FIRST, SECOND, and THIRD SERIES, with many Plates and Woodcuts. 3 vols. crown 8vo. 10s. 6d. each.

The Application of Cast and Wrought Iron to Building Purposes. By the same Author. Fourth Edition, with 6 Plates and 118 Woodcuts. 8vo. 16s.

Iron Ship Building, its History and Progress, as comprised in a Series of Experimental Researches. By Sir W. FAIRBAIRN, Bart. F.R.S. With 4 Plates and 130 Woodcuts. 8vo. 18s.

The Strains in Trusses Computed by means of Diagrams ; with 20 Examples drawn to Scale. By F. A. RANKEN, M.A. C.E. Lecturer at the Hartley Institution, Southampton. With 35 Diagrams. Square crown 8vo. price 6s. 6d.

Mitchell's Manual of Practical Assaying. Third Edition for the most part re-written, with all the recent Discoveries incorporated. By W. CROOKES, F.R.S. With 188 Woodcuts. 8vo. 28s.

The Art of Perfumery; the History and Theory of Odours, and the Methods of Extracting the Aromas of Plants. By Dr. PIESSE, F.C.S. Third Edition, with 53 Woodcuts. Crown 8vo. 10s. 6d.

Bayldon's Art of Valuing Rents and Tillages, and Claims of Tenants upon Quitting Farms, both at Michaelmas and Lady-Day. Eighth Edition, revised by J. C. MORTON. 8vo. 10s. 6d.

On the Manufacture of Beet-Root Sugar in England and Ireland. By WILLIAM CROOKES, F.R.S. With 11 Woodcuts. 8vo. 8s. 6d.

Practical Treatise on Metallurgy adapted from the last German Edition o Professor KERL's *Metallurgy* by W CROOKES, F.R.S. &c. and E. RÖHRIG Ph.D. M.E. 3 vols. 8vo. with 625 Wood cuts, price £4 19s.

Loudon's Encyclopædia of Agri culture: comprising the Laying-out, Im provement, and Management of Lande Property, and the Cultivation and Econom of the Productions of Agriculture. Wit 1,100 Woodcuts. 8vo. 21s.

Loudon's Encyclopædia of Gardening comprising the Theory and Practice Horticulture, Floriculture, Arboricultur and Landscape Gardening. With 1,0 Woodcuts. 8vo. 21s.

Religious and Moral Works.

The Outlines of the Christian Ministry Delineated, and brought to the Test of Reason, Holy Scripture, History, and Experience, with a view to the Reconciliation of Existing Differences concerning it, especially between Presbyterians and Episcopalians. By CHRISTOPHER WORDSWORTH, D.C.L. &c. Bishop of St. Andrew's, and Fellow of Winchester College. Crown 8vo. price 7s. 6d.

Christian Counsels, selected from the Devotional Works of Fénelon, Archbishop of Cambrai. Translated by A. M. JAMES. Crown 8vo. price 5s.

Ecclesiastical Reform. Nine Essays by various Writers. Edited by the Rev. ORBY SHIPLEY, M.A. Crown 8vo. [Nearly ready.

Authority and Conscience; a Free Debate on the Tendency of Dogmatic Theology and on the Characteristics of Faith. Edited by CONWAY MOREL. Post 8vo. 7s. 6d.

Reasons of Faith; or, the Order of the Christian Argument Developed and Explained. By the Rev. G. S. DREW, M.A. Second Edition, revised and enlarged. Fcp. 8vo. 6s.

Christ the Consoler; a Book of Comfort for the Sick. With a Preface by the Right Rev. the Lord Bishop of Carlisle. Small 8vo. 6s.

The True Doctrine of the Eucharist. By THOMAS S. L. VOGAN, D.D. Canon and Prebendary of Chichester and Rural Dean. 8vo. 18s.

The Student's Compendium the Book of Common Prayer; being Not Historical and Explanatory of the Litur of the Church of England. By the Rev. ALLDEN NASH. Fcp. 8vo. price 2s. 6d.

Synonyms of the Old Testamen their Bearing on Christian Faith and Pra tice. By the Rev. ROBERT B. GIRDI STONE, M.A. 8vo. price 15s.

Fundamentals; or, Bases of Bel concerning Man and God: a Handbook Mental, Moral, and Religious Philosopl By the Rev. T. GRIFFITH, M.A. 8 price 10s. 6d.

An Introduction to the Theolog of the Church of England, in an Exposit: of the Thirty-nine Articles. By the R T. P. BOULTBEE, LL.D. Fcp. 8vo. price

Christian Sacerdotalism, view from a Layman's standpoint or tried Holy Scripture and the Early Fathe with a short Sketch of the State of the Church from the end of the Third to Reformation in the beginning of the S teenth Century. By JOHN JARDINE, M LL.D. 8vo. 8s. 6d.

Prayers for the Family and f Private Use, selected from the Collect of the late Baron BUNSEN, and Tra lated by CATHERINE WINKWORTH. I 8vo. price 3s. 6d.

Churches and their Creeds. the Rev. Sir PHILIP PERRING, Bart. Scholar of Trin. Coll. Cambridge, University Medallist. Crown 8vo. 10s.

he Truth of the Bible; Evidence from the Mosaic and other Records of Creation; the Origin and Antiquity of Man; the Science of Scripture; and from the Archæology of Different Nations of the Earth. By the Rev. B. W. SAVILE, M.A. Crown 8vo. 7s. 6d.

Considerations on the Revision of the English New Testament. By C. J. ELLICOTT, D.D. Lord Bishop of Gloucester and Bristol. Post 8vo. price 5s. 6d.

An Exposition of the 39 Articles, Historical and Doctrinal. By E. HAROLD BROWNE, D.D. Lord Bishop of Ely. Ninth Edition. 8vo. 16s.

he Voyage and Shipwreck of St. Paul; with Dissertations on the Ships and Navigation of the Ancients. By JAMES SMITH, F.R.S. Crown 8vo. Charts, 10s. 6d.

he Life and Epistles of St. Paul. By the Rev. W. J. CONYBEARE, M.A. and the Very Rev. J. S. HOWSON, D.D. Dean of Chester. Three Editions:—

LIBRARY EDITION, with all the Original Illustrations, Maps, Landscapes on Steel, Woodcuts, &c. 2 vols. 4to. 48s.

INTERMEDIATE EDITION, with a Selection of Maps, Plates, and Woodcuts. 2 vols. square crown 8vo. 21s.

STUDENT'S EDITION, revised and condensed, with 46 Illustrations and Maps. 1 vol. crown 8vo. 9s.

vidence of the Truth of the Christian Religion derived from the Literal Fulfilment of Prophecy. By ALEXANDER KEITH, D.D. 37th Edition, with numerous Plates, in square 8vo. 12s. 6d.; also the 39th Edition, in post 8vo. with 5 Plates, 6s.

e History and Destiny of the World nd of the Church, according to Scripture. By the same Author. Square 8vo. with 40 Illustrations, 10s.

he History and Literature of the Israelites, according to the Old Testament and the Apocrypha. By C. DE ROTHSCHILD and A. DE ROTHSCHILD. Second Edition. 2 vols. crown 8vo. 12s. 6d. Abridged Edition, in 1 vol. fcp. 8vo. 3s. 6d.

vald's History of Israel to the Death of Moses. Translated from the German. Edited, with a Preface and an Appendix, by RUSSELL MARTINEAU, M.A. Second Edition. 2 vols. 8vo. 24s. Vols. III. and IV. edited by J. E. CARPENTER, M.A. price 21s.

England and Christendom. By ARCHBISHOP MANNING, D.D. Post 8vo. price 10s 6d.

The Pontificate of Pius the Ninth; being the Third Edition, enlarged and continued, of 'Rome and its Ruler.' By J. F. MAGUIRE, M.P. Post 8vo. Portrait, price 12s. 6d.

Ignatius Loyola and the Early Jesuits. By STEWART ROSE. New Edition, revised. 8vo. with Portrait, 16s.

An Introduction to the Study of the New Testament, Critical, Exegetical, and Theological. By the Rev. S. DAVIDSON, D.D. LL.D. 2 vols. 8vo. 30s.

A Critical and Grammatical Commentary on St. Paul's Epistles. By C. J. ELLICOTT, D.D. Lord Bishop of Gloucester and Bristol. 8vo.

Galatians, Fourth Edition, 8s. 6d.

Ephesians, Fourth Edition, 8s. 6d.

Pastoral Epistles, Fourth Edition, 10s. 6d.

Philippians, Colossians, and Philemon, Third Edition, 10s. 6d.

Thessalonians, Third Edition, 7s. 6d.

Historical Lectures on the Life of Our Lord Jesus Christ: being the Hulsean Lectures for 1859. By C. J. ELLICOTT, D.D. Fifth Edition. 8vo. 12s.

The Greek Testament; with Notes, Grammatical and Exegetical. By the Rev. W. WEBSTER, M.A. and the Rev. W. F. WILKINSON, M.A. 2 vols. 8vo. £2. 4s.

Horne's Introduction to the Critical Study and Knowledge of the Holy Scriptures. Twelfth Edition; with 4 Maps and 22 Woodcuts. 4 vols. 8vo. 42s.

The Treasury of Bible Knowledge; being a Dictionary of the Books, Persons, Places, Events, and other Matters of which mention is made in Holy Scripture. By Rev. J. AYRE, M.A. With Maps, 15 Plates, and numerous Woodcuts. Fcp. 8vo. price 6s.

Every-day Scripture Difficulties explained and illustrated. By J. E. PRESCOTT, M.A. I. Matthew and Mark; II. Luke and John. 2 vols. 8vo. price 9s. each.

The Pentateuch and Book of Joshua Critically Examined. By the Right Rev. J. W. COLENSO, D.D. Lord Bishop of Natal. Crown 8vo. price 6s.

PART V. Genesis Analysed and Separated, and the Ages of its Writers determined. 8vo. 18s.

PART VI. The Later Legislation of the Pentateuch. 8vo. 24s.

The Formation of Christendom. By T. W. ALLIES. PARTS I. and II. 8vo. price 12s. each.

Four Discourses of Chrysostom, chiefly on the parable of the Rich Man and Lazarus. Translated by F. ALLEN, B.A. Crown 8vo. 3s. 6d.

Thoughts for the Age. By ELIZABETH M. SEWELL, Author of 'Amy Herbert.' New Edition. Fcp. 8vo. price 5s.

Passing Thoughts on Religion. By the same Author. Fcp. 3s. 6d.

Self-examination before Confirmation. By the same Author. 32mo. 1s. 6d.

Thoughts for the Holy Week, for Young Persons. By the same Author. New Edition. Fcp. 8vo. 2s.

Readings for a Month Preparatory to Confirmation from Writers of the Early and English Church. By the same. Fcp. 4s.

Readings for Every Day in Lent, compiled from the Writings of Bishop JEREMY TAYLOR. By the same Author. Fcp. 5s.

Preparation for the Holy Communion; the Devotions chiefly from the works of JEREMY TAYLOR. By the same. 32mo. 3s.

Bishop Jeremy Taylor's Enti Works; with Life by BISHOP HEBE Revised and corrected by the Rev. C. EDEN. 10 vols. £5. 5s.

'Spiritual Songs' for the Sunday and Holidays throughout the Year. J. S. B. MONSELL, LL.D. Vicar of Egh and Rural Dean. Fourth Edition, Six Thousand. Fcp. price 4s. 6d.

The Beatitudes. By the same Auth Third Edition, revised. Fcp. 3s. 6d.

His Presence not his Memory, 18 By the same Author, in memory of his S Sixth Edition. 16mo. 1s.

Lyra Germanica, translated from t German by Miss C. WINKWORTH. Fi SERIES, the *Christian Year,* Hymns for t Sundays and Chief Festivals of the Chur SECOND SERIES, the *Christian Life.* F 8vo. price 3s. 6d. each SERIES.

Endeavours after the Christi Life; Discourses. By JAMES MARTINE. Fourth Edition. Post 8vo. price 7s. 6d.

Travels, Voyages, &c.

Six Months in California. By J.G. PLAYER-FROWD. Post 8vo. price 6s.

The Japanese in America. By CHARLES LANMAN, American Secretary, Japanese Legation, Washington, U.S.A. Post 8vo. price 10s. 6d.

My Wife and I in Queensland; Eight Years' Experience in the Colony, with some account of Polynesian Labour. By CHARLES H. EDEN. With Map and Frontispiece. Crown 8vo. price 9s.

Life in India; a Series of Sketches shewing something of the Anglo-Indian, the Land he lives in, and the People among whom he lives. By EDWARD BRADDON. Post 8vo. price 9s.

How to See Norway. By Captain J. R. CAMPBELL. With Map and 5 Woodcuts. Fcp. 8vo. price 5s.

Pau and the Pyrenees. By Count HENRY RUSSELL, Member of the Alpine Club. With 2 Maps. Fcp. 8vo. price 5s.

Hours of Exercise in the Alps. By JOHN TYNDALL, LL.D., F.R.S. Second Edition, with Seven Woodcuts by E. Whymper. Crown 8vo. price 12s. 6d.

Westward by Rail; the New Route to the East. By W. F. RAE. Second Edition. Post 8vo. with Map, price 10s. 6d.

Travels in the Central Caucas and Bashan, including Visits to Ararat a Tabreez and Ascents of Kazbek and Elbr By DOUGLAS W. FRESHFIELD. Squ crown 8vo. with Maps, &c., 18s.

Cadore or Titian's Country. JOSIAH GILBERT, one of the Authors of 'Dolomite Mountains.' With Map, l simile, and 40 Illustrations. Imp.8vo.31s.

The Playground of Europe. LESLIE STEPHEN, late President of Alpine Club. With 4 Illustrations on W by E. Whymper. Crown 8vo. 10s. 6d.

Zigzagging amongst Dolomit with more than 300 Illustrations by Author. By the Author of 'How we S the Summer.' Oblong 4to. price 15s.

The Dolomite Mountains. Ex sions through Tyrol, Carinthia, Carn and Friuli. By J. GILBERT and G CHURCHILL, F.R.G.S. With nume Illustrations. Square crown 8vo. 21s.

How we Spent the Summer; a Voyage en Zigzag in Switzerland Tyrol with some Members of the ALI CLUB. Third Edition, re-drawn. In ob 4to. with about 300 Illustrations, 15s.

Pictures in Tyrol and Elsewh From a Family Sketch-Book. By same Author. Second Edition. 4to. many Illustrations, 21s.

eaten Tracks; or, Pen and Pencil
Sketches in Italy. By the Author of 'How
we spent the Summer.' With 42 Plates of
Sketches. 8vo. 16s.

he Alpine Club Map of the Chain
of Mont Blanc, from an actual Survey in
1863—1864. By A. ADAMS - REILLY,
F.R.G.S. M.A.C. In Chromolithography on
extra stout drawing paper 28in. x 17in.
price 10s. or mounted on canvas in a folding
case, 12s. 6d.

istory of Discovery in our
Australasian Colonies, Australia, Tasmania,
and New Zealand, from the Earliest Date to
the Present Day. By WILLIAM HOWITT.
2 vols. 8vo. with 3 Maps, 20s.

isits to Remarkable Places:
Old Halls, Battle-Fields, and Scenes illustrative of striking Passages in English
History and Poetry. By the same Author.
2 vols. square crown 8vo. with Wood Engravings, 25s.

Guide to the Pyrenees, for the use
of Mountaineers. By CHARLES PACKE.
Second Edition, with Maps, &c. and Appendix. Crown 8vo. 7s. 6d.

The Alpine Guide. By JOHN BALL,
M.R.I.A. late President of the Alpine Club.
Post 8vo. with Maps and other Illustrations.

Guide to the Eastern Alps, price 10s.6d.

Guide to the Western Alps, including
Mont Blanc, Monte Rosa, Zermatt, &c.
price 6s. 6d.

Guide to the Central Alps, including
all the Oberland District, price 7s. 6d.

Introduction on Alpine Travelling in
general, and on the Geology of the Alps,
price 1s. Either of the Three Volumes or
Parts of the *Alpine Guide* may be had with
this INTRODUCTION prefixed, price 1s. extra.

The Rural Life of England.
By WILLIAM HOWITT. Woodcuts by
Bewick and Williams. Medium 8vo. 12s. 6d.

Works of Fiction.

arndale; a Story of Lancashire Life.
By a Lancashire Man. 3 vols. post 8vo.
price 21s.

he Burgomaster's Family; or,
Weal and Woe in a Little World. By
CHRISTINE MÜLLER. Translated from the
Dutch by Sir J. G. SHAW LEFEVRE, K.C.B.
F.R.S. Crown 8vo. price 6s.

opular Romances of the Middle
Ages. By the Rev. GEORGE W. COX, M.A.
Author of 'The Mythology of the Aryan
Nations' &c. and EUSTACE HINTON JONES.
Crown 8vo. 10s. 6d.

ales of the Teutonic Lands; a
Sequel to ' Popular Romances of the Middle
Ages.' By GEORGE W. COX, M.A. late
Scholar of Trinity College, Oxford; and
EUSTACE HINTON JONES. Crown 8vo.
price 10s. 6d.

artland Forest; a Legend of North
Devon. By Mrs. BRAY, Author of 'The
White Hoods,' 'Life of Stothard,' &c. Post
8vo. with Frontispiece, 4s. 6d.

ovels and Tales. By the Right
Hon. BENJAMIN DISRAELI, M.P. Cabinet
Editions, complete in Ten Volumes, crown
8vo. price 6s. each, as follows :—

'THAIR, 6s.	VENETIA, 6s.
NINGSBY, 6s.	ALROY, IXION, &c. 6s.
BIL, 6s.	YOUNG DUKE, &c. 6s.
ANCRED, 6s.	VIVIAN GREY, 6s.

CONTARINI FLEMING, &c. 6s.
HENRIETTA TEMPLE, 6s.

Stories and Tales. By E. M. SEWELL.
Comprising *Amy Herbert* ; *Gertrude* ; the
Earl's Daughter ; the *Experience of Life* ;
Cleve Hall; *Ivors* ; *Katharine Ashton* ; *Mar-
garet Percival* ; *Laneton Parsonage* ; and
Ursula. The Ten Works complete in Eight
Volumes, crown 8vo. bound in leather and
contained in a Box, price TWO GUINEAS.

Cabinet Edition, in crown 8vo. of
Stories and Tales by Miss SEWELL :—

AMY HERBERT, 2s. 6d.	KATHARINE ASHTON, 2s. 6d.
GERTRUDE, 2s. 6d.	
EARL's DAUGHTER, 2s. 6d.	MARGARET PERCI-VAL, 3s. 6d.
EXPERIENCE OF LIFE, 2s. 6d.	LANETON PARSON-AGE, 3s. 6d.
CLEVE HALL, 2s. 6d.	URSULA, 3s. 6d.
IVORS, 2s. 6d.	

A Glimpse of the World. Fcp. 7s. 6d.

Journal of a Home Life. Post 8vo. 9s. 6d.

After Life; a Sequel to the 'Journal of a Home
Life.' Post 8vo. 10s. 6d.

The Giant; a Witch's Story for English
Boys. Edited by Miss SEWELL, Author of
' Amy Herbert,' &c. Fcp. 8vo. price 5s.

Wonderful Stories from Norway,
Sweden, and Iceland. Adapted and arranged
by JULIA GODDARD. With an Introductory
Essay by the Rev. G. W. Cox, M.A. and
Six Illustrations. Square post 8vo. 6s.

The Modern Novelist's Library. Each Work, in crown 8vo. complete in a Single Volume :—

MELVILLE'S DIGBY GRAND, 2s. boards; 2s. 6d. cloth.

———— GLADIATORS, 2s. boards; 2s. 6d. cloth.

———— GOOD FOR NOTHING, 2s. boards; 2s. 6d. cloth.

———— HOLMBY HOUSE, 2s. boards; 2s. 6d. cloth.

———— INTERPRETER, 2s. boards; 2s. 6d. cloth.

———— KATE COVENTRY, 2s. boards; 2s. 6d. cloth.

———— QUEEN'S MARIES, 2s, boards; 2s. 6d. cloth.

TROLLOPE'S WARDEN 1s. 6d. boards; 2s cloth.

———— BARCHESTER TOWERS, 2s. boards; 2s. 6d. cloth.

BRAMLEY-MOORE'S SIX SISTERS OF THE VALLEYS, 2s. boards; 2s. 6d. cloth.

Becker's Gallus ; or, Roman Scenes of the Time of Augustus. Post 8vo. 7s. 6d.

Becker's Charicles : Illustrative of Private Life of the Ancient Greeks. Post 8vo. 7s. 6d.

Tales of Ancient Greece. By the Rev. G. W. Cox, M.A. late Scholar of Trin. Coll. Oxford. Crown 8vo. price 6s. 6d.

Poetry and The Drama.

Ballads and Lyrics of Old France; with other Poems. By A. LANG, Fellow of Merton College, Oxford. Square fcp. 8vo. price 5s.

Thomas Moore's Poetical Works, with the Author's last Copyright Additions :—

Shamrock Edition, price 3s. 6d.
People's Edition, square cr. 8vo. 10s. 6d.
Library Edition, Portrait & Vignette, 14s.

Moore's Lalla Rookh, Tenniel's Edition, with 68 Wood Engravings from Original Drawings and other Illustrations. Fcp. 4to. 21s.

Moore's Irish Melodies, Maclise's Edition, with 161 Steel Plates from Original Drawings. Super-royal 8vo. 31s. 6d.

Miniature Edition of Moore's Irish Melodies, with Maclise's Illustrations (as above), reduced in Lithography. Imp. 16mo. 10s. 6d.

Lays of Ancient Rome ; with Ivry and the Armada. By the Right Hon. LORD MACAULAY. 16mo. 3s. 6d.

Lord Macaulay's Lays of Ancient Rome. With 90 Illustrations on Wood, Original and from the Antique, from Drawings by G. SCHARF. Fcp. 4to. 21s.

Miniature Edition of Lord Macaulay's Lays of Ancient Rome, with Scharf's Illustrations (as above) reduced in Lithography. Imp. 16mo. 10s. 6d.

Southey's Poetical Works, with the Author's last Corrections and copyright Additions. Library Edition. Medium 8vo with Portrait and Vignette, 14s.

Goldsmith's Poetical Works, Illustrated with Wood Engravings from Designs by Members of the ETCHING CLUB. Imp 16mo. 7s. 6d.

Poems. By JEAN INGELOW. Fifteenth Edition. Fcp. 8vo. 5s.

Poems by Jean Ingelow. With nearly 100 Illustrations by Eminent Artists, engraved on Wood by DALZIEL Brothers. Fcp. 4to. 21s.

A Story of Doom, and other Poems By JEAN INGELOW. Third Edition. Fcp price 5s.

Bowdler's Family Shakspeare cheaper Genuine Edition, complete in 1 vol. large type, with 36 Woodcut Illustrations price 14s. or in 6 pocket vols. 3s. 6d. each.

Horatii Opera, Library Edition, with Copious English Notes, Marginal References and Various Readings. Edited by the Rev J. E. YONGE, M.A. 8vo. 21s.

The Odes and Epodes of Horace a Metrical Translation into English, with Introduction and Commentary. By Lor LYTTON. With Latin Text. New Edition Post 8vo. price 10s. 6d.

The Æneid of Virgil Translated int English Verse. By JOHN CONINGTON, M.A Corpus Professor of Latin in the University of Oxford. New Edition. Crown 8vo. 9s.

Rural Sports &c.

Encyclopædia of Rural Sports; a Complete Account, Historical, Practical, and Descriptive, of Hunting, Shooting, Fishing, Racing, &c. By D. P. BLAINE. With above 600 Woodcuts (20 from Designs by JOHN LEECH). 8vo. 21s.

The Dead Shot, or Sportsman's Complete Guide; a Treatise on the Use of the Gun, Dog-breaking, Pigeon-shooting, &c. By MARKSMAN. Fcp. with Plates, 5s.

A Book on Angling: being a Complete Treatise on the Art of Angling in every branch, including full Illustrated Lists of Salmon Flies. By FRANCIS FRANCIS. New Edition, with Portrait and 15 other Plates, plain and coloured. Post 8vo. 15s.

Wilcocks's Sea-Fisherman: comprising the Chief Methods of Hook and Line Fishing in the British and other Seas, a glance at Nets, and remarks on Boats and Boating. Second Edition, enlarged, with 80 Woodcuts. Post 8vo. 12s. 6d.

The Fly-Fisher's Entomology. By ALFRED RONALDS. With coloured Representations of the Natural and Artificial Insect. Sixth Edition, with 20 coloured Plates. 8vo. 14s.

The Ox, his Diseases and their Treatment; with an Essay on Parturition in the Cow. By J. R. DONSON, M.R.C.V.S. Crown 8vo. with Illustrations, 7s. 6d.

A Treatise on Horse-shoeing and Lameness. By JOSEPH GAMGEE, Veterinary Surgeon, formerly Lecturer on Principles and Practice of Farriery in the New Veterinary College, Edinburgh. 8vo. with 55 Woodcuts, 15s.

Blaine's Veterinary Art: a Treatise on the Anatomy, Physiology, and Curative Treatment of the Diseases of the Horse, Neat Cattle, and Sheep. Seventh Edition, revised and enlarged by C. STEEL. 8vo. with Plates and Woodcuts, 18s.

Youatt on the Horse. Revised and enlarged by W. WATSON, M.R.C.V.S. 8vo. with numerous Woodcuts, 12s. 6d.

Youatt on the Dog. (By the same Author.) 8vo. with numerous Woodcuts, 6s.

The Dog in Health and Disease. By STONEHENGE. With 73 Wood Engravings. New Edition, revised. Square crown 8vo. price 7s. 6d.

The Greyhound. By the same Author. Revised Edition, with 24 Portraits of Greyhounds. Square crown 8vo. 10s. 6d

The Setter; with Notices of the most Eminent Breeds now extant, Instructions how to Breed, Rear, and Break; Dog Shows, Field Trials, and General Management, &c. By EDWARD LAVERACK. With Two Portraits of Setters in Chromolithography. Crown 4to. price 7s. 6d.

Horses and Stables. By Colonel F. FITZWYGRAM, XV. the King's Hussars. With 24 Plates of Woodcut Illustrations, containing very numerous Figures. 8vo. 15s.

The Horse's Foot, and how to keep it Sound. By W. MILES, Esq. Ninth Edition, with Illustrations. Imp. 8vo. 12s. 6d.

A Plain Treatise on Horse-shoeing. By the same Author. Sixth Edition, post 8vo. with Illustrations, 2s. 6d.

Stables and Stable Fittings. By the same. Imp. 8vo. with 13 Plates, 15s.

Remarks on Horses' Teeth, addressed to Purchasers. By the same. Post 8vo. 1s. 6d.

Works of Utility and General Information.

Modern Cookery for Private Families, reduced to a System of Easy Practice in a Series of carefully-tested Receipts. By ELIZA ACTON. Newly revised and enlarged; with 8 Plates, Figures, and 150 Woodcuts. Fcp. 6s.

Maunder's Treasury of Knowledge and Library of Reference: comprising an English Dictionary and Grammar, Universal Gazetteer, Classical Dictionary, Chronology, Law Dictionary, Synopsis of the Peerage, Useful Tables, &c. Fcp. 8vo. 6s.

Collieries and Colliers: a Handbook of the Law and Leading Cases relating thereto. By J. C. FOWLER, Barrister. Second Edition. Fcp. 8vo. 7s. 6d.

The Theory and Practice of Banking. By HENRY DUNNING MACLEOD, M.A. Barrister-at-Law. Second Edition. entirely remodelled. 2 vols. 8vo. 30s.

M'Culloch's Dictionary, Practical, Theoretical, and Historical, of Commerce and Commercial Navigation. New Edition, revised throughout and corrected to the Present Time; with a Biographical Notice of the Author. Edited by H. G. REID, Secretary to Mr. M'Culloch for many years. 8vo. price 63s. cloth.

A Practical Treatise on Brewing; with Formulæ for Public Brewers, and Instructions for Private Families. By W. BLACK. Fifth Edition. 8vo. 10s. 6d.

Chess Openings. By F. W. LONGMAN, Balliol College, Oxford. Fcp. 8vo. 2s. 6d.

The Law of Nations Considered as Independent Political Communities. By Sir TRAVERS TWISS, D.C.L. 2 vols. 8vo. 30s. or separately, PART I *Peace*, 12s. PART II. *War*, 18s.

Hints to Mothers on the Management of their Health during the Period of Pregnancy and in the Lying-in Room. By THOMAS BULL, M.D. Fcp. 5s.

The Maternal Management of Children in Health and Disease. By THOMAS BULL, M.D. Fcp. 5s.

How to Nurse Sick Children; containing Directions which may be found of service to all who have charge of the Young. By CHARLES WEST, M.D. Second Edition. Fcp. 8vo. 1s. 6d.

Notes on Hospitals. By FLORENCE NIGHTINGALE. Third Edition, enlarged; with 13 Plans. Post 4to. 18s.

Notes on Lying-In Institutions; with a Proposal for Organising an Institution for Training Midwives and Midwifery Nurses. By FLORENCE NIGHTINGALE. With 5 Plans. Square crown 8vo. 7s. 6d.

The Cabinet Lawyer; a Popular Digest of the Laws of England, Civil, Criminal, and Constitutional. Twenty-third Edition, corrected and brought up to the Present Date. Fcp. 8vo. price 7s. 6d.

Willich's Popular Tables for Ascertaining the Value of Lifehold, Leasehold, and Church Property, Renewal Fines, &c.; the Public Funds; Annual Average Price and Interest on Consols from 1731 to 1867; Chemical, Geographical, Astronomical, Trigonometrical Tables, &c. Post 8vo. 10s.

Pewtner's Comprehensive Specifier; a Guide to the Practical Specification of every kind of Building-Artificer's Work: with Forms of Building Conditions and Agreements, an Appendix, Foot-Notes, and Index. Edited by W. YOUNG, Architect. Crown 8vo. 6s.

Periodical Publications.

The Edinburgh Review, or Critical Journal, published Quarterly in January, April, July, and October. 8vo. price 6s. each Number.

Notes on Books: An Analysis of the Works published during each Quarter by Messrs. LONGMANS & Co. The object is to enable Bookbuyers to obtain such information regarding the various works as is usually afforded by tables of contents and explanatory prefaces. 4to. Quarterly. *Gratis.*

Fraser's Magazine. Edited by JAMES ANTHONY FROUDE, M.A. New Series, published on the 1st of each Month. 8vo. price 2s. 6d. each Number.

The Alpine Journal; A Record of Mountain Adventure and Scientific Observation. By Members of the Alpine Club. Edited by LESLIE STEPHEN. Published Quarterly, May 31, Aug. 31, Nov. 30, Feb. 28. 8vo. price 1s. 6d. each Number.

Knowledge for the Young.

The Stepping Stone to Knowledge: Containing upwards of Seven Hundred Questions and Answers on Miscellaneous Subjects, adapted to the capacity of Infant Minds. By a MOTHER. New Edition, enlarged and improved. 18mo. price 1s.

The Stepping Stone to Geography: Containing several Hundred Questions and Answers on Geographical Subjects. 18mo. 1s.

The Stepping Stone to English History: Containing several Hundred Questions and Answers on the History of England. 1s.

The Stepping Stone to Bible Knowledge: Containing several Hundred Questions and Answers on the Old and New Testaments. 18mo. 1s.

The Stepping Stone to Biography: Containing several Hundred Questions and Answers on the Lives of Eminent Men and Women. 18mo. 1s.

Second Series of the Stepping Stone to Knowledge: containing upwards of Eight Hundred Questions and Answers on Miscellaneous Subjects not contained in the FIRST SERIES. 18mo. 1s.

The Stepping Stone to French Pronunciation and Conversation: Containing several Hundred Questions and Answers. By Mr. P. SADLER. 18mo. 1s.

The Stepping Stone to English Grammar: Containing several Hundred Questions and Answers on English Grammar. By Mr. P. SADLER. 18mo. 1s.

The Stepping Stone to Natural History: VERTEBRATE or BACKBONED ANIMALS. PART I. *Mammalia*; PART II. *Birds, Reptiles, Fishes.* 18mo. 1s. each Part.

INDEX.

SPOTTISWOODE AND CO., PRINTERS NEW-STREET SQUARE, LONDON.